English-Medium Instruction
and Translanguaging

BILINGUAL EDUCATION & BILINGUALISM
Series Editors: **Nancy H. Hornberger** *(University of Pennsylvania, USA)* and **Wayne E. Wright** *(Purdue University, USA)*

Bilingual Education and Bilingualism is an international, multidisciplinary series publishing research on the philosophy, politics, policy, provision and practice of language planning, Indigenous and minority language education, multilingualism, multiculturalism, biliteracy, bilingualism and bilingual education. The series aims to mirror current debates and discussions. New proposals for single-authored, multiple-authored or edited books in the series are warmly welcomed, in any of the following categories or others authors may propose: overview or introductory texts; course readers or general reference texts; focus books on particular multilingual education program types; school-based case studies; national case studies; collected cases with a clear programmatic or conceptual theme; and professional education manuals.

All books in this series are externally peer-reviewed.

Full details of all the books in this series and of all our other publications can be found on http://www.multilingual-matters.com, or by writing to Multilingual Matters, St Nicholas House, 31–34 High Street, Bristol BS1 2AW, UK.

BILINGUAL EDUCATION & BILINGUALISM: 126

English-Medium Instruction and Translanguaging

Edited by
**BethAnne Paulsrud,
Zhongfeng Tian and Jeanette Toth**

MULTILINGUAL MATTERS
Bristol • Blue Ridge Summit

DOI https://doi.org/10.21832/PAULSR7321

Library of Congress Cataloging in Publication Data

A catalog record for this book is available from the Library of Congress.

Names: Paulsrud, BethAnne - editor. | Tian, Zhongfeng – editor. | Toth, Jeanette – editor.

Title: English-Medium Instruction and Translanguaging/Edited by BethAnne Paulsrud, Zhongfeng Tian and Jeanette Toth.

Description: Bristol, UK; Blue Ridge Summit: Multilingual Matters, 2021. | Series: Bilingual Education & Bilingualism: 126 | Includes bibliographical references and index. | Summary: "This book offers a critical exploration of definitions, methodologies, and ideologies of English-medium instruction (EMI) and contributes to new understandings of translanguaging as theory and pedagogy across diverse contexts. It demonstrates the affordances and constraints that translanguaging processes present in relation to EMI classrooms"—Provided by publisher.

Identifiers: LCCN 2020036969 (print) | LCCN 2020036970 (ebook) | ISBN 9781788927314 (paperback) | ISBN 9781788927321 (hardback) | ISBN 9781788927338 (pdf) | ISBN 9781788927345 (epub) | ISBN 9781788927352 (kindle edition)

Subjects: LCSH: English language—Study and teaching—Foreign speakers. | Translanguaging (Linguistics) | Bilingualism.

Classification: LCC PE1128.A2 E5445 2021 (print) | LCC PE1128.A2 (ebook) | DDC 428.0071—dc23 LC record available at https://lccn.loc.gov/2020036969

LC ebook record available at https://lccn.loc.gov/2020036970

British Library Cataloguing in Publication Data

A catalogue entry for this book is available from the British Library.

ISBN-13: 978-1-78892-732-1 (hbk)
ISBN-13: 978-1-78892-731-4 (pbk)

Multilingual Matters

UK: St Nicholas House, 31–34 High Street, Bristol BS1 2AW, UK.
USA: NBN, Blue Ridge Summit, PA, USA.

Website: www.multilingual-matters.com
Twitter: Multi_Ling_Mat
Facebook: https://www.facebook.com/multilingualmatters
Blog: www.channelviewpublications.wordpress.com

The policy of Multilingual Matters/Channel View Publications is to use papers that are natural, renewable and recyclable products, made from wood grown in sustainable forests. In the manufacturing process of our books, and to further support our policy, preference is given to printers that have FSC and PEFC Chain of Custody certification. The FSC and/or PEFC logos will appear on those books where full certification has been granted to the printer concerned.

Typeset by Nova Techset Private Limited, Bengaluru and Chennai, India.
Printed and bound in the UK by Short Run Press Ltd.
Printed and bound in the US by NBN.

Contents

Transcription Key

text	utterance in English
text	original utterance in language other than English and translation from original utterance
text	original utterance in third language (other than English)
"text"	quoted or read text
TEXT	word spoken with emphasis
[text]	clarifying text not spoken by informants
(inaudible)	utterance that cannot be clearly heard
...	longer pause
text –	utterance that is cut off

Contributors

John Adamson is a Professor at the University of Niigata Prefecture in Japan. As Chief Editor of *Asian EFL Journal*, he is active in editorial work. Having received his EdD from the University of Leicester, he has pursued research in CLIL and EMI, self-access, academic writing and journal editing.

Bassey E. Antia is Professor of Linguistics at the University of the Western Cape, South Africa. His teaching and research interests span multilingualism (in higher education), language policy, terminology, health communication, corpus linguistics, decoloniality, political economy of English, French as a foreign language and translation studies. Some of his ongoing work addresses the diversification of languages and language varieties used in teaching, learning and assessment in higher education. Bassey has authored *Terminology and Language Planning: An Alternative Framework of Discourse and Practice*, edited *Indeterminacy in Terminology and LSP* and co-edited *Corpus Linguistics and African Englishes* (all published by John Benjamins).

Sovicheth Boun is an Assistant Professor of ESL and Literacy in the Department of Secondary and Higher Education, School of Education, Salem State University, USA. He serves on the Editorial Advisory Board of the *Journal of Language, Identity and Education* (*JLIE*) and the Editorial Review Board for the *International Journal of TESOL Studies* (*IJTS*) and the *Journal of Southeast Asian American Education and Advancement* (*JSAAEA*). Sovicheth's most recent book is the *Handbook of Bilingual and Multilingual Education*, co-edited with Wayne E. Wright and Ofelia García (Wiley-Blackwell, 2015).

Eowyn Crisfield is a teacher, teacher trainer and researcher with over 25 years' experience in languages in education. Her research and teaching are focused on improving language provisions in schools around the world, with special emphasis on developing ethical approaches to languages in schools, including home languages, EAL and host country languages. Eowyn has worked with the Aga Khan Academies since 2015, at both a network and school level. She is also a Senior Lecturer in TESOL at Oxford Brookes University, UK.

Fiona Dalziel is an Assistant Professor of English Language and Translation at Padova University, Italy, where she teaches on the BA and MA programmes in Modern Languages. Her research interests include: promoting metacognitive learning strategies and learner autonomy; teaching academic writing; English-medium instruction (EMI); and the use of drama in language learning, including that of adult migrants. While Head of the University Language Centre (2013–2018), Fiona introduced a support program for lecturers involved in EMI. She has been the coordinator of the Padova University English drama group for over 20 years.

Naoki Fujimoto-Adamson is a teacher-researcher based in Japan. She received her MEd from Leicester University and her MA in English language teaching (ELT) from Essex University, UK. Naoki's research interests are in the fields of team-teaching in Japanese secondary schools, the history of ELT in Japan and academic publishing.

Bridget Goodman is Associate Professor and Director of the MA in Multilingual Education program at Nazarbayev University Graduate School of Education (NUGSE), Kazakhstan. She earned an MSEd in teaching English to speakers of other languages (TESOL) and a PhD in educational linguistics at the University of Pennsylvania, USA. Bridget has been a member of the NUGSE Academic Writing Research Group, and PI of the project 'Development of students' multilingual competence in EMI postgraduate research programs in Kazakhstan' (2018–2020). Her research and supervision activities focus on EMI, translanguaging and genre knowledge in Eurasian countries.

Isla Gordon is the Early Years Principal for the Campus des Nations of the International School of Geneva, Switzerland. She was Junior School Principal of the Aga Khan Academy from 2014 to 2017. Isla's ties continue with the Aga Khan Development network as a member of the Aga Khan Academies Language Advisory Committee.

Marta Guarda is a research assistant at the University of Padova, Italy. She holds a PhD in applied linguistics and English studies from the same university and is currently conducting research on the language use and perspectives of students involved in EMI programmes. She is also involved in the activities of the University Language Centre's EMI lecturer support programme. Marta is one of the editors of a 2017 volume, *Sharing Perspectives on EMI* (Peter Lang), and the author of several research papers on the EMI phenomenon in Italian higher education.

Alexandra Holland is currently the Academic Development Manager for the Aga Khan Academies. Based in London, she works with schools in Kenya, India and Mozambique to build IB continuum programmes that are relevant to students living in the developing world, with an emphasis on bilingual primary education.

Ellen Hurst-Harosh is a sociolinguist and an Associate Professor in the Humanities Education Development Unit at the University of Cape Town, South Africa. She teaches discourse analysis and genre analysis. Her research focuses on African youth language practices including stylects and registers, as well as translanguaging pedagogies and the use of African languages in higher education.

Sulushash Kerimkulova is an Associate Professor at Nazarbayev University Graduate School of Education (NUGSE), Kazakhstan. She obtained her diploma of Candidate of Pedagogical Sciences from the USSR Academy of Pedagogical Sciences, Moscow, in 1987. With more than 40 years of teaching and research experience at higher educational institutions in Kazakhstan, Sulushash serves as a member of the national team of Higher Education Reform Experts under the Erasmus+ programme and is an expert at two national accreditation agencies. Her current research focuses mainly on reforms in higher education (internationalisation, quality assurance, governance) and in tri/multilingual education.

Kathy Luckett is Director of the Humanities Education Development Unit, Professor in the Centre for Higher Education Development and associate staff member of the Department of Sociology, University of Cape Town, South Africa. She teaches and supervises on the School of Education's Masters in Higher Education Studies and in the Department of Sociology. Kathy's research interests are: higher education policy around equity, access and language; sociology of knowledge and curriculum studies with a focus on the humanities; Africana; decolonial and postcolonial studies; and research methods that apply social/critical realism to educational evaluation.

Naashia Mohamed is a Lecturer in the School of Curriculum and Pedagogy within the University of Auckland's Faculty of Education and Social Work, New Zealand. Through her teaching and research, Naashia seeks to support minoritised language learners and reduce the educational gap they face. Her research addresses issues related to language education, sociolinguistics and language policy, with a particular focus on language, power and identity. Naashia has previously taught in school and university contexts in the Maldives, where she was also involved in school curriculum reform and teacher professional development.

D. Philip Montgomery is a former Instructor and Director of the Academic English program at NUGSE, with an MEd in educational policy from the University of Illinois Urbana-Champaign, USA. He was the founding Chief Editor of NUGSE Research in Education, and has written and presented on syllabus design, student-centred teaching and developing genre knowledge in EMI contexts. He is currently a PhD student at Michigan State University, USA.

BethAnne Paulsrud is Senior Lecturer of English at Dalarna University, Sweden. Her work as a teacher educator and researcher is informed by her many years of experience as a preschool and primary school teacher, as well as a mother tongue teacher. BethAnne's research focuses on multilingualism in educational policy and practice, English and English-medium instruction in Sweden, and family language policy. Her current research projects include an international comparative study of primary teachers' attitudes, beliefs and knowledge of multilingualism. She has previously co-edited two volumes on translanguaging and education (Multilingual Matters, 2017; Studentlitteratur, 2018).

Margie Probyn has taught English in an EMI secondary school, worked as a researcher and in-service teacher educator at Rhodes University and taught in the Education Faculty at the University of the Western Cape, South Africa. Margie is currently a researcher at the Centre for Multilingualism and Diversities Research at the University of the Western Cape with special research interests in language and science teaching and learning in multilingual classrooms; teacher education; language teaching and learning; language-in-education policy and practice; and language, access and social justice in education.

Jack Pun is an Assistant Professor in the Department of English at the City University of Hong Kong. He holds a doctorate in education from the University of Oxford, which explored the teaching and learning process in EMI science classrooms. Jack investigates how science students overcome their language challenges in studying science through English medium. His research interests are English as the medium of instruction (EMI), classroom interactions and English learners' language challenges and coping strategies.

Colin Reilly is a Senior Research Officer in the Department of Language and Linguistics at the University of Essex and a Teaching Associate in the School of Education at the University of Glasgow, UK. His research focuses on translanguaging, multilingualism, language policy and linguistic ethnography. Colin is currently working on the British Academy-Global Challenges Research Fund project, 'Bringing the outside in: Merging local language and literacy practices to enhance classroom learning and achievement', which investigates multilingualism and language policy in Botswana, Tanzania and Zambia.

Heath Rose is Associate Professor of Applied Linguistics at the University of Oxford and the coordinator of the EMI Oxford Research Group. His research explores the curriculum implications of the globalisation of English. Heath is author of *Global Englishes for Language Teaching* (Cambridge University Press, 2019).

Kari Sahan holds a PhD from the University of Oxford, Department of Education. Her research focuses on the policies and practices of English as a medium of instruction in higher education. Kari previously worked at the Turkish Fulbright Commission and as an English instructor at universities in Turkey.

Ute Smit is Professor of English Linguistics at the University of Vienna, Austria. Her research focuses mainly on English in and around the classroom in various educational settings. Her publications have appeared in renowned journals (e.g. *Applied Linguistics, International Journal of Bilingualism and Bilingual Education, Journal of Immersion and Content Based Language Education, TESOL Quarterly* and *System*) and with international publishers (e.g. John Benjamins, de Gruyter, Multilingual Matters and Palgrave). Ute was a co-founding member of the AILA Research Network on 'CLIL and Immersion Education' and is presently a board member of ICLHE (Integrating Content and Language in Higher Education) Association.

Zhongfeng Tian is an Assistant Professor of TESL Teacher Education/ Applied Linguistics at the University of Texas at San Antonio, USA. He holds a PhD in curriculum and instruction from Boston College. His research focuses on bilingual education, TESOL and translanguaging. He has co-edited a special issue, 'Positive Synergies: Translanguaging and Critical Theories in Education' (2019) with Holly Link, for *Translation and Translanguaging in Multilingual Contexts*. Zhongfeng is also the lead editor (with Laila Aghai, Peter Sayer and Jamie L. Schissel) of an edited volume, *Envisioning TESOL through a Translanguaging Lens: Global Perspectives* (Springer, 2020).

Jeanette Toth is a Senior Lecturer of English at Dalarna University, Sweden. Drawing on her years of teaching experience in Swedish compulsory schools and as a mother tongue teacher, she has investigated language ideologies in English-medium instruction (EMI) at the primary school level in Sweden. In addition to EMI, Jeanette's research interests include policies, practices and perspectives on language use in the classroom, particularly with regard to bilingual and multilingual education.

She has previously written about EMI in two edited volumes on translanguaging and education (Multilingual Matters, 2017; Studentlitteratur, 2018).

Wayne E. Wright is Associate Dean for Research, Professor, and the Barbara I. Cook Chair of Literacy and Language in the College of Education at Purdue University, USA. He is co-editor of the *Journal of Language, Identity, and Education* and Editor of the *Journal of Southeast Asian American Education and Advancement*. Wayne's recent books include *Foundations of Teaching English Language Learners: Research, Theory, Policy, and Practice* (3rd edn, 2019) and *Foundations of Bilingual Education and Bilingualism* (7th edn, 2021, with Colin Baker). He is a former Fulbright Scholar (Cambodia) and a recipient of the Charles A. Ferguson Award for Outstanding Scholarship.

Foreword

Exclusive English-medium instruction (EMI), especially one that also takes its norms for the 'E' exogenously, is an aberration in those countries that lie outside of the 'inner circle' of the UK, USA, Anglophone Canada, Australia, New Zealand, South Africa and parts of the Caribbean in Kachru's (1992) World Englishes model. Aberration is also arguably apt as a description for the practice of EMI in certain communities in these inner circle countries. Exclusive EMI in 'outer or expanding circle' countries and communities is a cultural travesty, one that highlights the hegemonic slant and reach of either or both colonial cultural politics and contemporary political economy.

On this view, then, EMI in content area pedagogy, even when it is initiated locally, is cut from the same ideological fabric of 'linguistic imperialism' as the 'monolingual fallacy' in the teaching of English in outer/expanding circle environments which Phillipson (1992) criticises. In both content and English language pedagogy, EMI guarantees that the inner circle has a huge market for educational resources and services, as well as a cheap and readily usable workforce. Because language, as critical language awareness reminds us, is more than a means of communication, EMI in outer/expanding circle contexts is easily able to shape local aspirations and serve as a local system of social selection for a global marketplace that is tied to the apron strings of the inner circle.

To take on the 'E' in EMI, as this collection does, is therefore much more than an exercise in documenting pedagogical practices. Taking on the 'E' is a major intervention in the ordinary course of colonial cultural politics and contemporary political economy in the classroom. The editors, BethAnne Paulsrud, Zhongfeng Tian and Jeanette Toth, as well as their authors are to be applauded for tackling this question through the lens of translanguaging. Obviously, translanguaging has by now established itself as, among others, theory, pedagogy and political action. It is therefore well suited to challenge the pride of place that has been traditionally accorded the 'E' in content or language pedagogy in multilingual outer circle contexts, or to push back on, and temper the influence of, an increasingly important 'E' in expanding circle countries and communities.

Contributors to this book provide accounts of translanguaging in primary, secondary and tertiary education, and do so from a breathtakingly impressive array of peripheral contexts in Hong Kong, Turkey, Malawi, Kenya, Japan, South Africa, Kazakhstan, Maldives, Italy and Cambodia. We learn about how school proprietors, teachers and students continue to go against the grain of micro- and macro-level policies to prise open spaces in which the hegemony of English is challenged.

There have been and there will be other ways of challenging English hegemony, but translanguaging has emerged as an important tool for semiotic glocalisation in the classroom. Glocalisation of meaning-making resources in the classroom allows a powerful language like English with global reach to interact symbiotically with local languages in the education of students, and in such a way that all that goes in lockstep with local languages and local meaning-making (e.g. embedded knowledge, perspectives, environment, workers) is not sacrificed on the altar of globalism.

On the other hand, translanguaging is caught up in something of a quandary. We know now that contemporary, neoliberal power works best, in Foucauldian terms, by concealing the dynamics of its exercise; in other words, 'when it is exercised through productive constraints [that enable] subjects to act *in order* to constrain them' (Tremain, 2005: 4, original emphasis). We also know now that multilingualism, even while being feted globally, is increasingly being pressed into the service of monoculturalism and other centre interests (Piller, 2016). In whatever flavour (such as translating, code-switching, or normalised and boundary-defying heteroglossic practice), translanguaging will not mount a serious challenge to the 'E' if it is merely an ancillary or a pathway to the 'E', operating largely within a 'flexible convergence' model of multilingual education (García, 2009a). The 'E' is not challenged when local languages are called to do duty only in ratified or unratified peer talk, in the teacher's explanation or simplification of content presented in 'E' or in the teacher's regulation of classroom behaviour. What these practices do in fact is to enact an ideology of language hierarchy in which features enregistered as 'non-E' are inferior to 'E'.

To correct the aberration that the 'E' in EMI represents in outer/expanding circle contexts, what the lens of cultural politics and political economy suggests is that, in the multiple ways it is understood, translanguaging go beyond ephemeral teacher-talk or notes on the board. It will have to set itself objectives that transcend enhanced understanding of lessons or the reconfiguring of power in interpersonal relations in the classroom. In some contexts, for translanguaging to serve as a rejoinder to a politicised 'E' in EMI, features enregistered as named local languages must be valued enough to become integral parts of the repertoire employed in presenting core content across subjects on offer, in writing course material and in providing assessment tasks (Antia & Dyers, 2019). Translanguaging must support a local educational material development industry. In all contexts, it will have to be generative of discourses and practices that stave off convergence, promoting 'flexible multiplicity' (García, 2009a) instead.

Without a doubt, this book is a treasure trove of material for reflecting on translanguaging as a project in theory construction, in pedagogical practice and in the political economy of languaging in a clearly circumscribed context.

Bassey E. Antia
University of the Western Cape, Bellville, South Africa

Introduction

BethAnne Paulsrud, Zhongfeng Tian
and Jeanette Toth

This volume presents a compilation of studies from across the globe, all investigating multifarious intersections of *translanguaging* and *English-medium instruction* (EMI). Although translanguaging involving the use of multiple languages may be seen as paradoxical in classrooms where instruction is nominally English-only, the phenomenon of translanguaging – as a theoretical perspective and a pedagogical practice – in such contexts is, in fact, not a new one. While employing English as the sole intended language of instruction has long been prevalent in widely diverse linguistic contexts, the ensuing reality has been a plethora of de facto policies as well as classroom materials and methods that rarely are monolingual. What is new in this volume is therefore not the fact that EMI and translanguaging may exist side by side, but rather that these contexts are now studied with an innovative understanding of the affordances available for learning, communicating, building identity, dismantling hierarchies, promoting social justice, and resisting monolingual ideologies when EMI and translanguaging are allowed to be juxtaposed.

In this introductory chapter, we begin with an overview of EMI and translanguaging, tracing their origins and current definitions. We then briefly present the chapters of the volume and how they relate to the intersections of EMI and translanguaging as both concepts and practices.

EMI: English-Medium Instruction

Although it is but one of many global languages, English has a particularly privileged status as it has in many cases become the de facto lingua franca in communication involving speakers of different languages. Increasingly, English is not only the language of choice for international business and media, but also as a medium of instruction in contexts where it is not a majority language. Perhaps due to the perceived socioeconomic value associated with the improved proficiency in English that stakeholders may attribute to the increased exposure to English, EMI programmes may be seen as a way of attracting students in a competitive global education market (Doiz *et al.*, 2011; Paulsrud, 2019). However, while Rose and

McKinley (2018: 113) make the point that 'internationalization is viewed at its worst as an economic ploy to drum up student numbers and tuition', it may also be considered 'a way to positively influence universities' global outlook'. Although educational institutions at the primary, secondary and tertiary level offer EMI for a variety of reasons, these programmes nonetheless provide a space where students from different linguistic and cultural backgrounds meet on common linguistic ground in shared learning experiences.

Definitions

The concept of EMI has not been easily or consistently defined in either research or practice. Related terms include the following: teaching English to speakers of other languages (TESOL; Pecorari & Malmström, 2018); integrating content and language in higher education (ICLHE; Pérez-Vidal, 2015); content and language integrated learning (CLIL; Nikula *et al.*, 2016); English-medium education in multilingual university settings (EMEMUS; Dafouz *et al.*, 2016); and English-medium education (EME; Gardner, 2012). Whereas TESOL is mainly concerned with teaching the English language, approaches such as ICLHE and CLIL focus on language as well as content, with an aim to integrate them in instruction. By contrast, EMI does not necessarily include such integration, as its 'overarching teacher focus is on content' (Macaro, 2018: 8). Little attention is thus given to language issues in EMI (Toth, 2018a), perhaps due to a general lack of specific language goals in many EMI programmes (Yoxsimer Paulsrud, 2014). After comparing several definitions across recent studies, Pecorari and Malmström (2018: 499) have identified 'four characteristics of EMI settings', which they summarise as follows:

(1) English is the language used for instructional purposes.
(2) English is not itself the subject being taught.
(3) Language development is not a primary intended outcome.
(4) For most participants in the setting, English is a second language (L2).

These characteristics can be considered to align with Macaro's (2018: 1) definition of EMI: the 'use of the English language to teach academic subjects (other than English itself) in countries or jurisdictions where the first language of the majority of the population is not English'. The term EMI has often been associated with secondary and tertiary education, yet this definition can be applied broadly to also include primary education as well, and is appropriate for all of the contexts addressed in this volume.

EMI in global research

In recent years, research on EMI has been gaining attention, with a number of edited volumes devoted to the topic (see, for example, Dimova *et al.*, 2015; Doiz *et al.*, 2013; Fenton-Smith *et al.*, 2017). The phenomenon of teaching subject content through the medium of English in contexts where it is not a majority language is not a new one, although internationalisation trends in education have raised concerns in the research community regarding how EMI programmes are equipped to meet the needs of learners. Shohamy (2013: 203) has highlighted a number of issues associated with learning content through 'a language that is not fully familiar to students'. These issues include equity in learning conditions for different student groups, bias in assessment through a second language, and outcomes of content learning versus development of language proficiency (Shohamy, 2013). Likewise, in their systematic review of EMI in higher education, Macaro *et al.* (2018: 36) state that there is as yet insufficient evidence that EMI benefits the development of English proficiency with no cost to students' content learning. They maintain that 'key stakeholders have serious concerns regarding the introduction and implementation of EMI' (Macaro *et al.*, 2018: 45), calling for studies of EMI classroom discourse that demonstrate 'the kind of practice which may lead to beneficial outcomes' (Macaro *et al.*, 2018: 36).

Although limited in number and scope, there have been a few such studies of EMI programmes in secondary education, where classroom discourse in which multiple languages (rather than English-only) are employed has been shown to potentially promote content learning (see, for example, Paulsrud & Toth, 2020; Yoxsimer Paulsrud, 2014). Similarly, research on EMI in Sweden at the primary school level has found that in spite of language hierarchies privileging the use of English in EMI, students' use of the local language – here, Swedish – allowed access to the EMI subject content and encouraged participation in the lessons (Toth, 2018a; Toth & Paulsrud, 2017). While Pecorari and Malmström (2018: 499) note that the practice of conducting instruction in English can be considered to be 'axiomatic' in EMI settings, practices that include the use of other languages may thus also be present in EMI classrooms, such as in the form of textbooks, support words and peer scaffolding (see, for example, Paulsrud & Toth, 2020; Toth & Paulsrud, 2017). In many cases, such practices reflect *translanguaging* as both theory and pedagogy.

Translanguaging

Owing to its potential to build on the dynamic bilingualism of learners (Lewis *et al.*, 2012b), the term *translanguaging* has caught the imagination of many bilingual educators and scholars across global contexts (e.g. Adrian Blackledge, Suresh Canagarajah, Angela Creese, Ofelia García, Nancy Hornberger, Li Wei, Angel Lin, Leketi Makalela) in the 21st century. Originally coined as *trawsieithu* when it was first developed in Welsh education circles in the 1980s (Williams, 1994), its definition and use have been extended from Welsh-English bilingual classrooms to classrooms across international contexts (e.g. Blackledge & Creese, 2010; Lin & He, 2017; Mazak & Carroll, 2016), as well as from classroom pedagogical practices to bilinguals' everyday meaning-making practices (e.g. García, 2009a; García & Li Wei, 2014). More importantly, the concept of trans-languaging has been infused with social justice purposes, with the possi-bilities of challenging linguistically structured inequalities and transforming language-minoritised students' learning environments (e.g. Flores & García, 2013; García & Sylvan, 2011). Similar to the increasing research interest on EMI, the past decade has also witnessed an ever-growing boom in educational research focusing on translanguaging. While a comprehensive review of the term translanguaging is beyond the scope of this chapter (for a full review see, for example, Conteh, 2018; García & Lin, 2017; Li Wei & García, 2016; Paulsrud *et al.*, 2017a; Poza, 2017; Vogel & García, 2017), we briefly explicate the concept here from two perspectives: translanguaging as theory and translanguaging as pedagogy.

Translanguaging as theory

As theory, translanguaging represents an epistemic shift from tradi-tional theorisations of bilingualism as two separate, bounded language systems. Instead, a translanguaging perspective affords a holistic, dynamic view of bilingualism (García, 2009a; Grosjean, 2010). Translanguaging focuses on the observable, communicative practices of bi/multilinguals and posits that they have a unitary linguistic repertoire composed of meaning-making features that are selected and deployed in different con-texts (García & Li Wei, 2014). Translanguaging theory takes the point of view of speakers themselves to describe bilinguals' flexible and fluid use of language features to mediate social and cognitive activities (García & Kleyn, 2016). Through this lens, bilingual speakers/writers are seen as creative and critical language users (Li Wei, 2011), using the totality of their linguistic resources 'without regard for watchful adherence to the socially and politically defined boundaries of named (and usually national and state) languages' (Otheguy *et al.*, 2015: 283).

Translanguaging was borne out of a need to empower speakers from language-minoritised communities, to protect their language rights as well as to affirm their complex discursive practices (García, 2009a; García & Kleifgen, 2018). Such mixing of different linguistic (and semiotic) codes to perform identity, creativity and criticality is thereby seen as a normative practice of bilingual speakers, instead of being stigmatised according to a monolingual norm in society (Li Wei, 2018). In this sense, translanguag-ing theory seeks 'to dismantle named language categories and counters ideologies that position particular languages as superior to others and the language practices of monolinguals as superior to those who are said to speak with linguistic resources that go beyond the strict boundaries of named languages' (Vogel & García, 2017: 6). As a theory, it thus challenges colonial and modernist-era structuralist ideologies of language standardisation (Makoni & Pennycook, 2007) by liberating and privileging language-minoritised speakers' bilingual performances and legitimising all their linguistic varieties.

Translanguaging as pedagogy

As pedagogy, translanguaging originally referred to requiring students to deliberately switch the language mode of input and output in bilingual Welsh/English classrooms (e.g. if students read a book in Welsh, then they wrote a text in English). Williams (2002) suggests that this type of language alternation strategy often uses the stronger language to develop the weaker language, thus contributing toward a potentially relatively balanced development of a child's two languages.

In recent years, García (2014) has argued for the use of translanguaging as both a constructivist and a transformative bilingual pedagogy in classrooms. As a pedagogy, it refers to 'the ways in which bilingual students and teachers engage in complex and fluid discursive practices that include, at times, the home language practices of students in order to "make sense" of teaching and learning, to communicate and appropriate subject knowledge, and to develop academic language practices' (García, 2014: 112). Translanguaging pedagogy seeks to create a heteroglossic, inclusive space for all learners to draw upon their full linguistic repertoires to acquire, understand and demonstrate knowledge (Khote & Tian, 2019). In this space, bi/multilingualism is acknowledged as a resource and teachers strategically incorporate students' cultural and linguistic funds of knowledge in academic tasks while also showing students 'when, where, and why to use some features of their repertoire and not others, enabling them to also perform according to the social norms of named languages as used in schools' (García & Kleyn, 2016: 15). Therefore, translanguaging pedagogy holds the promises of 'support[ing] young people in sustaining the cultural and linguistic competence of their communities while simultaneously offering access to dominant cultural competence' (Paris, 2012: 95). It empowers language-minoritised students by focusing on their marginalised voices and supporting their positive identity development. Ultimately, translanguaging pedagogy aims to advance a social justice agenda to ensure that all students are educated deeply and justly (Tian & Link, 2019), and that all linguistic resources are seen as legitimate for learning (Rosén & Wedin, 2015).

EMI and Translanguaging: The Present Volume

This volume comprises 11 theoretical and empirical studies, all addressing translanguaging in EMI settings across the globe. It commences with Sahan and Rose's problematisation of the 'English-only hegemony' in tertiary education offering EMI. A number of other chapters also address translanguaging in universities, offering studies spread over a wide context, from South Africa (Luckett & Hurst-Harosh) and Malawi (Reilly) in the Global South to studies of Asian contexts, such as Cambodia (Boun & Wright), Japan (Adamson & Fujimoto-Adamson) and Kazakhstan (Goodman, Kerimkulova & Montgomery). In addition to these studies, Dalziel and Guarda present an Italian perspective on translanguaging in a European tertiary setting, while Pun's study of science classes in Hong Kong affords an understanding of translanguaging at the secondary level. Meanwhile, the chapters focusing on the primary level offer unique considerations of EMI, as they expand the field beyond secondary and tertiary education. In their chapters, Crisfield, Gordon and Holland investigate a private school in Kenya, Probyn considers research on the primary level in the postcolonial South African context, and Mohamed explores translanguaging practices among young learners outside the school context in the Maldives.

One assumption associated with EMI is the belief that the more students are exposed to English in lessons, the more fluent they will become (Macaro, 2018: 88). According to Pecorari and Malmström (2018: 497), 'EMI presupposes and is enabled by the ability of all participants (e.g. teachers, students, administrative staff) to use English as a lingua franca'. Thus, the paradox is that the expectation that more exposure leads to greater proficiency also relies on the students having enough proficiency to manage the EMI lesson. This illogicality may be assuaged through pedagogical translanguaging practices that do not limit students to English as a language for learning, recognising that simply because students (or teachers) choose EMI does not mean that they have the ability to manage the EMI lesson. Jaspers (2018), however, warns us that the transformative claims of translanguaging pedagogies cannot be taken for granted because translanguaging research 'always needs to be considered against the background of *continuing inequalities, predominant discourses, local circumstances*, and *personal considerations*' (Jaspers, 2018: 7, emphasis added). In other words, it is essential to recognise that context matters and translanguaging pedagogies must be strategically and purposefully planned, designed and implemented considering multiple contextual factors at both macro and micro levels, such as imbalanced power dynamics among languages, learner background, programme context and lesson goals. In the studies in the volume, the authors do consider issues such as practices, policies, language ideologies, language hierarchies, attitudes, beliefs, social justice and the imagined self, with a focus on the particularities of their own contexts. The chapters here do not focus on outcomes of EMI programmes, nor on the proficiency of the stakeholders participating in such programmes per se, but rather on a diverse range of themes exploring what happens on EMI programmes when translanguaging is afforded space. Some of the many themes illustrating the crossroads of EMI and translanguaging are briefly presented below.

A translanguaging perspective may offer affordances rather than constraints for EMI practices in the classroom and, as **Adamson and Fujimoto-Adamson** state, both pedagogical challenges as well as opportunities. In their study of pedagogic practices of translanguaging, they relate how translanguaging strategies provide scaffolding for less proficient students, or deepened understanding for more proficient students, creating a responsive environment for teaching and learning. **Dalziel and Guarda** identify several functions of translanguaging in the classroom, such as task management and strengthened student cooperation, especially as speakers from different linguistic and cultural backgrounds interact. Likewise, **Goodman, Kerimkulova and Montgomery** describe how allowing flexible language use also encourages transfer of academic skills among university students. These findings reflect those of **Luckett and Hurst-Harosh** who, also in the tertiary context, see how student engagement can increase as opportunities for 'drawing on funds of contextual knowledge' expand.

As seen in numerous previous studies (e.g. Ali, 2013; Bolton et al., 2017; Borg, 2016; Coleman et al., 2018), the expectation (be it implicit or explicit) with EMI has often been that students are already highly proficient in English, and prepared for instruction to be solely through the medium of English. However, this is not always the case (Jiang et al., 2019), as students in EMI programmes still benefit from the flexible use of all of their linguistic resources for accomplishing lessons. Studies such as **Probyn**'s reveal how interventions that develop translanguaging pedagogies in the multilingual primary classroom can instead promote both epistemic access and identity affirmation, when teachers explicitly adopt heteroglossic orientations in classrooms. Likewise, **Pun**'s study illustrates how translanguaging spaces in the classroom encourage peer scaffolding for developing both content and language knowledge (see also Toth, 2018a).

Possible tensions between official and de facto language policies may arise due to the Englishisation of education (Coleman, 2006; Dafouz et al., 2016; Hultgren, 2018). **Reilly** notes that 'language-in-education policies through a monoglossic lens' do not reflect the realities of multilingual spaces, such as the university context in Malawi. **Sahan and Rose**, as well, argue against policies promoting English-only ideologies, and call for a resistance to monolingual educational practices in the EMI classroom. As a means to this, **Probyn** stresses the need for more targeted preservice and in-service teacher training, to ensure that teachers know how to develop positive, flexible translanguaging pedagogies and thus promote social justice in the diverse classrooms of many contexts (see also Paulsrud & Zilliacus, 2018).

Previous research on EMI in upper secondary schools has found that translanguaging offers a disruption of language hierarchies (Yoxsimer Paulsrud, 2014; see also García & Li Wei, 2014). According to Risager (2012), levels of language hierarchy can range from the macro to the micro. Studies in this volume reveal how translanguaging can unravel hierarchies, both those implemented by institutions governing school decisions and those created de facto in everyday lessons. In their chapter, **Boun and Wright** maintain that translanguaging practices bolster all languages in the EMI classroom (not just English), in order 'to support multiple languages and literacies, irrespective of the status and spread of such languages'. Furthermore, **Crisfield, Gordon and Holland** argue that translanguaging practices in an elite international school actually afford ethical bilingual education by granting greater status to the local language, Kiswahili.

Mohamed, in her study of young children using their linguistic resources creatively in storytelling, articulates: 'The English-first ideology promoted by schools is out of sync with the sociolinguistic reality of the everyday languaging in which young people in the 21st century engage.' She sees the possibilities for translanguaging practice to empower young children in their linguistic and cultural identities. This is echoed in **Reilly**'s study, where he concludes that 'the use of translanguaging allows students to effectively perform their identities as young, educated Malawians'.

This brief overview has only offered a glimpse of the rich understandings offered by new research at the crossroads of EMI and translanguaging. Our aim with this volume is to address the gap in publications by presenting a global view of EMI in relation to translanguaging theory and pedagogy. The studies within are of interest to those who are curious about the roles of languages in the EMI classroom and who want to know more about EMI settings where students and teachers are allowed – or even encouraged – to use their entire linguistic repertoires for communicating and learning.

1 Problematising the E in EMI: Translanguaging as a Pedagogic Alternative to English-only Hegemony in University Contexts

Kari Sahan and Heath Rose

Introduction

Despite an increasing body of research that challenges native speaker hegemony, English-only ideologies remain strong in language policy and education, including English-medium instruction (EMI). First language (L1) use in second or foreign language (L2) classrooms has been energetically debated in the field of second language acquisition (SLA) for decades, and most language education researchers now agree on the benefits that other languages can offer learners in instructed educational contexts. This understanding, however, has yet to transfer to many EMI settings, especially those that have developed separately from language teaching curricula. Policies guiding the implementation of EMI in higher education are often motivated by top-down political ideologies that insist on English-only or English-always use in the classroom (Kirkpatrick, 2017). These policies are often driven by the belief that immersive settings better fulfil the language development aims of EMI programmes, even if such aims are not explicitly stated in EMI curricula. Rose and Galloway (2019: 195) note that 'a language development objective is not openly declared in definitions of EMI, which makes it distinct from other forms of content-related language teaching models', but many institutions hold an 'expectation that English-language proficiency will develop in tandem with subject discipline knowledge'.

In this chapter, we argue that the 'E' in EMI should not be interpreted to mean English-only. We assert that teachers and students should be

1

encouraged to use and embrace their multilingual resources, including the entirety of their linguistic repertoires. We support this claim by drawing first on research examining L1 use in the EMI classroom. Noting that the majority of this research has investigated code-switching, we then argue that the fluidity of language use in EMI classes may be better characterised as translanguaging. Rather than categorising languages as discrete entities, translanguaging frames language use as a performative act in which users construct and interpret meaning based on the resources available in their linguistic repertoires (Canagarajah, 2013a). Thus, multilingualism is a strength compared to monolingualism, as it multiplies the linguistic resources available to users. Given the inherently multilingual nature of the EMI classroom, translanguaging captures how teachers and students move freely across language boundaries. We also argue that translanguaging practices should be embraced as a pedagogical tool and a natural feature of multilingual communication, in order to combat ideologies of EMI as English-only and English-always. We illustrate our points by drawing upon examples from recent research, and we present examples from one of the author's own empirical research studies on EMI practices at universities in Turkey.

L1 Use and Multilingual Practices in EMI

Research within foreign language education has suggested that L1 use has a facilitative effect on L2 learning (Anton & DiCamilla, 1998; Cook, 2001; Swain & Lapkin, 2000). Ferguson (2009: 231) proposes that the L1 serves 'as a communicative and pedagogic resource in bilingual contexts, especially where pupils struggle to understand difficult subject matter whilst simultaneously learning a foreign language, one that is nominally the official medium of instruction'. With this in mind, previous studies have focused on the use of L1 in EMI contexts, with much of this research conducted from the perspective of code-switching (Airey, 2012; Lo & Macaro, 2012; Tarnopolsky & Goodman, 2014). Such studies have sought to analyse the purpose of switches between linguistic codes, often comparing the role of L1 with that of English. Airey (2012) describes EMI at Swedish universities as a situation of parallel language use, whereby course material is assigned in English but lectures are often given in Swedish. Similarly, drawing from the findings of an ethnographic study of EMI at a Swedish university, Söderlundh (2013) suggests that language choice is governed by emergent norms in the classroom. She found that English was typically used for 'on-task' discussions and the L1 was used for closed discussions between L1 speakers, and that code-switching occurred most commonly for single word translations. Tarnopolsky and Goodman (2014) found that the L1 was used in EMI classrooms in Ukraine for facilitative functions such as establishing rapport, disciplining students and improving comprehension through explanations of content-specific terminology.

Similarly, in a study based in Hong Kong, Evans (2008) found that teachers used their shared L1 when talking to students individually or discussing non-academic topics, and that code-switching served to introduce and clarify new vocabulary items. These findings suggest that EMI classrooms often do not achieve 'the English-only immersion programme envisaged by policymakers' (Evans, 2008: 495), as L1 use appears to be a common practice across global EMI contexts.

The use of L1 in EMI classrooms should not be surprising. Li Wei and Martin (2009) argue that code-switching is a natural bilingual behaviour but attracts attention in the classroom because language education policies tend to be shaped by top-down monolingual ideologies that discourage multilingual practices (see, for example, Probyn, this volume). The literature on code-switching in EMI classrooms is valuable as it highlights the pedagogical functions of L1 and supports our assertion that the EMI classroom is inherently a multilingual space. However, this research is limited in that it analyses language use in categorical terms, which does not necessarily capture how teachers and students move freely across language boundaries in bilingual classrooms. Fitting within the multilingual turn in SLA (see May, 2014), we suggest that translanguaging is an appropriate framework to capture the range of multilingual practices in the EMI classroom.

How is Translanguaging Different from Code-Switching?

Creese and Blackledge (2015: 26) assert that a 'translanguaging approach to teaching and learning is not about code-switching, but rather about an arrangement that normalises bilingualism without diglossic functional separation'. In other words, translanguaging is not a theoretical alternative to code-switching; rather, it proffers an ontological, epistemological and axiological shift in thinking about language use and bilingualism in the classroom. Translanguaging is norm-emergent and based in the practices of the individual rather than imposed by prescriptive standards: it 'takes as its starting point the language practices of bilingual people' (García & Li Wei, 2014: 22), thereby challenging assumptions of monolingual normativity. García (2009a: 45) states that translanguaging practices are the *multiple discursive practices* in which bilinguals engage in order to *make sense of their bilingual worlds*' (original emphasis). In other words, translanguaging is the practice of bringing together and enacting linguistic features that belong to multiple named languages and, in doing so, it reveals the arbitrary nature of those named language boundaries. Translanguaging 'leads us away from a focus on languages as distinct codes to a focus on the agency of individuals engaged in using, creating, and interpreting signs for communication' (Creese & Blackledge, 2015: 26). The distinction between code-switching and translanguaging is thus ideological (Lewis *et al.*, 2012a) in that code-switching assumes clear boundaries between named languages, which are distinct and separate from one another. As its starting point, however, translanguaging recognises named languages as social constructs.

García and Li Wei (2014: 22–23) illustrate the difference between a traditional understanding of code-switching in bilingualism and a translanguaging perspective on language use with the example of the language function on an iPhone: the language settings on an iPhone allow users to select a particular language, such as English or Spanish. This is a code-switching epistemology whereby one language is selected at a given time and users can 'switch' between languages by adjusting the settings on their phone. A translanguaging epistemology, however, is more analogous to text messaging whereby users may select features from their entire linguistic repertoire, including emojis and other visual features, to encode their message. Whereas the language settings on the phone limit the user to a single named language, the language practices of the user when texting are more dynamic and fluid. A translanguaging epistemology is built on this premise: rather than being limited to the constraints of a single language, bilinguals select from their entire linguistic repertoire to construct meaning.

While traditional conceptions of bi-/multilingualism view the bilingual as an individual with the ability to communicate, to varying degrees, in two or more distinct, autonomous languages, translanguaging instead perceives of the multilingual linguistic resources of the bilingual as a single, continuous linguistic repertoire (García & Li Wei, 2014). In other words, the bilingual is not two monolinguals added together. As such, translanguaging allows for a space to overcome the notion of code-switching resulting from linguistic deficit. From a translanguaging perspective, bilinguals do not code-switch because they do not perform language practices based on monolingual norms. Rather, 'both languages are used in a dynamic and functionally integrated manner to organise and mediate mental process in understanding, speaking, literacy, and not least, learning' (Lewis *et al.*, 2012a: 655).

Translanguaging offers an ontological perspective that emphasises the fluidity of language use rather than the rigid boundaries of named languages, which it acknowledges as social constructs rather than objective or 'natural' occurrences. '[L]anguages do not exist as real entities in the world and neither do they emerge from or represent real environments; they are, by contrast, the inventions of social, cultural and political movements' (Makoni & Pennycook, 2007: 2). Research on translanguaging considers the entirety of an individual's linguistic repertoire and understands language use as an individual's autonomous ability to enact elements of that linguistic repertoire.

Why Translanguaging in EMI?

By challenging assumptions of monolingual norms, translanguaging allows for an explicit focus on social justice and applies a critical lens to traditional approaches of understanding language use in bilingual classrooms. Thus, we suggest that translanguaging offers an appropriate framework through which to understand language use in the EMI classroom, an inherently multilingual space, and to challenge the ideological notion that EMI education should be English-only. Because 'translanguaging as a concept tries to move acceptable practice away from language separation' (Lewis *et al.*, 2012a: 659), it has powerful implications for teachers and students in EMI settings, where it would allow bilinguals to utilise the entirety of their linguistic resources for the purposes of teaching and learning. Language education policies that codify monolingualism through a one-language-at-a-time ideology reinforce the perception of bilingualism as two separate linguistic systems and code-switching as a result of this separation. However, a shift in pedagogy that perceives language use in terms of a continuous and integrated linguistic repertoire rather than as separate, inherently distinct languages normalises multilingual practices. Put simply, translanguaging normalises the practice of multilinguals learning subject matter multilingually.

In the context of EMI, this is particularly important as EMI is often implemented in a top-down fashion as a result of globalising political and economic forces. These forces inherently privilege certain groups over others (such as monolingual English speakers over non-native English speakers), and these inequalities are exaggerated with respect to socioeconomic differences, including access to English and English language learning resources, which are not evenly distributed across geographic and socioeconomic lines. An ideological stance that insists upon English-only use in EMI education posits English as the only gatekeeper to knowledge, and students who have not had the privilege of high-quality English education are denied access to certain forms of knowledge or career advancement. However, a position towards EMI that embraces translanguaging as a normalised classroom practice envisions the potential for students to learn through the medium of English, thus gaining access to global scientific discourses, while also acknowledging the diversity of linguistic resources in the EMI classroom and the value of knowledge in other languages.

A translanguaging perspective is powerful in EMI contexts because the EMI classroom is inherently a bi-/multilingual space. If the primary aim of EMI is content teaching and learning, translanguaging encourages the use of all linguistic resources available to teachers and students – including but not limited to English – to make sense of academic content knowledge. EMI policies are often justified on the basis of English's status as the global lingua franca and as the language of science and academia. In addition to improving university rankings and attracting international students and staff (Wächter & Maiworm, 2015; Wilkinson, 2013), policy makers argue that EMI allows students to access the plethora of scientific research published in English. Thus, English is framed as *the* language of science. However, Mazak and Herbas-Donoso (2014: 31) suggest that the tension 'between English as the only language of science and the reality of multilingual people "doing" science multilingually ... creates a sociocultural context ripe for translanguaging' in EMI classrooms. From a translanguaging perspective, EMI is not English-only because the teachers and students are not English-only monolinguals. They are able to access subject content matter and engage with scientific ideas beyond those available in English-only. Translanguaging research seeks to understand how multilinguals enact their multilingual linguistic repertoires to construct meaning.

Examples from Research in EMI Contexts

In the following section, we review empirical studies on translanguaging practices in EMI classrooms in order to illustrate that translanguaging is not merely an ideologically driven construct, but one that is built on a growing body of research to support its use in subject learning. The research reviewed in this section illustrates how translanguaging in EMI classrooms resists a monolingual mindset that only validates English as the language of learning. As Lin and He (2017) note, research on EMI classroom practices that go beyond the monolingual medium of instruction principle is still limited. This is particularly true of research conducted in university classrooms.

At the primary and secondary school levels, researchers have examined translanguaging practices in EMI classrooms to highlight the fluidity of language use for the purposes of teaching and learning. Toth and Paulsrud (2017) describe the translanguaging practices of two observed EMI science teachers at a primary and upper secondary school in Sweden. The findings from their research suggest that the language choices of teachers and students facilitate content learning in contexts where teachers and students have 'varying access to a range of linguistic resources' (Toth & Paulsrud, 2017: 191). They conclude that translanguaging allows for collective scaffolding, whereby students co-construct meaning with one another, and contributes to the development of scientific knowledge in both the L1 and the L2.

Similarly, Lin and He (2017) conducted an ethnographic study into the multilingual practices in an EMI/CLIL science classroom at a secondary school in Hong Kong. Their study consisted of 13 recorded classroom observations, which were analysed 'by identifying the scenarios of translanguaging in the CLIL classroom' (Lin & He, 2017: 231). The study was conducted in an educational context where the official school policy adhered to a monolingual ideology but where the teacher created a space of multilingual engagement. The authors present excerpts of classroom interaction which indicate the social and pedagogical benefits of L1 use in the EMI classrooms. From their analysis of classroom interaction, the authors conclude:

> If [the student]'s contribution [in the L1] ... had been successfully forbidden (by the English-only rule imposed by the school's official EMI policy) or discouraged by the teacher (who said, 'but I don't know your language'), this collectively constructed meaning-making chain, which turned out to have a valuable pedagogical scaffolding function, would not have been possible. (Lin & He, 2017: 232)

Even though the nature of these multilingual exchanges sometimes involved linguistic resources not shared by all participants – in some cases, not shared by the teacher – Lin and He (2017) argue that translanguaging serves a valuable pedagogical function, allowing students to engage in deeper meaning-making processes (see also Pun, this volume).

Less empirical research has been conducted on translanguaging practices at the university level, so the question remains as to how applicable the translanguaging practices found in secondary school contexts might be to tertiary classrooms, which traditionally consist of more lecture-style instruction. In a study on lecturers' attitudes towards EMI in Korea, Kim *et al.* (2018) investigated the attitudes of teaching staff in the humanities and social science departments at three technical (science and engineering) universities through questionnaires ($n = 37$) and interviews ($n = 9$). They found that lecturers reported confusion over the dual aims of content and language learning in EMI education, with one participant describing EMI as a situation of trying to 'catch two rabbits at a time' or, more accurately, 'catching none after chasing two' (Kim *et al.*, 2018: 117). While the EMI lecturers in this study reported the benefits of EMI in terms of internationalising the university, the participant lecturers suggested that content learning should be the primary aim of university-level EMI classes, noting that subject lecturers are content specialists who often have little or no training in language teaching. Further, the participants suggested that the L1 plays a key role in EMI classes and indicated that they preferred using the L1 when necessary in their own lectures. From here, Kim *et al.* (2018: 113) conclude that translanguaging can help students develop their academic skills in both languages and provide a 'meaningful and creative pedagogical approach to the education of truly bilingual persons'. However, what this study lacks is empirical evidence on how the L1 is used in the classroom and how it might play a facilitative role in content learning.

Nonetheless, Kim *et al.*'s (2018) conclusion that lecturers and students should be allowed more linguistic freedom in the implementation of EMI addresses the tension between the dual yet ambiguous aims of EMI: if content learning is to be prioritised over language learning, a translanguaging perspective on EMI might offer a theoretical and pedagogical alternative to English-only medium of instruction because it allows teachers to scaffold discipline-specific knowledge in the L2 with the help of the L1 and because it encourages students to engage with content material using all of their linguistic resources. Given that the primary concern of EMI education is content learning, an insistence on English-only instruction appears ideologically (mis)guided rather than pedagogically sound.

Much of the research investigating translanguaging practices in university settings has focused on bilingual university contexts. In an ethnographic case study consisting of classroom observations and interviews, Mazak and Herbas-Donoso (2015) describe the translanguaging practices of a science lecturer at a bilingual university in Puerto Rico. In this particular course, Spanish was the primary medium of instruction for lectures but the textbook and other course materials were printed in English. The authors use the case study to illustrate the tension between linguistic hierarchies and local realities: English materials are selected for content teaching because English is 'the' language of science and academia, but the classroom is not an English-only space because of the students' linguistic background and the local sociopolitical context. Thus, the researchers argue that the bilingual classroom is a space where bilingual teachers and students perform science bilingually. They illustrate the fluidity of language use in a bilingual science classroom with examples from their data:

> For example, we observed the professor speaking Spanish cognates of English terms while gesturing toward the written English text on a PowerPoint slide. This behavior is not a 'code-switch,' yet there is clearly a bilingual proficiency being evoked in that moment that is more appropriately captured through the notion of translanguaging. (Mazak & Herbas-Donoso, 2015: 703)

Because a code-switching perspective perceives languages as discrete entities, it is limited in its ability to capture the continuity with which bilingual teachers and students move across language boundaries, making meaning of English terms in the L1. Mazak and Herbas-Donoso (2015: 698) conclude that 'translanguaging served to apprentice the Spanish-dominant students into English for scientific purposes'. Reflective of the hegemonic status of English in academia, students were introduced to scientific discourse in English while also enacting linguistic resources in the L1 for meaning-making.

In their ethnographic study, Wang and Curdt-Christiansen (2019) find similar translanguaging practices at a bilingual university in China. Through classroom observations, interviews and document analysis, they investigate the translanguaging practices of teachers and students in a business management programme in China. The authors describe a situation of flexible bilingual language use and conclude that the use of two languages provides a richer understanding of content material. Wang and

Curdt-Christiansen (2019) argue that the recognition of bilingual education at this particular university gave rise to the practice of translanguaging in the classroom.

The empirical studies presented in this section illustrate how translanguaging validates bilingual practices in EMI contexts. While an official policy recognising bilingual education – as Wang and Curdt-Christiansen (2019) suggest – might provide more institutional legitimacy to multilingual practices, translanguaging occurs naturally in the interaction of bilingual speakers who share linguistic resources. Even in settings where official policy does not make concessions for bilingual models of education, bilinguals enact the entirety of their linguistic resources in the co-construction of meaning. In the following section, we attempt to illustrate this point by exploring cases from our own empirical research at universities in Turkey where the fluidity of language use in EMI classrooms is evident, even in contexts without explicit bilingual language policies.

A Case Study from Turkey

The research on translanguaging conducted by Mazak and Herbas-Donoso (2014, 2015) and Wang and Curdt-Christiansen (2019) is situated within universities with explicit bilingual language policies. In many EMI contexts, official language policy is often reflective of monolingual norms that envision a single (named) language of instruction in the classroom. English is selected as the language of instruction because of its hegemonic position as the language of science and business. Although policy envisions a monolingual classroom, we argue that the bi-/multilingual reality of the EMI classroom lends itself to multilingual teaching and learning, which can be understood through the lens of translanguaging. In order to illustrate this point made alongside other theoretical points made thus far, we will briefly present examples from our recent research on EMI in university-level engineering classrooms in Turkey.

The data presented in the following examples were collected as part of a larger research project led by one of the authors in May 2017 from undergraduate EMI classes in a mechanical engineering department at a state university in Turkey. The participant teachers were three EMI lecturers with at least five years' experience in lecturing through EMI. They were all Turkish nationals and L1 Turkish speakers who held doctoral degrees in mechanical engineering. Participation was voluntary, and consent was obtained from the participant teachers prior to the observations. The teachers' names have been anonymised in this study. Each lecturer's class was observed twice, resulting in a total of nearly 14 hours of classroom observations. The lessons were audio-recorded and transcribed for analysis. The following examples consist of one excerpt from each of the three lecturers' classes to demonstrate the fluidity of language use in EMI classrooms.

Excerpt 1.1 takes place in the middle of a third-year course called Strength of Materials. In the excerpt, the teacher (Burak) is solving a mathematical problem on the board. He elicits student responses to complete the equation:

Excerpt 1.1 *Solving an equation in Burak's class*

Speaker	Original (English, Turkish)	English translation
Teacher	Plus or minus?	
Student	Two **teta değil.**	**It's not** two **theta.**
Teacher	Sorry?	
Student	**Öyle değil, hocam.**	**It's not like that, teacher.**
Teacher	**Evet.**	[checks equation on board] **Yes.**
Student	**Hocam, bu** sigma x prime **birşey.**	**Teacher, this is** sigma x prime **something.**
Teacher	**Bir dakika,** you are right. So we have square root of x, okay, square root of sigma x minus sigma y over two, squared, plus tau squared, squared. This is the equation of maximum and normal stresses. We also obtained maximum shear stresses.	**One minute,** you are right. So we have square root of x, okay, square root of sigma x minus sigma y over two, squared, plus tau squared, squared. This is the equation of maximum and normal stresses. We also obtained maximum shear stresses.

Here, the teacher poses a question in English regarding the sign ('positive or negative') of the next term in the equation. The student responds in Turkish, not with the answer to the teacher's question but with a correction to what is written on the board ('it's not two theta'). The student's statement suggests that he is enacting multiple 'codes' at this point in the lesson: he is listening to the teacher in English while also reading the numerical equation on the board and enacting his L1 Turkish resources to process content information. When he notices an error in what the teacher has written, he volunteers this information in Turkish. In stating the correction, the student uses the phrase 'sigma x prime', in which the letter 'x' is pronounced in English and the term 'prime' is preferred over its Turkish equivalent. The student prefers to enact scientific terminology in English, suggesting that he is familiar with English academic discourse, although he discusses the issue of what is written on the board in Turkish. The teacher responds with two brief utterances in Turkish – *evet* (yes) and *bir dakika* (one minute) – before continuing the lecture in English. Furthermore, the student uses the Turkish honorific, *hocam*, a respectful term meaning teacher and used for university lecturers. In choosing to address his lecturer as *hocam*, the student reaffirms cultural practices specific to the local context. In this teacher–student exchange, meaning is negotiated in L1 Turkish while the language of content instruction remains English, illustrating the fluidity of language use in the classroom.

The process of meaning-making in multiple language 'codes' can also be seen in the following example, Excerpt 1.2, which is an excerpt from a second-year statics course. The teacher, Hamza, presents the students with an example problem in which they are asked to find the acceleration of a cart. The following exchange occurs as the student is trying to solve the problem:

Excerpt 1.2 *Solving a problem in Hamza's class*

Speaker	Original (Turkish, English)	English translation
Student	C uh o ivmede … eh altı düşükse … tamamen …	C uh at that acceleration … eh, if six is low … it's entirely …
Teacher	What's that?	
Student	Şu eksi üç galiba şu ivme sola giderse …	That's negative three, I think, if that acceleration goes to the left …
Teacher	Çok güzel bir soru.	That's a very good question.
Student	Az seviyede, orası aynı ivme değil, altı …	At a low level, it's not the same acceleration there, six …
Teacher	İşte bu problem için spesifik– For this problem, it is okay. But in reality, if you are, uh C, it's going to be the same answer. Okay? It's going to be the same answer, but if this C is let's say attached to another part, which is the second example in your book, then you need to do it like zero point two times uh cosine 60 i minus zero point two times 60 j. But these i's and j's are for this exit point.	Well, for this problem, it is specific– For this problem, it is okay. But in reality, if you are, uh C, it's going to be the same answer. Okay? It's going to be the same answer, but if this C is let's say attached to another part, which is the second example in your book, then you need to do it like zero point two times uh cosine 60 i minus zero point two times 60 j. But these i's and j's are for this exit point.

Here, the student translanguages to make sense of the problem regarding the acceleration of the cart. Although the problem was presented in L2 English, the student uses her entire linguistic repertoire to understand the problem and apply scientific concepts. As she works through the problem, she articulates her thoughts in Turkish. It is clear from the teacher's reaction ('that's a very good question') that the student is engaged deeply with the course material. However, the student does not limit her engagement to the L2. Rather, she thinks aloud in the L1, speaking her thoughts as they occur in short phrases rather than fully developed sentences. Although the student does not pose a direct question in the L1, it is clear from the exchange that the teacher has understood her developing thought process and engages to negotiate meaning. The teacher begins his explanation in the L1 before switching to the L2, perhaps out of respect for official policy that dictates that English should be the medium of instruction. However, the teacher permits the student to participate in the L1.

Arguably, if the teacher had adhered to a strict English-only policy, this student would be limited in her interaction, as she would not be allowed to enact the range of linguistic resources she appears to be using to make sense of the content material. By allowing the student to translanguage, discussing in the L1 a concept that was presented in the L2, the teacher has created a space for deeper content learning.

In the previous two excerpts, we have seen instances of translanguaging practices by students to engage with the lesson and content material. In Excerpt 1.3, the teacher, Yakup, translanguages to present course content in a second-year lecture on thermodynamics:

Excerpt 1.3 *Thermodynamics lecture from Yakup's class*

Speaker	Original (English, Turkish)	English translation
Teacher	Extended surface, we said. Okay. Let me show you how its construction is. This is a tube, okay? So, hot water flows through the tube. Now. Fin. I put fins over the lines, I mean, pipes. Fins. Uh. It's a very thin metallic sheet. Uh. **Aynen kitabınız, ders kitabınızın yaprakları gibi ince bir–**	Extended surface, we said. Okay. Let me show you how its construction is. This is a tube, okay? So, hot water flows through the tube. Now. Fin. I put fins over the lines, I mean, pipes. Fins. Uh. It's a very thin metallic sheet. Uh. **Just like your books, as thin as the pages of your textbooks.**
Student	**Hocam siz** blade **demiyor musunuz?**	Teacher, don't you say blade?
Teacher	Huh?	
Student	**Yani şey** blade **yani.**	I mean, like, blade, you know.
Teacher	**Yok, fin diyoruz,** transferle **birlikte, fin. Bunların adı fin. Evet. Dolayısıyla hava bu finlerinarasından akacak. İnce sık sık yerleştirilmiş finler, çapraz yönden akacak. Su boruların içerisindenakacak. Tamam mı? Eh geçirdiğiniz su, sıcak su ise havayı ısıtıyorsunuz demektir. Soğuk su,** chilled water **deriz buna. Soğuk su geçiriyorsunuz, havayı soğutuyorsunuz demektir. Eşanjör dediğimiz şey bu. Bunu ısı transferi derslerinde anlatacağım size.** So, we have heating coil which is a uh. Thin tube. [writing] Heat exchanger. [writing] It is called thin tube exchanger.	No, we call this **fin**, together with transfer it's **fin**. Their name is **fin**. Yes. So the air is going to flow between the fins. Thin, tightly placed fins, it's going to flow between them diagonally. The water flows through the pipes. Okay? Eh, the water that you're sending, if it's hot water, it means you're heating the air. Cold water, we call this chilled water. If you're sending chilled water, it means you're cooling the air. This is the thing we call exchanger. I'll explain this to you in the heat transfer courses. So, we have heating coil which is a uh. Thin tube. [writing] Heat exchanger. [writing] It is called thin tube exchanger.

In this excerpt, the teacher Yakup moves across language boundaries to present content knowledge. The teacher describes the structure of the extended surface in English, offering the term 'fin' to describe an aspect of its construction. Although the explanation later flows to L1 Turkish, the teacher retains the term 'fin', using it rather than its Turkish equivalent (*kanatçık*). The student asks for clarification, offering an English term he knows ('blade') to describe thin pieces of metal, similar in structure to the concept under consideration. In doing so, the student draws upon the resources available in his linguistic repertoire, and the teacher explains the bounds of domain-specific terminology ('with transfer it's fin'). Similarly, the teacher introduces the concept of 'chilled water'. Rather than directly translating the Turkish equivalent to 'cold water' or omitting an English translation, the teacher provides a discourse-specific term ('we call this chilled water'). Both teacher and student move fluidly across language boundaries, enacting the entirety of their linguistic repertoires to make meaning of scientific concepts. Notably, the teacher and student use scientific terminology in English, the language of the larger scientific community, while discussing scientific concepts in Turkish, the local language of their community.

These examples are typical of the language practices observed in EMI classes in this mechanical engineering department in Turkey. As teachers and students move fluidly across language boundaries, their translanguaging practices suggest that they enact the range of their linguistic resources for meaning-making. Language use is fluid, with scientific concepts presented and discussed in both the L1 and the L2 (see also Toth & Paulsrud, 2017). By translanguaging, the teacher scaffolds scientific and discipline-specific concepts, thus 'apprenticing' students into academic discourses in English while still building knowledge in the students' L1 (Mazak & Herbas-Donoso, 2014). In these examples, English is not *the only* language of science, nor is it *the only* medium of instruction. Rather than adhering to a top-down policy of monolingualism, teachers and students are enacting the entirety of the linguistic resources available to them in the teaching and learning of content knowledge.

Conclusion

In this chapter, we have argued that EMI should not be English-only instruction and we have illustrated through examples from our own research that it is not, in practice, English-only. The vast majority of EMI students and teachers are not monolingual, and to treat them as such deprives them of their real identities as multilingual language users. Given the inherently multilingual nature of the EMI classroom, we have suggested that translanguaging is an appropriate framework to capture the range of multilingual practices in which teachers and students engage during processes of teaching and learning. A translanguaging framework captures how teachers and students move freely across language boundaries. In EMI contexts, translanguaging practices reflect the importance of English as a lingua franca for academia and science as well as the particulars of the local sociocultural context, including the identity of teachers and students. Translanguaging practices illustrate how meaning is constructed in multiple languages simultaneously, with language flowing in conversational exchange to negotiate meaning of complex academic concepts. In short, translanguaging captures how multilinguals do science multilingually.

EMI is a multilingual endeavour, and should be viewed as such even when official policies advocate otherwise. Multilingual practices, like translanguaging, resonate with current movements in applied linguistics and language educational research, which are undergoing a multilingual turn in their theoretical perspectives. Rather than viewing the use of the L1 as a sign of deficit in English knowledge, we as teachers and researchers need to ensure that EMI stakeholders view the practices of translanguaging as a useful tool for successful education. This is especially relevant when the outcomes of curricula centre on the learning of subject knowledge, rather than the English language – as is the case for most EMI contexts.

Future research into translanguaging needs now to focus on how translanguaging can be used in EMI to better achieve the outcomes of subject learning. By mapping the functions and ways in which language boundaries are crossed, researchers might better understand the ways in which translanguaging can be used as an educational tool in multilingual classroom environments. Whether it is to maintain social or cultural norms, as in our first example of the student's use of an L1 honorific form to address the teacher; or to allow students the space to think aloud in the languages of their choosing, such as in our second example; or to discuss subject-specific L2 vocabulary by moving freely between the L1 and L2, as in our third example; translanguaging affords learners a freedom that an English-only ideology may stifle.

It may well be the case that some teachers and learners choose to adhere to majority-English language practices in their EMI studies. We want to emphasise that this perspective is not necessarily wrong, so long as it is an individual choice which is based on the freedom to apply one's multilingual resources when needed. Thus, to interpret the 'E' in EMI to mean English-only or English-always will inevitably constrain the educational environment and take away this freedom from teachers and students, and thereby erode students' learning potential.

2 Translanguaging in EMI in the Japanese Tertiary Context: Pedagogical Challenges and Opportunities

John L. Adamson and Naoki Fujimoto-Adamson

Introduction

This chapter explores the concept of translanguaging (TL) in, and in preparation for, English-medium instruction (EMI) in the Japanese tertiary context. It draws upon our studies into the perceptions and use of TL by teachers, language advisors and students at one newly established university. Without a precedent of a top-down language policy influencing these participants' determination of language policies, we have conducted several longitudinal studies through the first years of the university in EMI classes, in English classes adopting a content and language integrated learning (CLIL) approach to prepare students for EMI, and in a self-access learning centre (SALC) where bilingual language advisors support student learning for CLIL and EMI. This latter site of learning (SALC) was established to provide students with an autonomous space for self and collaborative language study, particularly in light of the emphasis the university places on EMI and academic English. As it was envisaged that our mostly monolingual Japanese students would struggle with the academic challenges of university-level EMI, use of the SALC has been strongly encouraged as it is a space where advice about language and lesson content can be exchanged. For that purpose, SALC advisors are cognisant with both language and EMI curriculum content.

As a backdrop to the studies referred to in this chapter, we would like first to provide a brief description of the university where they were conducted. Established in 2009 as a mixed four-year university, its main field of study is international studies and regional development (ISRD) with an annual intake of approximately 180 students, all of whom take compulsory first-year academic English classes. EMI courses in their major field (e.g. Chinese policy, economics, environment) are taught by Japanese and non-Japanese faculty. There is also a secondary school English language teacher minor in which English and Japanese faculty teach applied linguistics mostly in English. Two other smaller fields (nutrition and child studies) run smaller programmes with lower enrolment ($n = 80$), with fewer compulsory English classes and no EMI. In this sense, the newness of the university and the absence of a top-down, institutional language policy provide a unique opportunity to create a small evidence base to guide our own language policies.

Findings presented here are synthesised from our research into EMI instructor perceptions of student language and skills needs (Brown & Adamson, 2012, 2014), student perceptions of an academic English lecture course adopting a CLIL approach and analysis of students' English reports related to that class (Adamson & Coulson, 2014, 2015), EMI course materials encouraging strategic TL (Fujimoto-Adamson & Adamson, 2018), and SALC language use (Adamson & Fujimoto-Adamson, 2012). Collectively, these data provide insights into TL use and perceptions across various language, content and non-classroom 'learning spaces' (Savin-Baden, 2007: 13) key to students taking, or preparing for, EMI in the university. We view these perspectives critically as representing both pedagogical challenges to and opportunities for the development of language(s) policy in our particular context.

Turning to literature underpinning this study, we see TL, EMI, CLIL and self-access as key themes which inform our language practices and policies.

Reflections on Translanguaging

While much research into TL considers the wider issues of how languages are used in society and work in an age of increasing migration (Canagarajah, 2013b), our study is more concerned with the pedagogic practices of TL (Blackledge & Creese, 2010). TL research in educational contexts is particularly important for us as it considers, as García and Kano (2014: 271) outline, how non-Anglophone students use metalinguistic resources from their first language (L1) 'literacy practices' to negotiate second language (L2) writing processes. Rather than seeing languages employed in TL as 'additive' (García & Kano, 2014: 259), this type of bilingualism is regarded as a means to 'shuttle' between languages and literacies (Canagarajah, 2006: 26).

In this sense, TL transcends code-switching research which sees languages as separate systems and instead views the use of languages as emanating from the same 'linguistic repertoire' (Velasco & García,

2014: 7). Lee and Canagarajah (2018: 46) illustrate this in a study of a South Korean researcher who created a 'bricolage' of a research paper by organising bilingual resources physically around him. Similarly, Gallagher and Colohan's (2017) investigation into student TL in content instruction determined it as beneficial compared to not accessing the L1. The discoursal practice of TL in EMI was observed by Cross (2016: 15), who saw the L1 and L2 'oscillate' so students could concentrate on content, but Cross warned of the tension among some students as to whether L1 use was appropriate. Indeed, such tension between L1 and L2 literacy practices may entail the 'risk' (Thesen, 2014: 6) of the L1 being unaccepted in that learning context. However, few studies consider teacher proficiency in the students' L1 in TL, apart from Toth and Paulsrud (2017) who contrasted two EMI teachers with different competences in the local language (Swedish). Significantly, the teacher with limited proficiency in Swedish engaged his class in TL by utilising students proficient in English to aid struggling students, which holds resonance for our study where non-Japanese instructors nevertheless engaged in TL.

In terms of the site of TL practice, as Japan-based tertiary practitioners, TL represents a localised means to counteract the bias of monolingual, Anglophone disciplinary norms in this linguistically peripheral setting and to allow students and teachers greater opportunities to participate. This is achieved by offering student determination in language use, a stance aligned with Canagarajah's calls for 'local norms of relevance' in language policy (Canagarajah, 2005: xxvii). To exemplify this in our context, Brown and Adamson (2012, 2014) investigated the shift from strict monolingualism towards localising disciplinary pedagogy in our EMI provision to converge with the realities of diverse language proficiencies among our Japanese students and instructors.

EMI/CLIL in the Japanese Tertiary Context

Looking at the larger issues underpinning our university's moves into delivering content through English, EMI in Japan has spread in a non-uniform manner, primarily among elite universities funded by government initiatives to become 'global' (Ministry of Education, Culture, Sports, Science and Technology, hereafter MEXT, 2011) and thereafter among less prestigious institutions struggling to recruit students in a society with a declining birth rate. This critical situation for non-elite institutions, such as ours, is compounded by a reluctance towards long-term overseas study among the Japanese (Burgess, 2014) who see more relevance in domestic study (Imoto, 2013). Furthermore, Stigger (2018) notes that language policies from MEXT for EMI programmes in Japan remain unclear, with the consequence that local EMI practice rests upon instructor and student willingness and proficiency in English

(Ishikawa, 2011; Yonezawa, 2011). Despite some influx of foreign students, most students are monolingual Japanese, so questions arise as to whether disciplinary and pedagogic processes should adhere to those of an Anglophone university rather than local, pragmatic norms. This recalibration of language policy needs to be made in light of Brown and Iyobe's (2014) report in which only 5% of Japanese undergraduate students attend any EMI classes. Fundamentally, as Phan (2013) notes, Japanese faculty still imagine EMI typically as study abroad in Anglophone contexts, so when EMI in Japanese universities does take place, the overall purpose of English-only instruction – the monolingual 'E' in EMI – needs to be problematised (Brown & Adamson, 2014; see also Sahan & Rose, this volume). Commonly, Japanese students may not intend to embark upon content studies in an Anglophone context, but still wish to study EMI in their home country yet in a more linguistically accessible manner. As a natural consequence, English preparation courses for Japan-based EMI adopting a CLIL approach must also mirror local EMI practices in terms of language policy and move from the emphasis on language learning alone to the 'dual focus' (Coyle *et al.*, 2010: 1) on both language and content needs.

When Japanese enrol in EMI or CLIL instruction at the tertiary level, few studies look at TL practice. One key exception is Moore's (2017) study into Japanese tertiary learners' perceptions of L1/L2 use which reveals that more proficient students used their L1 less as they viewed the use of Japanese negatively. Less proficient students were inclined to use their L1 more as they wished to participate in tasks despite a lack of English ability and confidence. These findings contrast with findings from Adamson and Coulson (2014, 2015) in which lower proficiency students in a CLIL lecture course felt empowered by L1 use and by the opportunity to utilise their L1 content knowledge in writing tasks. Although Moore (2017) notes the role of improving L2 proficiency in student perceptions, Adamson and Coulson's studies see both proficiency and content knowledge as key to how students perceive course effectiveness for the local EMI goals for which their lecture course was designed. These content-focused goals concur with Lasagabaster's (2013) and Merino and Lasagabaster's (2015) advocacy of student L1 use in CLIL instruction, and suggest that interdisciplinary collaboration between content and language faculty has the potential to make CLIL instruction bilingual in nature. Furthermore, it questions the temporary role of L1 for the purpose of L2 production (Swain & Lapkin, 2013), instead positioning TL as a long-term strategy.

Positioning Self-Access as a Learning Space

Much literature surrounding self-access focuses on the integration of a SALC with the institution's educational curricula to maintain a sense of relevance (Gardner & Miller, 1999; Thompson & Atkinson, 2010). Other research has addressed its resources (Reinders & Lewis, 2006), autonomy (Little, 1995), and language advising by centre staff (Reinders *et al.*, 2004). While these aspects of self-access use retain significance for our centre, of particular importance is its language policy, since a SALC as a 'learning space' fundamentally differs in direction and purpose from a classroom environment (Savin-Baden, 2007: 13). As a SALC promotes autonomous study, advisors typically guide users in strategy use and goals in language learning, yet, as Candas (2011) warns, overly rigid self-direction may require occasional advisor intervention to shift personal policy, termed as 'organising circumstance' (Spear & Mocker, 1984: 4). In terms of language policy for a centre, some research advocates a monolingual 'English-only' policy (Gardner & Miller, 1999) to provide opportunities for target language use, whereas others counter this 'two solitudes' approach to language acquisition by integrating L1 use (Blackledge & Creese, 2010; Jacobson & Faltis, 1990) as used in multilingual contexts. Levine's (2011) stance in support of student use of their L1 sees it as a means to exercise their sense of autonomy. From the practical perspective of reducing anxiety among lower proficiency students, Lin (2005: 46) sees employment of the students' L1 as 'local, pragmatic coping tactics' and Martin (2005: 80) as promoting 'safe' language practice. Against this body of research in favour of L1 use in self-access, however, students may harbour rigid beliefs concerning language acquisition, and regard TL as inappropriate (Setati *et al.*, 2002a).

In light of the issues raised in the literature on TL, EMI/CLIL and self-access, our research objective is to reveal patterns of TL by teachers and students across the various 'learning spaces' (Savin-Baden, 2007: 13) on campus – EMI courses, CLIL language courses and a SALC – and to explore how language policies are locally determined.

A Synthesis of Studies

This synthesis of our studies involves analysis of data from multiple methods. Brown and Adamson's (2012, 2014) research into the compulsory first-year *kiso semi* class – a programme intended to prepare all students for the general academic demands of university study – involved interviewing content faculty about how the English language programme could support EMI. The semi-structured interviewing approach was intentionally adopted as it offered the interviewers the ability to delve further into questions (Kvale, 1996). In SALC research, recordings of student-to-student and language advisor-to-student interaction were made and questionnaires were distributed to all first-year university students about their perceptions and use of the centre (Adamson *et al.*, 2012). Discourse analysis of SALC interactions was conducted to see how TL unfolded in student- and advisor-determined interaction without teachers.

Further to this, perceptions of the centre were taken from annually conducted questionnaire research. English language class data were gathered over several years from questionnaires distributed in a lecture preparation class, a programme designed to prepare first-year students for the upcoming demands of EMI. These questionnaires focused on language use and student perceptions of how effective the class was for their EMI and other language programmes. EMI findings drew upon teacher materials and methods of instruction, and teacher perceptions of TL using those materials and methods in a collaborative autoethnography (CAE) (Chang *et al.*, 2013). CAE is a process of joint-narrativisation of experiences and beliefs among participants which encourages a co-construction of discourse. In this sense, it is potentially more probing than individual narratives as participants can support and challenge each other and ask for deeper explanations in a dialogue.

Collectively, this multi-methods study represents for us the opportunity to reflect critically upon these findings from the initial years since the university's establishment. In this sense, the methods constitute an 'intrinsic' case study (Stake, 1995) as the findings help to inform our current and future TL practices and policymaking. Informed consent was given by all participants across the studies. In the case of the CAE, the participants were the authors ourselves, so we have decided to reveal our identities in keeping with the reflective nature of that particular study. All other participants' identities are anonymised.

Evolving Findings from the Learning Spaces

We present our findings in a thematic and chronological manner to illustrate how our practices and perceptions of TL have evolved longitudinally.

Kiso semi findings

After the foundation of the university in 2009, Brown and Adamson (2014) conducted interviews with EMI content faculty from 2011 to 2012. As English language teachers, we wished to ascertain how our English language provision could prepare students for the demands of EMI. EMI instructors also taught a compulsory first-year *kiso semi* to equip students with academic skills, so they gave us insights from content instruction and also from their perspectives as instructors of general academic literacy. In interviews with them in English ($n = 7$: six Japanese and one non-Japanese), they recommended that English classes in the same first year expose students to both Japanese and English reading materials and that our monolingual English language provision shift as recorded in Excerpt 2.1 below with a Japanese teacher (JT):

Excerpt 2.1 *Interview with a Japanese teacher (Brown & Adamson, 2014: 12)*

JT: Students must base written work on multiple sources both Japanese and international, apply research skills, synthesize information, and understand differences between Japanese and international sources.

EMI faculty teaching *kiso semi* also expected students to 'develop an awareness of the difference between multiple [reading] sources, both Japanese and international', showing unexpected awareness of the benefits of drawing upon student linguistic repertoires, not simply for language learning benefits, but for content knowledge (Gallagher & Colohan, 2017). One remarked that Japanese and Western researchers tended to view international issues from different perspectives which needed to be highlighted in English classes. This finding led us to question the 'E' in English language preparation classes for EMI and showed an unexpected pragmatic propensity towards TL among content faculty.

SALC findings

Concurrent with this research into early expectations for the English language provision, research was also conducted into student use and perceptions of the new SALC. Adamson and Fujimoto-Adamson (2012) made several recordings of actual language use in the SALC and also asked all first-year students ($n = 240$) to give feedback on the centre in an annual questionnaire (Adamson *et al.*, 2012).

In terms of actual language(s) use in the SALC, three recordings were made. Firstly, three students were recorded interacting with advisors for approximately 15 minutes. The discourse analysis referred to code-switching terminology (intersentential and intrasentential) as it provides useful terms to explain the mechanical aspects of interaction in the L1 and L2. Intersentential switching between languages was the norm for students when discussing SALC tasks with advisors, as in Excerpt 2.2:

Excerpt 2.2 *Student intersentential code-switching*

Speaker	Original (Japanese)	English translation
Student	これはやらなくてもいいですか？	We don't need to do this, right?

However, advisors spoke exclusively in English with them. Interestingly, when the talk shifted off-task, intrasentential code-switching became more frequent among the students, as for example in Excerpt 2.3:

Excerpt 2.3 *Advisor intrasentential code-switching*

Speaker	Original (Japanese, English)	English translation
Advisor	We had 焼肉 for dinner.	We had **grilled beef** for dinner.

or in Excerpt 2.4:

Excerpt 2.4 *Advisor intrasentential code-switching*

Speaker	Original (Japanese, English)	English translation
Advisor	We had **なんか** ... a difficult time at the bus station.	We had **sort of** ... a difficult time at the bus station.

(**なんか** means 'sort of', to express vagueness in Japanese.) This appeared to show that inter- and intrasentential L1/L2 usage was theme-dependent. The second recording of an advisory session between a student and advisor about English writing over roughly 10 minutes was linguistically demanding so both spoke mostly Japanese, with English used only intrasententially to pinpoint specific language; for example, the advisor explained pronoun use as follows in Excerpt 2.5:

Excerpt 2.5 *Advisory intrasentential use of specific words*

Speaker	Original (Japanese, English)	English translation
Advisor	Travel agency **とか**, Paris の前に a はいらないよね, at じゃなくて in ね.	**When you use words like** travel agency etc., you don't need 'a' in front of Paris, not 'at', but 'in', OK.

In a third recording lasting about 45 minutes, six male students in an English circle injected Japanese words into their conversation for challenging lexis or concepts, such as ソーラン節 (traditional sea shanty songs), 正月 (New Year) and 雑煮 (traditional New Year soup). In contrast, longer stretches of Japanese sentences were observed when students wished to repair interaction on the point of breakdown, for example, when one student said in Excerpt 2.6:

Excerpt 2.6 *Student repair of interaction*

Speaker	Original (Japanese, English)	English translation
Student 1	よし、たまるぜポイントが。	**OK, I'm collecting points.**
Student 2	Yes, but no Japanese is allowed.	

Interestingly, as can be seen above, at this juncture another student replied, 'Yes, but no Japanese is allowed', revealing a student-imposed language policy to resist what was perceived as too much L1 use, which concurs with Setati *et al.* (2002a).

In the first years of the SALC's operation (2009–2011), questionnaires were distributed to all first-year students ($n = 240$) concerning their use of the centre and language policy (Adamson *et al.*, 2012). Turning firstly to language policy responses, in its first few years, the centre was divided into language zones by bold lines on the floor and signs ('English only' for most of the centre and 'Japanese or English allowed' for the area in front of the three language advisor desks). Responses regarding this policy showed that most students engaged in TL with each other despite the 'English only' rule, with one student remarking that 'the border is meaningless'. Another asked why advisors did not 'force people to speak English'. Such views were an indication that while some students regarded TL as their right in a non-classroom 'learning space' (Savin-Baden, 2007: 13) and as a means to exercise autonomy (Levine, 2011), others believed in enforced monolingualism as in the 'two solitudes' approach (Cummins, 2005a: 590; Gardner & Miller, 1999; Setati *et al.*, 2002a).

Lecture class findings

As in the findings from the *kiso semi* study, it was recommended to tertiary faculty in similar contexts that the ability to synthesise Japanese and English reading materials should be promoted; the focus of research then shifted to how English language classes embraced TL practices. In Adamson and Coulson (2014, 2015), attention was directed to English lecture classes as much EMI was delivered through lectures with large (from 50 to over 100) student numbers. The first-year lecture class was delivered to all 180 students in international studies and regional development and was intended to prepare students for the academic rigors of EMI. To achieve this, the student cohort was split proficiency-wise into two classes over one full academic year. The same course content of lecture listening practice and note-taking was combined in a multimodal manner with related reading in Japanese and English to culminate in an end of course report (1800 words minimum) in English. This report comprised summaries of notes accumulated over the year and critical synthesis of readings, as advocated by Lasagabaster (2013) and Merino and Lasagabaster (2015). Both lower and higher proficiency classes mirrored each other in content but were taught at differing pace and depth. Initially, with the divergence in language proficiency, it was expected that outcomes in report writing would differ according to language abilities.

Our 2014 study looked at bilingual questionnaire data (2011–2014) from biannual surveys into student perceptions of the course in terms of their own language improvement, the effectiveness of the course in preparing them for EMI, and – important for TL insights – the bilingual readings related to lecture content. Findings from the first and second semesters showed differences among students of lower proficiency in the first semester who were less positive about their language improvement and the effectiveness of the course for EMI compared to the higher proficiency group. By the end of the year, however, the lower proficiency students exhibited much higher levels of confidence about their language improvement and course effectiveness, whereas the higher proficiency group dipped slightly. As bilingual readings came more into effect in the second semester when writing their report, findings revealed both groups had positive attitudes towards bilingual reading content related to their report. A pattern emerged over three years, suggesting that initial class division based on pre-course language proficiency did not correlate with student perceptions of self-efficacy and course effectiveness. As the grading of students was based on both language and content foci (Coyle *et al.*, 2010), the final grades differed from language assessment alone. This was reflected in the surprising drop in confidence among higher proficiency students in the second semester who perhaps expected their grades to be higher due to initial self-perceptions of language ability. Overall, these findings suggested to us that the CLIL approach to assessment and the integration of TL readings were making the course more authentic and relevant to the students' local EMI.

Accompanying the questionnaire findings, data were also collected in 2012, asking a small number of students ($n = 35$) to make simple literacy maps illustrating what sources of advice and materials they drew upon for their final report. Literacy maps are similar to mind maps and show visually in bubbles the key people, materials and even classes that have informed students in their particular study. As TL practice could not be observed in non-class settings, it was felt that such student self-reporting of their literacy brokering could yield useful insights into language use in more autonomous contexts.

Findings compiled from the maps revealed where and from whom information was drawn apart from the lecture class teachers and materials; for example, other non-lecture class sources were used which clearly did not require English language use, as in 'online', 'friends and family' and Japanese 'content teachers'. Although maps could be drawn by a limited number of students (only one class could be accessed), findings indicated that the students' personal literacy networks were pragmatically focused on gathering relevant information and guidance in a manner similar to the 'bricolage' observed by Lee and Canagarajah (2018: 46). TL and access to L1 'literacy practices' (García & Kano, 2014: 271) can be assumed to have played a major role in this process.

To assess the role of TL in the final report required a focus on the final written product. In Adamson and Coulson (2015), we extended the analysis of the questionnaire findings and literacy maps to an investigation of L1 and L2 citation practice over three years (2011–2014) for 271 reports. We analysed reports firstly in terms of the average number of L1 references, the overall average number of references (L1 and L2), the percentage of L1 references used each year and the percentage of students using three or more L1 references. We also investigated if high grades correlated with L1 references. We see this analysis of end references as insightful to TL in the final product of academic writing.

The requirements for this report were that up to six references were encouraged and that L1 references were viewed as positive if the article content was relevant to the topic and could contrast well with English articles. Although no direct negativity was expressed on this aspect of TL policy, as Cross (2016) observed, we noted some scepticism among the student body when we announced that L1 sources were allowed. Analysis of the number of end references from 2011 to 2014 showed that the average number of L1 (Japanese) references used had actually dropped from two to one per report. Overall, the average total number of references used per report was steady at around three to four. The percentage of L1 references then naturally showed a dip from an initial 48% to 36%. Those using three or more references also showed a decrease from 36% to 15%.

Examining the differences between the two proficiency groups, it was observed that lower proficiency students frequently used L1 references, perhaps because of the ease of reading in their L1, yet in contrast to Moore's (2017) findings, higher proficiency students also were observed to read in the L1, possibly for the same reason. Upon questioning, it was found that this was because their L1 reading content often contrasted with views in L2 readings. Over the three years of analysis between final report grades and the number of L1 references, no clear pattern of higher L1 use correlated with the grade.

EMI findings

Moving now onto EMI practices, we investigated how we, as English language teachers, engaged in TL when teaching our own content courses, discourse analysis and sociolinguistics (Fujimoto-Adamson & Adamson, 2018: 209), and particularly how TL shaped language support for students of mixed proficiency. We drew upon examples of classroom practice to show how TL was not used simply to enhance understanding, but how L1 use was integrated into course content. One example illustrating this is from a sociolinguistics class in which students are required to reflect on gender bias in their own L1 writing system. In Japanese, the character for woman – 女 – is found in the words for 'jealous', 'hate' and 'noisy', all carrying negative connotations. Students are asked to reflect on and discuss whether they regard this as sexist.

Further to this L1 integration into course content, we also stressed the visual simplification of potentially difficult course content, a strategy mirroring the scaffolding of content proposed by Goodman (2014). In our discourse analysis materials on the topic of speech events, a continuum is drawn on the board which requires students to mark how formal or casual they feel common speech events in Japanese are (for example, talking to their mother on the phone, giving a graduation speech, speaking to an old teacher from school). Subsequent class discussion focuses on the students' relative positioning on the continuum of the speech events.

We termed this TL and content scaffolding as 'hybrid' practice in EMI (Fujimoto-Adamson & Adamson, 2018: 201), to encourage less proficient students in class participation, and also to make content comprehensible to all students. We reflected upon these practices together in a CAE (Chang *et al.*, 2013) in which we jointly narrated our experiences teaching applied linguistics/EMI as English language practitioners over one year.

CAE findings

In our findings, five key themes emerged from our narratives. The first was the shift for us from teaching English as a foreign language (EFL) to EMI. Both John (an English speaker from the UK) and Naoki (a Japanese speaker) expressed the challenge involved in this pedagogical 'shift' from language teaching to teaching their applied linguistics courses in English, with Naoki in particular recognising the necessity of preparing students for L2 dissertation writing in the years beforehand.

The second theme focused on the adaptations inherent in this shift. John commented on the necessity of simplifying not only his language input in EMI, but also the actual content itself. This is an indication that, as Ishikawa (2011) and Yonezawa (2011) note, EMI in Japan needs to undergo fundamental changes compared to content instruction in Anglophone contexts.

Delving more into how this can be achieved in their teaching practices in the third theme of scaffolding, John explained how he lists key language at the side of the board so that students can be reminded visually of that language constantly during content instruction. Naoki stressed the importance of modelling previous students' essays, not perfectly written ones from Anglophone scholars. The manner of these adaptations for John and Naoki shows their emphasis on 'scaffolding' of language which may be traced to their language teaching sensitivities and knowledge of their own students' linguistic difficulties, some of whom were previously taking their English classes.

The fourth theme addressed the important area of TL in EMI, with John and Naoki concurring that the students' use of Japanese was an essential means to 'language' their way into comprehension and participation. John stressed firstly how Japanese can be used, albeit imperfectly, to manage the flow of lessons, explain key concepts and give feedback. He encourages discussions in either Japanese or English on content which embraces their own Japanese language use in society. He felt this approach affords greater agency to lower proficiency students when trying to cope with the possibly daunting task of studying sociolinguistics and discourse analysis themes through English. Naoki's use of Japanese slightly differed in that she uses a Japanese textbook for sociolinguistics to 'deepen' comprehension but then to encourage guided discussions in English on what they have read, a point which John referred to as similar to 'safe' language practice (Martin, 2005: 80) to reduce student anxiety. Naoki replied that using a Japanese textbook in this way is also a means to de-centre mono-lingual Anglophone practice.

The final theme in their CAE turned to the instructors' reflections about student perceptions of their EMI practice. John's reflections revealed some doubt as to why students choose his EMI classes: an 'easy option' due to his inclusion of Japanese in his lessons, 'curiosity' about a foreigner using and allowing Japanese in class or an opportunity to prac-tise English, rather than a true interest in the subject itself. He felt other faculty might regard the content of his EMI classes as too simple com-pared to those delivered in Japanese. Naoki was more positive, noting that her classes in EMI are optional so students must have a 'genuine' interest in the content.

Reflecting on these findings in the CAE, from a wider perspective, other Japan-based EMI practitioners may find some resonance with our experiences as its practice becomes more popular and students opt not to study abroad yet still long for English-speaking opportunities (Stigger, 2018).

Challenges and Opportunities in TL Practices

Looking back at the findings related to TL practices for this university, we see in this one particular case various challenges and opportunities. Among these, of particular note is evidence of TL as practised in the pro-cess of writing reports through L1 (Japanese) reading and consultation with non-classroom stakeholders (the literacy maps and Naoki's use of a sociolinguistics textbook). It is also apparent in various stages of planning for L2 production and embedded in teacher materials, as seen in the use of Japanese script for gender awareness-raising. Important here is not simply the integration of L1 language and content themes into EMI but, as Goodman (2014) recommends, also the scaffolding of L2 (English) con-tent to make content in the L2 accessible for less proficient students. In Fujimoto-Adamson and Adamson (2018: 201), we argue that this sensitiv-ity towards language and content comprehension by language teachers offering EMI in applied linguistics creates a 'hybridity' in TL practice. Our findings also refer to non-classroom contexts (SALC) where, in con-trast to Gardner and Miller's (1999) advice, language policies are now set by students, not centre advisors or teachers. This exhibits the importance of viewing TL as student-determined, even though, as seen in Adamson and Fujimoto-Adamson (2012), students showed stricter views towards TL use than advisors or teachers. In this sense, the autonomy inherent in the non-classroom 'learning space' (Savin-Baden, 2007: 13) cannot be a guarantee of expectations of TL held by instructors or advisors. Extracts from advisor-to-student talk appeared to show more pragmatic use of the L1 when discussing metacognitive themes, but those episodes were more likely to be determined by advisors, the more dominant interactants, than students. Further ambivalent findings were seen regarding citation practices where L1 use was possibly linked to difficulties in L2 reading among lower proficiency students (Adamson & Coulson, 2015); this differed from higher proficiency students whose rationale for L1 reading was to contrast content with L2 readings.

Despite these unexpected findings from SALC student interaction and citation practices, it became evident that TL was not simply a short-term strategy choice (Swain & Lapkin, 2013), but possibly a longer term policy particularly for instructors and advisors. Perhaps this can be explained by its origin in the *kiso semi* research (Brown & Adamson, 2014) where content faculty made recommendations for English provision. This needs-related evidence was not passed down from institutional management, so was illustrative of a more bottom-up policy.

Considerations are also needed about student beliefs in our context towards language learning. Some exhibited clear monolingual views about L2 learning (Cummins, 2005a), particularly among higher proficiency students who may regard any lesson with a non-Japanese instructor as an opportunity for L2 practice, rather than content learning (Adamson & Coulson, 2014, 2015; Moore, 2017). This is complicated by feelings of inferiority, as expressed by John (see Fujimoto-Adamson & Adamson, 2018), who believed his TL stance in EMI approach may have been an 'easy option' for students and less academically valid. Nevertheless, from our CAE, his engagement in TL was not offset by a lack of Japanese fluency, which resonates with Toth and Paulsrud's (2017) observations.

Teaching mixed proficiency levels in one EMI programme perhaps best encapsulated the challenges and opportunities of TL practice (Adamson & Coulson, 2014, 2015), as the empowerment among lower proficiency students towards its use contrasts with higher proficiency students' feelings of disappointment that their initial confidence in their language abilities did not necessarily match their final grades. Here the intersection of EMI's content-driven goals, CLIL's focus on language and content, and beliefs about TL becomes apparent, not in its clear delineation of findings between proficiency groups but in its messiness and organic nature. Our longitudinal studies reveal mixed, complex and at times unexpected findings. Limitations of our institutional case study clearly lay in the selective nature of examining programmes and contexts in the university only accessible to us as practitioners; however, from the viewpoint of conducting intrinsically motivated case study research (Stake, 1995) at the local level, the findings still continue to inform us and to raise awareness of TL, despite occasional manifestations of resistance and reluctance. Perhaps most important in this process is the emphasis on determining relevant policies towards TL which have been researched, not assumed.

3 Malawian Universities as Translanguaging Spaces

Colin Reilly

Introduction

Language policies in Malawi have undergone numerous changes since the end of the colonial period under British rule (1891–1964). Kayambazinthu (1998: 388) states that the core issue facing language policy creation and implementation in post-colonial Malawi is twofold: acknowledging the 'practical usefulness' of English as a language of modernity and 'world civilisation' while also recognising that there is a need to maintain a sense of 'cultural identity' for Malawians and ensure 'ease of communication with the masses'. The most recent language-in-education policy moves towards an English-only approach and places English as the sole language to be used as the medium of instruction (MOI) in Malawian education. The primary justification for this is to increase the English language skills found within the nation. Globally, while there is a growing trend towards the adoption of English-only MOI in tertiary education (Dearden, 2014), translanguaging has also been found to occur in universities worldwide (Mazak & Carroll, 2016; see also Dalziel & Guarda, this volume). This chapter will focus on the tertiary education system in Malawi and aims to highlight the contrasts between policy and practice, discussing the ways in which multilingualism manifests within this ostensibly English-only EMI context. This will be achieved through addressing two research questions: (1) To what extent can Malawian universities be considered as translanguaging spaces? (2) How do stakeholders view the adoption of a translanguaging language policy?

This chapter will begin by providing an overview of the language-in-education policy situation in Malawi, illustrating the rationale behind the current English-only language-in-education policy and providing a contextual foundation for the present study. The value of using translanguaging as a concept to understand the linguistic practices within Malawian tertiary education will then be highlighted. This is followed by the results of a linguistic ethnography of Malawian universities which reveals the ways in which translanguaging is used for pedagogical and social purposes. Finally, stakeholder attitudes towards the adoption of a multilingual policy within Malawian universities will be discussed. This will highlight the relationship between policy and practice within this multilingual EMI context. The chapter ends with a discussion of the potential value of translanguaging as a concept within language policy in Malawi.

Language in Malawi

While Malawi is a multilingual country, there are debates surrounding the exact number of languages therein. There are linguistic, social and political issues concerning whether particular varieties should be treated as languages or dialects (Kayambazinthu, 1998: 370), with claims that languages in Malawi are 'said to vary between twelve and thirty-five' (Makoni & Mashiri, 2006: 65). The most recent census in Malawi with a focus on languages was conducted by the National Statistical Office in 1998, and asked respondents to state what language was commonly used for communication within their household. The results (National Statistical Office, 1998) reported information on 12 Malawian languages and two foreign languages as well as other unspecified languages. This census indicated that the most commonly spoken language in the home was Chichewa (also called Chewa), with 57.2% of the population stating that this was the most commonly used language in their homes. The next most commonly spoken language was Chinyanja (also called Nyanja) with 12.8% of the population, followed by Chiyao (also called Yao) with 10.1%. All other languages were reported as commonly used languages by less than 10% of the population and five Malawian languages were reported as the most commonly used language by less than 1% of the population. English was reported as the most commonly used language by 0.2% of the population in Malawi. While important sociolinguistic surveys have been conducted by the Centre for Language Studies in Malawi (1999, 2006, 2009), there has been no similar large-scale survey of language use since the 1998 census and as a result the contemporary situation is unclear. The positions that languages have in Malawi are also debated; however, English is regarded as the de facto official language of the country with Chichewa acting as the de facto national language.

An emerging language variety has also been identified by Moto (2001). This has been described as Malawi's 'new language' (Moto, 2001), also known as 'Chibrazi' ('language of brothers') (Huiskamp, 2016; Kamanga, 2014, 2016). University students were among the initial groups thought to speak this variety (Jalasi, 1999; Lekera, 1994). Moto (2001) and Kamanga (2014, 2016) suggest that the speech community extends beyond university students and note that its use is widespread in Malawi. It has been shown to be a variety which incorporates linguistic resources from

English, French, Chichewa and other Malawian languages as well as Shona and Latin (Moto, 2001). Used by speakers to express solidarity and create and perform a shared social identity (Kamanga, 2014; Moto, 2001), it challenges the boundaries between named languages in the country and represents speakers' flexible and creative use of their linguistic repertoires.

Language-in-Education Policies in Malawi

Language-in-education policies in Malawi have been characterised by the dilemma of when to use Malawian languages and when to introduce English (Kayambazinthu, 1998: 389). Here, policies will be briefly discussed to illustrate the context in which this study is embedded. Mtenje (2013: 96) notes that during the colonial period, policy stipulated that more widely spoken Malawian languages were used in the first two years of education, followed by English. Since independence there have been three major milestones in language-in-education policies in the country. In 1969, Chichewa was introduced as the MOI for the first four years of schooling, after which English was to be used as the MOI (Chilora, 2000: 2; Mtenje, 2013: 96; Williams, 2011: 44). This was part of the new government's goal to promote unity and to ensure that Chichewa became a dominant language in the country. Then, in 1996, a policy directive was introduced which stated that children should be taught in their mother tongue for the first four years of primary school after which time English should be used as the MOI. This directive was announced without consultation with educationalists or linguists and it is unclear how many languages would be catered for as, at the time, there were only resources for Chichewa (Kishindo, 2015). The directive retains the prominent position of English within the education system but also actively calls for the inclusion of multiple Malawian languages. This policy was never fully implemented and was viewed unfavourably by the general public who wanted their children taught through an English MOI, believing this to be the best way for them to acquire English language skills (Kamwendo, 2008; Matiki, 2001; Msonthi, 1997).

Despite the lack of effective policy implementation, the 1996 mother tongue language policy directive has been blamed for the low standard of education in Malawi (Kishindo, 2015). The perception that the mother tongue directive is to blame for the poor quality of education, and perceived low standards of English, has influenced the newest iteration of the language-in-education policy in Malawi: the English-only policy. This new policy was introduced as part of the New Education Act 2013 in Malawi, with the main aim of improving the education system in the country. The Malawi Law Commission, the body which developed the New Education Act, criticised the absence of clear language-in-education policy legislation within previous education acts and explicitly stated that 'there is need to have a provision on language of instruction in schools' (Law Commission, 2010: 63). The New Education Act contains the following legislation prescribing the MOI:

(1) The medium of instruction in schools and colleges shall be English.
(2) Without prejudice to the generality of subsection 1, the Minister may, by notice published in the Gazette, prescribe the language of instruction in schools. (Malawi Government, 2013: 42)

The introduction of the New Education Act was followed by a policy announcement in March 2014 by the Minister of Education, Luscious Kanyumba, who stated that 'the New Education Act mandates pupils to be taught in English from Standard One' (*Nyasa Times*, 2014). This policy was to be implemented in the following academic year, beginning in September 2014. In reality this new policy only officially affected the MOI for the initial four years of education, as policy since the 1960s has stated that English should be used from Standard Five. Malawian linguists have directly given evidence to the government establishing that the policy has negative pedagogical implications, as it will not be 'linguistically accessible' for the majority of students (Kamwendo, 2015: 35; see also Kishindo, 2015; Miti, 2015; Simango, 2015). Currently, the policy still stands, although it is unclear if any widespread, practical implementation has taken place, as there is a lack of awareness of the new policy among education stakeholders and no clear implementation plan (Chavula, 2019; Kamtukule, 2019). Kretzer and Kumwenda (2016) note that currently most schools in the country still use Chichewa and English.

When announcing the new English-only language policy in 2014, the Minister of Education noted:

It is the wish of government to see most of the pupils speak and write good English while at primary level. English speaking has been a problem to our pupils even those who completed secondary education. (*Nyasa Times*, 2014)

With the intended goal of improving English language provision so that there are more students who 'speak and write good English', the new policy forefronts a strict English-only EMI approach as the most desirable for education in the country. The prestige that is afforded to English in Malawi as an official language and as a global lingua franca has led to this positioning as the sole language suitable for use within the education system. Indeed, English is widely viewed as synonymous with education and negative attitudes towards the use of Malawian languages pervade the primary, secondary and tertiary levels (Kamwendo, 2003; Kayambazinthu, 2000; Matiki, 2001). Against this background in which, at a policy level, English-only instruction is being promoted as the best option within Malawian education, the remainder of this chapter will discuss the reality of language use and language attitudes within tertiary education and, using a translanguaging framework, assess the extent to which Malawian universities can be considered as translanguaging spaces. This will then address whether a strict English-only policy is feasible, or indeed beneficial, in practice within Malawian universities.

Translanguaging

This chapter draws on the concept of translanguaging spaces (Li Wei, 2011, 2018), which are spaces created for and by translanguaging, within which speakers can creatively and freely transform and transcend traditional notions and practices of communication. Within these spaces, identity and linguistic practices are fluid and can be constantly (re)constructed by speakers. Analysing the sociolinguistic situation within Malawian universities using the concept of translanguaging spaces allows several factors to be evaluated, including the following: the extent to which individuals use translanguaging as they navigate their experience within the university; how the use of translanguaging is viewed within the university space; and how translanguaging is regulated within the university space. In translanguaging spaces, varied linguistic resources are viewed as valuable, which allows critical and creative linguistic practices to occur (Bradley et al., 2018). This creativity allows speakers to transcend traditional social and linguistic boundaries and to create new ways of communicating (Zhu Hua et al., 2017). Communication within these spaces can challenge monolingual ideologies (Li & Luo, 2017); in multilingual contexts, translanguaging spaces in education can create classrooms which remain 'linguistically real' for students, reflecting the reality of their linguistic practices (Langman, 2014: 198) and their wider social reality (Dewilde, 2017). The concept of translanguaging spaces can be used to analyse the ways in which individuals navigate their multilingual realities within the EMI context of Malawian universities.

The standardisation and categorisation of named languages within Africa can be considered as a 'reflex of colonialism' (Lüpke, 2015: 3). The construction of arbitrary language boundaries does not reflect the reality of communication and the 'fluid use of language in multilingual settings in Africa' (Heugh, 2015: 281) and conceptualising languages as discrete, bounded entities represents a monoglossic view of language which can be considered a product of coloniality (Makoe & McKinney, 2014). Translanguaging offers an opportunity to challenge traditional language ideologies emanating from the Global North (Childs, 2016) and offers a valuable conceptual tool to describe the language practices of multilinguals. Within the African context, Makalela has developed the concept of Ubuntu translanguaging which provides a speaker-centred view of language use and describes the complex and translingual communication strategies particular to Africa (Makalela, 2016b). As in previous conceptualisations of translanguaging, the focus for Ubuntu translanguaging is on the rich and complex linguistic repertoires that individuals possess, rather than on the divisions between languages. Makalela (2016a: 191) forges a connection between translanguaging and the 'African value system of ubuntu that is understood within this frame of reference: *I am because we are; we are because I am*'. The values of co-existence and interconnectedness are reflected in Ubuntu translanguaging as '*a language is because another language is*' (Makalela, 2016a: 191). In this way, Ubuntu translanguaging provides a lens to examine language practices which forefronts the fluidity of languages and, at the same time, presents an opportunity to decolonise, disrupt and transcend language ideologies from the Global North.

• The ways in which language and language use are viewed are important factors in the establishment and success of language policies. Spolsky (2004) states that language policy consists of three main components: language practices, language beliefs and language management/planning. This final component can consist of the creation of specific rules and official legislation for how language is used. Often, this legislation is oriented around 'notions of language as homogenous, standardised, codified entities with clear boundaries' (Erling *et al.*, 2017: 142). This orientation is not necessarily appropriate in highly multilingual communities and has been suggested as one of the main causes of the failure to produce effective and inclusive language policies in Africa (Makoni & Mashiri, 2006). This failure is primarily because a monoglossic and bounded view of language does not accurately reflect individual and community language practices or language beliefs. To understand the language practices and beliefs within Malawian universities, this study conducted a linguistic ethnography of them, which will now be discussed.

A Linguistic Ethnography of Malawian Universities

The National Council for Higher Education (NCHE) guidance for universities states that the entrance requirements for an undergraduate degree should be 'a good Malawi School Certificate of Education (MSCE) or its equivalent with at least six credit passes including English' (NCHE, 2015: 35). In the NCHE's criteria for accreditation they also state these benchmarks:

Students completing programmes at undergraduate and postgraduate levels demonstrate good communication skills in English. (NCHE, 2014: 15)

Students successfully completing an undergraduate programme demonstrate competence in written and oral communication in English. (NCHE, 2014: 18)

English is thus a key language for getting into university and one of the functions of university education is to ensure that students can effectively communicate in English. However, Kamwendo (2003) notes that external examiners for the University of Malawi expressed concerns regarding the overall falling standards of English language skills among students. Additionally, while positive attitudes exist towards the use of English within universities, students and staff are critical of the limitations that an English-only EMI approach can have (Reilly, 2019).

The study presented in this chapter was conducted over a four-month fieldwork period in Malawi in 2016. The data collection adopted a linguistic ethnographic approach and a range of data collection methods were used: interviews, focus groups, participant recordings and participant observation. These multiple forms of data collection allow a comprehensive picture of language use and language attitudes to emerge.

The study of multilingual interactions in multilingual education environments is complex and can best be investigated through an interpretive, ethnographic approach. This allows the local actions and subjective attitudes of individuals to be studied while at the same time analysing how these are related to broader social contexts and norms within specific institutions and within national and international contexts (Copland & Creese, 2015; Unamuno, 2014). For this study, an ethnographic approach offers a way to investigate how individuals navigate the complex multilingual interactions within education and how the ways in which multilingualism manifests relate to the broader social context (Pérez-Milan, 2015, 2016).

Translanguaging in this chapter aligns with Makalela's Ubuntu translanguaging, which offers a conceptualisation of language which more closely corresponds to multilinguals' lived experience, language practices and views of their own language use (Makalela, 2013; Mazak, 2016). Using translanguaging spaces as a conceptual tool for understanding the spaces of Malawian universities highlights the ways in which individuals' linguistic practices are related to wider social structures and, in addition, the ways in which these language practices are transcending and challenging both traditional conceptualisations of language and these social structures themselves.

Data were collected at all the public universities in Malawi and one private university. Participant recording involved 20 participants (18 students and two staff) from one institution. Each participant was given a small dictaphone and lapel microphone, allowing them to record themselves during the course of one day at university. Participants repeated this over multiple days to ensure that recordings could be collected in a range of contexts. In total, 300 hours of audio data were collected. Analysis involved listening to 30-minute segments of different contexts (e.g. lectures, seminars, socialising) and transcribing sections in which translanguaging took place. Interviews took place at all eight research sites and, in total, 92 individual interviews were conducted (27 academic and administrative staff and 65 students). Eight student focus group interviews were conducted with between two and seven participants in each group. One focus group interview was conducted in each institution with students who had previously participated in an individual interview. Interviews and focus groups were semi-structured in nature, and included questions which provided information on general university experiences, self-reported language use across a range of contexts, and language attitudes. Where necessary, senior management in individual universities approved data collection and, for all data collection, participants were required to give written consent and were able to withdraw their participation at any point during, or after, data collection. During focus groups, participants were asked to agree to ensure that the discussions remained confidential.

Interview and focus group data were transcribed and underwent a process of qualitative coding using *NVivo* software. A three-stage coding process was conducted. In the first stage the data were used to develop codes reflecting the major topics and viewpoints which were present in the interviews and focus groups, and the transcripts were coded accordingly. In the second stage all transcripts and codes were reviewed and codes were added/altered where appropriate. In the third stage each individual code and corresponding coded sections of all transcripts were reviewed, and related codes were grouped together to establish key themes relating to how individuals use and view their linguistic resources. Where translations were required these were first conducted by the author, checked by a Chichewa language translator and tutor (ensuring the anonymity of participants) and, when required, checked again by the participants involved. The excerpts discussed below have been chosen as they give particular insight into individuals' orientation towards multilingual language practices. A translanguaging framework is adopted when discussing the data within the study, as this forefronts the creativity and criticality of individuals' language use, and focuses on how individuals are challenging traditional language ideologies in their communication. Whether the spaces under discussion are translanguaging spaces was evaluated using Li Wei's (2011) initial description of translanguaging spaces as spaces created both for and by translanguaging.

Translanguaging in Malawian Universities

This section will discuss the use of, and views towards, translanguaging in the social and academic domains of Malawian universities. Initially, examples will be given of translanguaging practices taken from participant recordings. This will be followed by qualitative interview and focus group data in which individuals discuss their own language practices.

Translanguaging in the social domain

This section will begin by presenting an example of translanguaging taken from a participant recording.

Excerpt 3.1 *Student in social domain*

Original (Chichewa, English)	English translation
Nda chonde. Ankangowerenga, anayankha mesa after kumutukwana. Ndinapita kumu texta kuti "now watch me whip now watch me nae nae". Nangotipatsa kuti imeneyo mpaka "now watch me whip" chibakera chija "now watch me nae nae" the hand, koma pamene paja analakwitsa ndi ndani. Be honest eti? Texting me eti?	Who? Please. He was just reading, he replied after cussing him. I went to text him that "now watch me whip now watch me nae nae" and just gave us that one until "now watch me whip" that blow "now watch me nae nae" the hand, but who messed up here? Be honest, not so? Texting me not so?

In Excerpt 3.1 a female student is telling a story about texting a male student, which subsequently resulted in a confrontation with the male student's partner. In the excerpt the female student is discussing aspects of the text exchange and seeking feedback on her actions. In doing so, she mentions the lyrics to a popular US hip-hop song by Silentó ('now watch me whip … now watch me nae nae'). Translanguaging allows this student, drawing on her entire linguistic repertoire, to recall and tell a story to her friends which involves a minor local drama developing in her personal life, and to make references to popular global culture. The student is able to creatively use her linguistic resources to narrate her own story, highlight her identity as a student embedded within the Malawian context and international context and actively create a translanguaging space through her language practices.

Clearly emerging from students' self-reported language use is that, for them, the social scene in university is one that is not monolingual. Instead they 'mostly use Chichewa and English' (Speaker #3 Focus Group 1) and it is 'mostly a mix of both' (Speaker #4 Focus Group 4). While the major focus emerging from interviews is on the use of English and Chichewa, students do highlight that additional Malawian languages will be used on campus, such as one student who notes that when talking to their friends the language would 'just change in Tumbuka' (Speaker #2 Focus Group 5). The visibility of complex multilingual repertoires within the university is due to the students' natural way of communication. As one student notes, 'you usually mix' because 'it's fun, most people are used to that' (Student #10). For students to communicate monolingually in the social domain would then not be indicative of the language practices to which they are accustomed and would not accurately reflect the multilingual reality of their linguistic repertoires.

One student reports that 'I feel like I don't run out of words … if I run out of a word in Chewa [an alternative way to refer to Chichewa] then I go to English, if I run from English then I go back to Chewa' (Student #38). A key theme which emerges when students rationalise their language practices is that by being able to draw on their entire linguistic repertoire, students are able to successfully communicate their ideas in a way that is comfortable to them.

Individuals exhibit an awareness of the creativity displayed in their language practices, stating that they use words that 'don't really exist but then we had to make them up' (Student #54), they are 'not real words in Chichewa' but 'a mixture of English and Chichewa' (Staff #64). They describe the practices that they engage in which allow them to challenge and go beyond the boundaries of named languages as they take 'a Chichewa word [and] turn it into an English word' (Staff #35) or when they 'Chichewalise the English word' (Speaker #3 Focus Group 1). Individuals are able to challenge and creatively transcend the boundaries between named languages in their language practices. This is clearly expressed in Excerpt 3.2, in which a student discusses the way that language is used socially.

Excerpt 3.2 *Interview with student #29*

It's a language I mean we can't call it Chichewa we can't call it English maybe Anglo-Chichewa something like that, yeah we can call it that name but it's ... a language that you are able to express yourself ... but also your feelings, you can best express yourself and also it's better understand, like, people can understand what you're trying to communicate and in doing that not only people are subjected to Chichewa or English they ... are able to learn some of the vocabulary of both languages, so it's like we are connecting this and this to make one thing.

This student expresses a clear awareness of the blurred and fuzzy boundary between the named languages within their linguistic repertoire. Rather than speaking in any one language, they are able to draw from and across their linguistic resources, to communicate in innovative and creative ways which disrupt the boundaries between named languages.

The use of translanguaging emerges within the social domain partly as a consequence of the sociolinguistic rules that students place on one another. Students report that they will be stigmatised if they are not perceived to be fluent English speakers as they will be 'humiliated' if they 'look like someone who doesn't know English around the campus' (Speaker #3 Focus Group 2). However, the use of English can also be stigmatised within the social domain. One student reports that her social group 'would speak a lot of English outside [of class]' and as a result, other students would 'look at you like "oh these pompous little kids"' (Speaker #5 Focus Group 3). Due to this stigmatisation, translanguaging becomes an effective way for students to communicate socially. One student notes that 'we need both English and Chichewa so that we should be known that this person belongs to Malawi but he is also an educated person' (Speaker #2 Focus Group 2), with another stating that using both languages plays a key role in their identity as 'there is a sense of identity there, sure you identify ah this is a Malawian but at the same time you're show-ing that you know also English' (Student #9). Within the social domain, translanguaging plays a crucial role in students performing their identities as students and is an essential skill which individuals must possess to effectively integrate on the social scene. To perform one's identity as a student involves participating in the creation of a translanguaging space within the social domain of the universities.

Translanguaging in the academic domain

Translanguaging also occurs within the academic domain. Excerpt 3.3 is taken from a participant recording session with a staff member who lectures in economics.

Excerpt 3.3 *Lecturer in academic domain*

Original (Chichewa, English)	English translation
When you talk of a limited company a limited company **ineyo ndikuyambitsa kampane yanga** called **kaya** 'Zanimuone', 'Ekwendeni', 'Embangweni', 'Emzuzu' company limited **eti?** That company **ndi ineyo** we are two different entities. **Kampane izipanga** run **chilichonse payokha inenso ndizipanga** run **chilichonse pandekha.**	When you talk of a limited company a limited company, **I am starting my company** called, such as, 'Zanimuone', 'Ekwendeni', 'Embangweni', 'Emzuzu' company limited **not so?** That company **and me we are two different entities. The company will be running everything on its own I too will be running everything on my own.**

Here translanguaging is used to clarify key technical terms such as 'lim-ited company' and to provide examples to allow students to more fully engage with the explanations. Translanguaging, as used here within the academic domain, allows for more effective teaching and learning as it enables the lecturer to explain concepts in more detail and in a way that students will more easily understand. This lecturer thus creates a translan-guaging space within his own classroom, legitimising the use of the multi-lingual repertoires which he and his students possess. This emerges as a key reason individuals give for the use of translanguaging inside the classroom. It 'makes the content much easier for the student to understand' (Speaker #34 Focus Group 2) and 'the whole mixing up thing ... it's easier that way' (Student #49). One staff member notes that it is particularly useful 'when you are bringing in some new concepts' (Staff #39).

Translanguaging plays a particularly key role when lecturers seek to provide examples for their students. This partially stems from the fact that the resources that are used within universities in Malawi are textbooks produced in Western countries containing examples which are not locally relevant. As such 'it is up to the lecturer concerned to contextualise ... so that it becomes meaningful' (Staff #39). Through the use of translanguaging, lecturers are able to draw on international academic knowledge while also making this contextually relevant for students. As one student notes, 'when you are talking of the ... typical local examples ... it's better to be using both languages' (Student #6 Focus Group 2). Translanguaging also serves classroom management functions within the academic domain. It can be used 'as an icebreaker' (Staff #44) within the class, to create a relaxed environment. One staff member notes that when their students are losing concentration they can 'bring them back to life' through deviating from a monolingual MOI (Staff #35). Students attest to this as well, stating that if a lecture was delivered monolingually, in only English, 'most people doze off ... it's like everyone is sleeping' (Speaker #4 Focus Group 2).

Much like the social domain, there are rules concerning the use of translanguaging in the academic domain. Due to the power dynamics within the classroom, staff members have the power to dictate how language is used within their classroom. This leads to a context in which some lecturers will allow the use of translanguaging within their classes while others will not. Students note that this can be 'a challenge' as 'some lecturers will say "okay you can speak Chichewa" ... but then it's others who say "English"' (Speaker #4 Focus Group 1). Staff will also differ in their own practices as some 'know that we only speak English not Chichewa here, but some of them don't know that, they'll mix it and mix Chichewa and English' which can be 'really confusing' for students (Speaker #2 Focus Group 1). Students are then required to adapt the ways in which they engage with and participate in their learning based on the linguistic rules that particular lecturers enforce. Some students view the practices of some lecturers as hypocritical and 'bad' as 'they're speaking to us in Chichewa and they don't allow us to speak to them in Chichewa' (Student #92). The extent to which academic domains are translanguaging spaces therefore becomes blurred. Certain individuals have the power to legitimise the language practices within a particular space; while they may engage in translanguaging practices themselves, they may nonetheless stigmatise others' translanguaging practices. These individuals with power thus control the extent to which others are able to have equitable opportunities to participate in the construction of, and have access to, a translanguaging space.

Attitudes towards a multilingual policy

Interview participants were asked to state their own ideal language policy for university. Eighty-eight interview participants provided responses to this question. The results, illustrated in Figure 3.1 (rounded to the nearest percent), show that 48% opt for a monolingual English-only policy. Other monolingual answers include Chichewa-only (1%) and

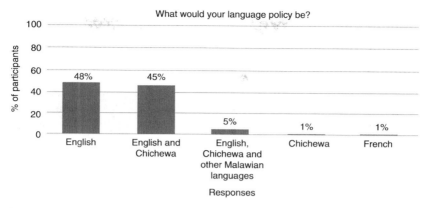

Figure 3.1 Responses to 'What would your language policy be?'

French-only (1%). However, 50% of respondents opt for a multilingual policy, with 45% opting for a policy that includes English and Chichewa and 5% opting for a policy that includes English and Chichewa plus additional Malawian languages. What emerges is support from around half of the participants for a monolingual English-only policy and, from the other half, support for a multilingual policy that incorporates both English and Malawian languages.

Favourable attitudes towards a multilingual policy emerge as this more accurately reflects the multilingual reality of individuals' repertoires and their everyday lives. As one student notes, 'one language isn't enough, not one language … it's not enough' (Speaker #4 Focus Group 6). For these individuals a monolingual, English-only policy presents a rigid, constraining option which does not allow them to make full use of their linguistic repertoire. Instead a policy 'which is flexible' (Student #62), and in which there is 'wiggle room' (Staff #6) is viewed as a more desirable option.

Students suggest that a multilingual policy would be one that would enable them to 'understand the things seriously' (Speaker #7 Focus Group 4). It is viewed as a 'win-win game' with 'English being an international language, Chichewa being a national language' (Speaker #4 Focus Group 1). They can both 'benefit from Chichewa … and benefit from English' (Speaker #2 Focus Group 7). A multilingual policy then allows students to be exposed to and engage with their learning in both of the languages that they view as being valuable in their lives.

Conclusion

This chapter has provided an overview of the changing language policies within Malawi and discussed the role translanguaging plays in Malawian universities. The prestige value which is associated with English due to its role in high-level domains within Malawi, and its importance as a global lingua franca has led to it being positioned as the sole language that is suitable for use as a MOI within education in Malawi. However, this does not reflect the language practices or language attitudes displayed among students and staff within universities in the country.

The question as to what extent Malawian universities can be viewed as translanguaging spaces is debatable. Following Li Wei's (2011, 2018) definition, translanguaging spaces are created both *for* and *by* translanguaging. Given that there is evidence of translanguaging occurring in universities, they can be considered spaces created *by* translanguaging. Spaces are created within the university in which students and staff can creatively and critically use language in a way that transcends boundaries of named languages and allows individuals to utilise their multilingual repertoires to more effectively socialise and engage with learning. However, since there is no official legislation which accommodates for translanguaging and translanguaging practices may be stigmatised and forbidden by particular individuals, they are not necessarily spaces created *for* translanguaging. Regarding the functions of translanguaging within Malawian universities, the use of translanguaging allows students to effectively perform their identities as young, educated Malawians and is an essential skill for integration in the social arena. Translanguaging also offers opportunities to increase students' engagement with course content and to create positive interpersonal relationships between students and staff. Ensuring students have the necessary skills to succeed in both global and local contexts is at the foundation of the language-in-education policy dilemma in the country. Viewing language-in-education policies through a monoglossic lens in which either Malawian languages or English are used as the MOI does not reflect the reality of language use at the tertiary level.

With regard to the question of how stakeholders view the adoption of a translanguaging language policy, it can be stated that there is clear evidence of support for a language policy which moves away from a strict English-only EMI approach and allows space for engaging with the multilingualism present within the universities. Given the multilingual reality of the university spaces and the positive attitudes towards a multilingual language policy, Malawian universities do have the potential to become spaces created both for and by translanguaging. Integrating a translanguaging perspective into language policies could have a positive impact in Malawi as it would more accurately reflect the linguistic practices of individuals, encourage a positive attitude towards multilingualism and challenge the dominance of former colonial languages (Bagwasi, 2017; Early & Norton, 2014; Makalela, 2016a, 2016b; Makoe & McKinney, 2014). Moving towards policy which adopts a translanguaging view of language could offer a more effective and inclusive approach to language-in-education policy in Malawi.

4 Translanguaging Pedagogies in the Humanities and Social Sciences in South Africa: Affordances and Constraints

Kathy Luckett and Ellen Hurst-Harosh

Introduction

In this chapter, we focus on translanguaging as an educational approach in which multiple languages and registers are used and encouraged in teaching, learning and assessment practices, within a higher education institution in South Africa which has an English-medium language policy. Through the application of aspects of Legitimation Code Theory and Appraisal Analysis, the chapter outlines the affordances of translanguaging as a pedagogic strategy, particularly how it permits students to utilise their full linguistic repertoires to make meaning, express their feelings and judgments and draw on 'cultural knowledge' through the use of their first or home languages, leading to high levels of student engagement.

Context and History

Today, as has been the case historically, the majority of the South African population speak languages other than English as their home language (see Table 4.1). Nevertheless, English is dominant in government, the media and, importantly, education. The status of English in South Africa originates with the presence of early Christian missionaries and British colonisation of the Cape, both in the late 18th century. During and

Table 4.1 South African home languages 2011

Language	Speakers	Percentage
Zulu	11,587,374	22.7%
Xhosa	8,154,258	16.0%
Afrikaans	6,855,082	13.5%
English	4,892,623	9.6%
Northern Sotho	4,618,576	9.1%
Tswana	4,067,248	8.0%
Sotho	3,849,563	7.6%
Tsonga	2,277,148	4.5%
Swati	1,297,046	2.5%
Venda	1,209,388	2.4%
Ndebele	1,090,223	2.1%
Sign language	234,655	0.5%
Other languages	828,258	1.6%
Total	**50,961,443**	**100.0%**

Source: Census 2011 (Lehohla, 2012) (most recent census data – the next census will be in 2021).

after apartheid, English was the preferred lingua franca of the anti-apartheid liberation movement who rejected the imposition in schools of Afrikaans, which was considered the language of the apartheid government. English came to be seen as the language of liberation – the South African Freedom Charter (1955) was written in English, and English was the language of the African National Congress, the political party that formed the first government after the end of apartheid. As a result, English became the primary medium of instruction (MOI) in the post-apartheid education system. Meanwhile, African languages were associated with the inferior Bantu education system (education provided for Africans under the policy of separate development during apartheid).

Despite policy attempts to rectify the status of African languages, including the recognition of nine African languages as official languages and the implementation of home language instruction in the first four years of schooling, English-medium instruction (EMI) remains dominant in all higher levels of education. Today at Grade 1 (ages five to six), English and Zulu are the most common MOI (22% and 23% of schools, respectively, in 2007; Department of Basic Education, RSA, 2010: 14). However, by Grade 4 (usually ages eight to nine), the majority of schools state their MOI to be English (79% in 2007; Department of Basic Education, RSA, 2010: 16). English is the primary language of instruction in nearly all high schools and higher education institutions around the country. Policy at the institutional level and at the level of national higher education policy tends to promote monolingualism(s) and currently constrains language practice in the academy. This needs to be adjusted in order to challenge the dominant monolingual Anglonormative bias (Makalela, 2018; McKinney, 2017).

The implementation of translanguaging pedagogies in this context is partly a response to recent events in South Africa's higher education landscape, particularly a series of student protests beginning with #RhodesMustFall (RMF). RMF was a movement originating at the University of Cape Town (UCT) which sought to decolonise the academy through a number of strategies, notably the removal of the statue of Cecil Rhodes, a colonial imperialist, which occupied a dominant position on UCT's main campus. Subsequent national #Fallist student protest movements from 2015 to 2018 similarly aimed at transforming higher education in South Africa, which was perceived as colonial, elitist and white. There has also been increased pressure from other stakeholders (the state, civil movements, black academic staff and so on) for transformation of the academy which has been notably slow to respond to the recommendations in the 1997 White Paper (Department of Education, 1997) and more recently a report on transformation in higher education (Ministry of Education, 2008).

RMF and subsequent student movements were relatively silent on the subject of languages. As Gambushe (2017) writes:

> During and after the fall of Rhodes, students spoke loudly about the need to decolonize the curriculum and transform higher education. Interestingly, in the process of talking about the need for decolonization and transformation, very little was said about language, about the question of the hegemony of English and the role of African languages in decolonization. (Gambushe, 2017)

Nevertheless, challenging the hegemony of English has long been considered critical for the decolonising project. At the end of the apartheid era, as the transition to a majority democratic government was taking place, Luckett (1993) advocated multilingualism in language planning for social justice in South Africa. It is interesting to reconsider these arguments now in light of the current debates. In 1993, Luckett described Churchill's (1986, cited in Corson, 1990: 144–145) ladder of multilingualism and evaluated South African education in those terms. Churchill outlined an ascending ladder of stages of multilingualism. Luckett suggested that most schools in South Africa were at Level 1 (supplementary teaching in English is provided for indigenous groups), with universities 'somewhere between Levels 2 and 3' (Luckett, 1993: 46) wherein policy responses include multicultural teaching strategies. Furthermore, Luckett (1993: 46) suggests, 'If the promotion of multilingualism and language equality is to be our goal in a new language plan, then the task ahead is to move our education system from Levels 1–4 to Level 6', in other words, to move from deficit approaches that provide access to English for indigenous groups, towards recognition of, and development of, African languages as official languages and mediums of instruction at all education levels. Today, the education system appears to have progressed somewhat, with most primary schools at Level 5 (provision of African languages as medium of instruction in the early years of schooling). However, in South African high schools and universities post-1994, the project of multilingualism has been set aside in favour of English access.

Current Policy in South Africa

Kotzé (2014: 15) shows that despite a constitution recognising 11 languages, in the intervening 20+ years since democracy in South Africa 'a tacit policy of monolingualism has been in evidence'. Kotzé argues that the political will for multilingualism is there, yet lacking at the level of implementation. In schooling, he suggests that a stalemate situation in terms of legislation has led to the continuation of the policy implemented in 1976 under apartheid of switching to English after four years of home language instruction, which has led to drastic results in terms of school pass rates.

The lack of implementation is often supposed to be a result of attitudes towards vernacular languages and the reported belief among teachers and parents that English should be the medium of education as early as possible, and that vernacular languages slow down the development of English (Kotzé, 2014: 22). However, a great deal of research suggests that learning in a home language is of considerable benefit and linguistics has clearly demonstrated that all languages have equal meaning-making capacity (McKinney, 2017: 5). Kotzé (2014) correlates the preference for English with the desire for (European) modernity and 'progress'. In Hurst (forthcoming), English is correlated with the global or international, is presented as universal and is considered as an important asset for work, offering convenience as a global lingua franca. However, Heugh (2013: 226) notes that the data on parents' demands for English are lacking and, in fact, the majority supported mother tongue education according to one national survey.

There is a corresponding assumption that African languages are not sufficiently 'developed' to operate in the academic space. This discourse is reflected in South Africa's Language Policy for Higher Education (LPHE; Ministry of Education, 2002) which, as Maseko (2014: 29–30) describes, 'acknowledges the current position of English and Afrikaans as languages of research and scholarship, but makes a point that it will be necessary to work within the confines of the status quo until such time as other South African languages have been developed to a level where they may be used in all HE functions'. Maseko (2014: 30) furthermore outlines how the LPHE 'mandates universities to undertake projects that focus on the development of all South African languages, such that they can be used across disciplines and as formal academic languages at HE level'. However, she then considers another report, the report on the Development of Indigenous Languages as Mediums of Instruction in Higher Education (Ministry of Education, 2003), which indicates that current language practice in higher education is 'not nearly adequate to bring the indigenous African languages to the fore and to have them used fully as mediums of instruction ...'. She argues that the report confirms the view of many other scholars that for languages to grow they need to be in use.

Pedagogies are being implemented in South African higher education contexts that often draw on the linguistic capital of students to bring their meaning-making resources into the classroom and, in addition, these pedagogies often require the employment of multilingual staff, including tutors. Some higher education institutions in South Africa have gone further; for example, the University of KwaZulu-Natal has implemented a policy in which all students must learn isiZulu, the dominant regional African language. This, however, can be critiqued as imposing bilingualism rather than building on more recent understandings of linguistic repertoires and language resources that cut across traditional descriptions of bounded languages (Parmegiani & Rudwick, 2014).

In language-in-education policy and curricula, there is still a dependence on the concept of 'named languages that are clearly bounded and hermetically sealed off from each other' (McKinney, 2017: 42). According to McKinney (2017: 42), the monolingual orientation, particularly Anglonormativity (the hegemony of English), is borne out in school practice and in policy where 'schools and teachers' typically treat named languages as autonomous objects that must be kept separate from each other. A shift from a policy emphasis on mono- or bilingualism and the imposition of discrete languages in the curriculum, to an acknowledgment of the messiness of actual language practice, would be an important one. Language policy needs to respond to bottom-up practice, and this is a crucial shift, particularly for pedagogy. In reality, change is happening at the pedagogic level in higher education, just because of who people are and how they use language on a daily basis. Real language use in South Africa often involves various forms of language mixing, code-switching, borrowing and unofficial varieties and registers of the various South African languages. Yet McKinney (2017) argues that speakers of non-dominant registers and hybridised languages are typically positioned as incompetent and deficient, whereas in fact if language were seen as a resource, speakers' multiple resources would no longer be seen as a barrier to learning.

According to McKinney (2017: 4), '... decisions about which language resources should count in schooling, which languages to use as languages of instruction, and how language should be taught are key to achieving social justice in education'. Following Fraser (2008), who argues for economic redistribution, cultural recognition and political representation for a multi-dimensional approach to social justice, McKinney (2017: 4–5) suggests that pedagogical choices are crucial and that learners need their (language) resources to be recognised. This was also promoted by Hurst *et al.* (2017: 93), who state that pedagogies that affirm and validate students' linguistic capital are empowering for multilingual students because they give voice to those students 'who occupy a liminal space and are often disregarded and devalued by the centre/the university'.

One approach to language pedagogy which emphasises language as resource and repertoire is that of translanguaging.

Translanguaging Pedagogies in the South African Context

Despite the emphasis on 'developing' African languages for academic use, many practitioners are implementing translanguaging or multilingual pedagogies in their teaching at university level, in spite of a lack of policy directives in this regard, and often in direct contravention of university/institutional policies (Kotzé, 2014: 16). Kotzé (2014: 24) suggests in South Africa that changes can be made at an institutional level by making use of existing multilingualism within the system. Translanguaging – language practices in which speakers blend and switch between languages, dialects and registers in everyday talk – is being adopted and encouraged as a pedagogic approach in multilingual contexts, in order to draw on students' full repertoires and properly recognise their language/linguistic resources (Hurst *et al.*, 2017; see also Probyn, this volume).

We consider translanguaging to be a decolonial move wherein 'decolonial theory gives epistemic privilege to the lived experience of subordinated groups' (Luckett *et al.*, 2019: 31). Decolonial theorists apply the concept of modernity/coloniality to the politics of knowledge production and they see the same patterns of power working to determine who produces knowledge, who owns it and who legitimates it. They are critical of the ways in which the North claims and validates only one form of knowledge, not only de-legitimating the knowledges of others, but 'undermining the very conditions for epistemic life' (Gordon, 2014: 85). In decolonial theory, Grosfoguel (2013: 74) outlines how the modern episteme has been institutionalised and universalised through the modern university system, the modern disciplines and the five hegemonic (ex-colonial) European languages. As a result, the onus is on speakers of non-European languages to 'catch up' and adapt to, in the case of South Africa, 'Anglonormativity' (McKinney, 2017), including native speaker levels of proficiency in English. Luckett *et al.* (2019: 37) claim that student assessment marks both the 'cognitive content' of student answers, and the hidden curriculum – 'all that is culturally arbitrary and contingent in the curriculum, for example, the degree to which their work meets the grammatical standards of native speakers of English'. They argue that persistent dominance of colonial languages in postcolonial contexts continues to delegitimise previously colonised peoples.

Makelela (2015: 15) suggests that translanguaging pedagogy applied in classrooms involves 'fuzziness and blurring of boundaries between languages' and posits that this is 'indexical tó the pre-colonial African value system of ubuntu', where *ubuntu* refers to 'human, cultural and linguistic interconnectedness' (Makalela, 2015: 21; see also Reilly, this volume). He argues that translanguaging can enhance epistemic access in multilingual spaces. It can also enable the affirmation and recognition of students, which is crucial on the otherwise alienating Anglonormative campuses in South Africa. According to van der Walt (2015: 362), 'The use of students' home or community languages can narrow the distance between the lecturer and the students, thereby making students more receptive and less anxious'. Translanguaging also offers an opportunity for sharing 'language, culture, intersubjectivities, interpretive horizons and frames of reference' with students (Luckett *et al.*, 2019: 38). Makalela (2015: 21) identifies another affordance of translanguaging, wherein enabling the use of students' full linguistic repertoires can support identity formation.

The following section describes our own pedagogical approach in a first-year course which forms the basis for this study.

Context for Data Collection

The data used for this analysis are an essay, a formal marked assignment that is set as part of a course in the extended degree programme in the Humanities Faculty at the University of Cape Town, a historically white university where a culture of Anglonormativity persists. The faculty includes both arts and social sciences departments, and the extended degree programmes involve a four-year degree structure for the bachelor of arts and bachelor of social sciences degrees, as opposed to the standard three-year structure. The four-year programme is intended to cater primarily for students coming from disadvantaged schools for purposes of redress for past inequalities effected during apartheid and structurally reproduced through the continued poor quality of education for black people living in townships and rural areas. For this reason, students on the four-year programme fall into the 'black' (inclusive demographic 'black' is used here to refer to all students who would not have been classified 'white' during apartheid) demographic group. Many of these students speak one or more languages in addition to English, with many students' home language being an African language or Afrikaans. However, many students are also first language (L1) English speakers and a few are monolingual in English.

Because of the racialised outcome in historically white universities of government policies for funding for educational development, extended degree programmes have been critiqued during the recent student

protests for their separate and therefore stigmatising state-funded structures, which are seen to perpetuate a deficit model of education for previously disadvantaged groups (Luckett & Shay, 2017). However, the
extended degree programme that hosts the course considered here has
sought to move away from deficit models and implement pedagogies that
respond to calls for decolonisation. One of the main pedagogic strategies
is the implementation of multilingual/translanguaging pedagogies. These
pedagogies are also being taken up in a number of departments in the
faculty in collaboration with the Education Development Unit, which
runs the extended degree programmes. Thus, education development in
the faculty is impacting on the mainstream curriculum – what gets taught
and how – which has long remained untouchable, ring-fenced as the
domain of disciplinary expertise and often defended by the liberal ideology of academic freedom (Baijnath, 2017). Until recently, the academic
curriculum and pedagogies, particularly in historically white universities
in South Africa, have continued to uncritically reproduce 'colonial difference' – the idea that the 'colonized' need to 'catch up' and adapt and
assimilate into Eurocentric social and cultural norms. This misrecognises
black students' linguistic and cultural capital and positions them as 'disadvantaged', 'underprepared' and in need of development. This situation
was noticed by students and was a key driver of the student protests
described above (Sebidi & Morreira, 2017). The implementation of translanguaging pedagogies is seen by both staff and students as a decolonising move, in its recognition of black students' linguistic and cultural
capital and its challenge to the hegemony of English as the only language
of academia.

Data Used in the Analysis

The essay that provided the data for the analysis below forms part of
the required coursework submissions for an introductory course on the
extended BA degree. It emphasises the development of critical analysis
skills including discourse analysis, visual analysis and genre analysis.
The essay is called 'My Language History' and it elicits information on
students' language backgrounds as one of the aims of the course – to
surface and value students' linguistic resources. Throughout the course,
students are encouraged to submit work and participate in class discussions and online tasks in languages other than English. Students are
encouraged to submit the Language History essay in the language or
languages of their choice, including translanguaging/code-switching
between languages and dialects or registers. It is important to note that
given that this is likely to be the first time these students are given this
opportunity, especially for written work in an environment where high
levels of proficiency in the English MOI is simply assumed as the norm,

all instances of language use in a language other than English in our sample can be assumed to be marked.

The essay itself is strongly framed or staged in terms of students' responses. The task outlines how students should respond by first describing their language history from birth to school, through school, and then from school to university. Many of the essays thus follow the recommended chronological structure and narrative genre. Additionally, the essay is not a typical academic essay task but is more subjective and experiential, asking students to draw on their personal narratives and write in the first person. It is perhaps easier for students to draw on their other languages in this less formal academic genre; for this reason, we see more translanguaging in this essay than in the other more formal essays on the course, despite students being allowed to submit all essays in languages of their choice. Despite the relatively personal nature of the essay, however, every year only a handful of students submit in a language or mix of languages other than English, so the data here are illustrative of pedagogic possibilities of translanguaging, rather than representative, because the data sample is relatively small.

Methodology

This data analysis required a methodology that would demonstrate the kinds of meanings students make when they are given permission to write using their full linguistic repertoires. To do this we turned to Maton's (2014) Legitimation Code Theory (LCT), which provides concepts for determining the principles that legitimate and organise knowledge in particular fields. One such concept is semantic density (SD), which is used to describe the extent to which meanings are condensed into language, symbols or practices (Maton, 2014: 129). Maton distinguishes between epistemological density and axiological density. The former is a typical characteristic of academic texts and captures the degree of condensation, integration or complexity of epistemic relations within abstract concepts and between these and their referents as an index of their explanatory power. The latter captures the degree of intensity with which meanings about social relations and practices are charged with social, moral, political or aesthetic value. Maton (2014: 166) explains, 'In social science where axiological cosmologies dominate, theories are assessed not for their explanatory power but in terms of their underlying models of humanity and society'. He defines cosmologies as the 'belief systems' that constitute social fields, underlying 'the ways that actors and practices are differently characterized and valued' (Maton, 2014: 162). Cosmologies are used to give 'constellations' of meanings in a field their axiological power or charge – their intensity of feeling, value or moral judgment – an axiological charge can be positive/neutral/

negative. Constellations are comprised of clusters, which in turn are condensations of stances that subjects take to communicate axiological meanings.

Given the nature of our data – students' language histories and language attitudes – we focus on social relations rather than epistemic relations in our analysis: that is, on our subjects' relations and attitudes to social groups and their languages and on the ways in which their attitudes or stances are constituted by certain belief systems and sets of values (cosmologies). We used Maton's concept of axiological semantic density (ASD) – or axiological condensation – found in stances, clusters and constellations and charged by cosmologies to analyse the rationales or moral reasoning for students' claims, positions and attitudes about language, particularly when they could draw on their full linguistic repertoires. We formed a proposition that these essays would tap into their 'structures of feeling' and so we wanted to focus on analysing meanings about social relations rather than the normal focus in academic writing, namely epistemic relations.

In order to operationalise the concept of axiological condensation, we moved from units of meaning (realised in chunks of text) to the underlying cosmologies that provide their axiological charge. We started with individual multilingual knowers (our students) who, as described above, learn in a formally monolingual context. We then coded their translanguaging essays into 'stances' (units of axiological meaning). These stances were then grouped into 'clusters' around the particular languages referred to by the students and discussed in the essays. The clusters were then grouped into 'constellations' which, according to Maton (2014), give coherence and value to the stances. We identified four 'constellations' to work with in our analysis: language attitudes, language and identity, language education policy and language and cultural knowledge. As noted above, constellations are charged positively or negatively by extra-linguistic cosmologies or belief systems. We used this idea of 'axiological charge' to code the stances in our data as being positively or negatively charged (see below).

Method

For this project we selected 13 essays from the Language History assignments in one year. In all cases students had given signed consent for us to use their essays for research purposes on condition of anonymity. Our purposive sample was determined on the basis of the following three criteria: the essays all met the requirements of the task; they were written in at least two languages, including examples of translanguaging (mostly English, isiXhosa and Afrikaans; the latter are the two official regional languages for our province, the Western Cape); and the essays captured students' attitudes to language. In our sample we ended up with

13 essays: six in English and isiXhosa; two in English, isiXhosa and Sesotho; three in English and Afrikaans; one in English, Afrikaans and isiXhosa; and one in English, Afrikaans and Arabic. We then employed two of our tutors, fluent in isiXhosa and Sesotho, and Afrikaans and Arabic, respectively, to work with us on translating all clauses into English to ensure that we properly understood the nuances of students' writing in languages other than English. Thereafter, we selected key phrases or stretches of text making up one unit of axiological meaning in which students expressed their stances (feelings and judgments) towards language practices. In all we identified 103 stances for analysis. Most stances were expressed in a mixture of English and isiXhosa or of English and Afrikaans. Table 4.2 shows the dominant language used for each stance that we analysed.

After immersing ourselves in the data, we identified the following constellations of axiological meaning in the essays: attitudes towards specific languages; attitudes towards language and identity; attitudes towards language-in-education policy; and attitudes towards language and cultural knowledge. Within each of these four constellations we grouped the stances selected for coding into language clusters. Note, the clusters were based on the language that was the target of the students' attitude or stance (as opposed to the language in which the stance was written, although we did keep track of that as well). The language clusters identified were English, isiXhosa, Afrikaans, L2 (English or Afrikaans) and Multilingualism (note that not all language clusters applied to each constellation). Appendix A shows the constellations and language clusters that we used to sort and compare the data. Some stances were coded twice, either because our stances (units of analysis) were too 'clumpy' and insufficiently disaggregated, or because we found that our coding categories sometimes overlapped.

Developing a Translation Device

In LCT a 'translation device' is a tool that shows how the researcher has moved between selected concepts in theory and their data. Translation

Table 4.2 Showing dominant language used per stance in data sample (13 essays)

Dominant language used per stance	N	%
English	64	62.1%
isiXhosa	22	21.4%
Afrikaans	14	13.6%
Sesotho	2	1.9%
Arabic	1	1.0%
Total stances in sample	**103**	

Table 4.3 A section of the translation device for coding axiological condensation using concepts from appraisal theory

Constellations	Clusters of stances towards languages within constellations	Axiological charge Affect +	Axiological charge Affect −	Axiological charge Judgment +	Axiological charge Judgment −
Language Attitudes	Home Lang (English)	Subject holds very positive feelings or emotions towards a person, social group or social practice, including a language.	Subject holds very negative feelings or emotions towards a person, social group or social practice, including a language.	Subject holds a person, social group or their behaviour – including language practice – in high esteem and with respect and/or judges their linguistic/cultural practices to be of high social/moral/ethical worth.	Subject holds a person, social group or their behaviour – including language practice – in low esteem and/or judges their linguistic/cultural practices to be questionable, immoral/unethical/socially unjust.
	Home Lang (isiXhosa)				
	Home Lang (Afrikaans)				
	L2 (English/Afrikaans)				
	Multilingualism				

devices are designed for specific studies and are not expected to be generalisable across studies. Once we had established our units of analysis (stances, clusters and constellations), we had to find a way of coding their 'axiological charge'. For this we borrowed concepts from Appraisal theory in Systemic Functional Linguistics (SFL). Appraisal is used in SFL for construing interpersonal meanings in the stratum of discourse semantics (Martin & White, 2005). We did not conduct a rigorous SFL analysis, but rather borrowed from Appraisal theory its three master categories for Attitude: Affect/Judgment/Appreciation, and adapted these as dimensions for our translation device. We limited ourselves to Attitude and did not use Graduation or Engagement. Affect captures subjects' attitudes regarding their feelings and emotions towards people and social practices and includes finer categories relating to desires and fears about well-being, security and satisfaction. Judgment captures subjects' evaluations of people and their behaviour, expressing esteem, respect, moral worth or social sanction. Judgment can draw on shared community, socialised or institutionalised values (Martin & White, 2005: 46). Appreciation captures attitudes towards things, phenomena and objects including approval and aesthetic value.

We set up our translation device to code each stance for types of Attitude in Appraisal theory described above and for contrasting values of ASD within them, namely a positive or negative charge. After coding all stances, we found that very few expressed attitudes of Appreciation, that is, evaluations of objects or things, and so this category was dropped. A section of our translation device is presented in Table 4.3.

Data Analysis with Examples

In this section we discuss the significant findings in our analysis of the data using the four coding categories derived from Appraisal theory: Affect(+)/Affect(−)/Judgment(+)/Judgment(−).

Firstly, for the cluster **Language Attitudes** relating to **Affect**, the analysis showed that there was no significant positive axiological charge for home language and, surprisingly, isiXhosa scored lowest (1.7% Affect+). Instead, students' stances showed higher positive feelings towards multilingualism (6.8% Affect+). It is noteworthy that the negative feelings expressed towards multilingualism (5.1% Affect−) had to do with its effect on subtracting from their use of their home languages and thus home language proficiency. Significant findings in this category included **Judgment** related to valuing a language for its social esteem or worth or condemning it for its failure to be practised ethically or morally. The strongest positive evaluation (23.7% Judgment+) was for multilingual practices, suggesting that students see multilingualism as the future for South African language practice, as illustrated in Excerpt 4.1.

Excerpt 4.1

Original (English)
You can fit in in any conversation, and it comes with lots of opportunities both in the social or formal places. And I feel as though/people in University should have the choice of writing essays and examinations in whichever language they choose.

Many stances, such as that in Excerpt 4.2, opposed the imposition of English or Afrikaans as second languages (25.4% Judgment−).

Excerpt 4.2

Original (English, isiXhosa)	English translation
Since high school I have been taught [...] that the more fluent you are in English the more intelligent you will be [...]. **Yandenza ndijongele phantsi ulwimi lwesiXhosa.**	Since high school I have been taught [...] that the more fluent you are in English the more intelligent you will be [...]. **This made me look down upon the language of isiXhosa.**

Under the **Language and Identity** cluster, for stances relating to **Affect**, unsurprisingly the strongest positive feelings were expressed for students' home languages and how these conveyed their 'true' identities (10.0% Affect+), as shown in Excerpt 4.3. Furthermore, there were no stances that expressed a negative charge for the relation between home language and identity.

Excerpt 4.3

Original (isiXhosa)	English translation
Ndithanda isiXhosa ngaphezukwawo onke amalwimi endiwaziyo ngokuba lelona lizwi endikwaziyo ukuzivakalisa ngalo.	I like isiXhosa above all languages because it is the voice in which I am able to express myself.

This was reinforced by the high proportion of stances positioned positively under **Judgment** (25% Judgment+), as in Excerpt 4.4.

Excerpt 4.4

Original (English, isiXhosa)	English translation
We usually say **esixhoseni umntu ngumntu ngabanye abantu, mna ndithi, umntu ngumntu ngelwimi lwakhe.**	We usually say **in isiXhosa a person is a person through other people but me, I say a person is a person through their home tongue/language.**

What was significant was the relatively high positive score for the relation between multilingualism and identity (20% Judgment+), suggesting that some students identify strongly with being multilingual rather than belonging to a particular ethnic group, as illustrated in Excerpt 4.5.

Excerpt 4.5

Original (isiXhosa)
Ukufunda amanye amalwimi kunceda ukukwaza unxibelelana nabanye abantu, kwaye uye ungumntu ukwazi uncinge ngendlela ezahlukeneyo.

English translation
Learning other languages helps in interacting with other people and often you as a person know how to think in different ways.

Another significant finding around language and identity was the negative positioning of English in the students' essays (12.5% Affect−) and (22.5% Judgment−), as shown in Excerpt 4.6.

Excerpt 4.6

Original (English)
This constant use of the English is (…) altering my attitude, mannerisms,/ and ultimately is making me feel like I'm turning into someone else.

We coded Excerpt 4.7 linking English with a middle-class or educated identity as carrying a negative charge for English under both Affect(−) and Judgment(−).

Excerpt 4.7

Original (isiXhosa, English)
Ekasi bendingathand ukukhumsha kakhulu ngoba bendingafuni bengathi ndizenza ngcono. Whenever I did speak English, I would use the same accent that was used in the community (…) because I wanted to fit in and did not want to be called a coconut.

English translation
In the township I didn't like speaking English a lot because I didn't want to be as if I am making myself superior. Whenever I did speak English, I would use the same accent that was used in the community (…) because I wanted to fit in and did not want to be called a coconut.

Not many stances fell into the **Language Education Policy** cluster and there were no very significant findings for **Affect**. What stood out for **Judgment** was the strong support for the use of home languages (isiXhosa and Afrikaans) as languages of learning at school (35.3% Judgment+), as seen in Excerpt 4.8.

Excerpt 4.8

Original (isiXhosa)
Isifundo sezibalo besisifunda ngolwimi lwesiXhosa, ulwimi lwesiXhosa belubaluleke ngendlela emandla (…) besilusebenzisa nangendlela esiye sicinge ngayo.

English translation
The study of numeracy we studied it in isiXhosa, the language of isiXhosa was important in a powerful way (…) as we used it for the way we used to think.

Excerpt 4.9 is one of the high proportion of stances that positioned the use of second languages (English or Afrikaans) as MOI negatively (29.4% Judgment−).

Excerpt 4.9

Original (English)
I remember one of my teachers in Grade 12 who used to teach in English saying "Kids listen! Listen! You must not laugh as if you are uneducated, not walk like you are ill disciplined and don't talk English like blacks." I did not see then the dominance (…) that English has over black people and learning institutions.

Finally, there were a small number of stances that fell into the cluster for **Cultural Knowledge**. Interestingly, there were no negative charges related to this cluster and all related to valuing home languages as carriers of cultural knowledge and practice. Stances such as Excerpt 4.10 expressed high levels of social esteem, respect and value for the cultural knowledge carried in those languages (90.0% Judgment+).

Excerpt 4.10

Original (isiXhosa)	English translation
Nje ngomXhosa okhulele ezilalini, sikhuliswe phantsi kwamasiko ahamba nezi thethe, kwaye ehlonitshiwe kakulu ngo tatomkhulu (…). Ndikhumbula ebuntwaneni bam ndenzelwa imbeleko nto leyo eyenziwa imbeleko (…). Yazo izinyanya zakowenu zokwamkela (…) zikukhusela kwimimoya emdaka. Izinyanya zizo qa ezikwazi ukuthetha no Qamata uThixo wamaXhosa.	As an isiXhosa who grew up in rural areas we were raised under traditions and customs, which were respected a lot by the grand-fathers (…). I remember in my childhood a dedication ceremony was made for me (…). The ancestors of your family will welcome you (…) and protect you from bad spirits. Ancestors are the only ones able to speak to Qamata the God of the Xhosa people.

Lastly, we analysed the language(s) used most for particular constellations and type of axiological charge. Fairly predictably, for both Affect and Judgment, when students discussed Language Attitudes towards their home languages and Cultural Knowledge they were more likely to employ their home languages, and when they discussed the use of English and multilingualism, they were more likely to use English again for both Affect and Judgment. This highlights the affordances of translanguaging in enabling students to draw on more contextual knowledge from their life experiences and cultural backgrounds.

Cosmologies

As noted above, cosmologies are sets of beliefs and values that charge constellations and clusters of meanings in a particular field by providing the social/political/moral reasoning or belief system that legitimates their positioning in a particular field. In this discussion we point to the key cosmologies that students drew on to give their stances high axiological charge.

Firstly, unsurprisingly in a postcolonial context with a history of centuries of settler oppression, there is evidence that students were drawing on attitudes generated by a subculture of resistance to the dominant settler culture (and English) by subordinated groups or classes. This was the most common cosmology that informed students' attitudes and was clearly part of their home cultures, as shown in Excerpt 4.11.

Excerpt 4.11

Original (Afrikaans)	English translation
Dit as asof my ma en my juffrou twee verskillende tale gepraat het (…). Ek het net daar besluit dat ek my ma se "taal" by die huis gaan praat en my juffrou se "taal" by die skool.	It was as if my teacher and mother spoke two different languages (…). I decided then I will only speak my mother's "language" at home and my teacher's "language" at school.

Some students advocated resistance to domination at a political/institutional level. A more defiant cosmology of resistance that fewer students appeared to be drawing on was an Africanist or anti-/de-colonial political discourse, as expressed in Excerpt 4.12.

Excerpt 4.12

Original (English)
English offered me no choice in terms of intellectual [development], the only pathway was to go over English in order to make it in life. English divided me from my own culture, shut down a dream of being African, pure Xhosa. English twisted me upside down and disconnected me from my own history, (…) in what way can an African experience be expressed properly into another language?

In contradiction to the cosmologies of resistance, there was evidence that some students adopted a pragmatic or instrumental rationality to legitimate their support for learning in English, as shown in Excerpt 4.13. We suggest that this attitude draws on the hegemonic discourse of globalisation in which English is viewed as the language of access to professional work and social mobility. Unsurprisingly, all stances derived from this cosmology were written in English.

Excerpt 4.13

Original (English)
English is a universal language. Therefore as I grow, and become better using this language I am doing myself a favour.

However, we also noted that some students drew on what could be termed an Afropolitan cosmology – a worldly rejection of a return to the past, an embracing of modernity through multilingualism – but a rejection of its Eurocentric version.

In summing up, we can infer that the opportunity given in these essays for students to use translanguaging in the languages of their choice gave them licence to express their feelings and attitudes towards language, identity and culture in ways that are normally repressed in their English medium-only essays on other courses. In particular, we suggest that they felt it was legitimate to draw on cosmologies of resistance and anti/decolonisation from their homes and political backgrounds that may have been constrained when writing in an English-only environment.

Conclusion

A great deal has changed since Luckett's (1993) argument regarding the need for multilingualism in all levels of South African education. Yet current policy still needs to refocus on the implementation of multilingualism in higher education language policies, and the position of English needs to be challenged. There is a need to use African languages in university spaces to contest persistent coloniality and extend the affordances of translanguaging. Rather than waiting for African languages to 'develop', they should be used immediately in university contexts, in spite of policy.

Our analysis reveals that the affordances of translanguaging are strongest when students are talking about home – about identity and cultural knowledge. Translanguaging opens up opportunities for students to draw on their capital and for their cosmologies to be shared and legitimised. Although the essay we analysed is not a highly academic abstract essay, the analysis shows that the students were emotionally engaged, which is conducive to learning. This frames the essay as an act of recognition, as opposed to endless acts of misrecognition. We are not claiming that translanguaging allows students higher levels of academic abstraction (epistemological semantic density) – merely that this first step in incorporating translanguaging pedagogies shows high levels of engagement (i.e. high levels of ASD which encourages motivation and engagement) and enables the possibility of students drawing on funds of contextual knowledge.

What is valued in the humanities and social sciences is the ability to set up relationships between abstract concepts and particular contextualised instances. Neither abstract concepts nor highly contextualised narratives are enough on their own; rather, relating one to another – the concept and the data – is the goal. For this reason, enabling students to draw on contextual knowledge such as identities and cultural knowledge through translanguaging is key to developing the postcolonial humanities.

Acknowledgments

We would like to thank Msakha Mona and Tammy Wilks for their assistance with translation for this project. We are grateful for funding from the UAE-based research cluster Languaging and Higher Education in Bilingual Contexts, led by David Palfreyman at Zayed University.

Appendix A: Showing Summary of Data Analysis

Constellations	Clusters of stances towards languages within constellations	Axiological charge Affect +		Axiological charge Affect –		Axiological charge Judgment +		Axiological charge Judgment –	
		N	%	N	%	N	%	N	%
Lang Attitudes	Home Lang (English)	3	5.1%	0		2	3.4%	1	1.7%
	Home Lang (isiXhosa)	1	1.7%	0		1	1.7%	0	
	Home Lang (Afrikaans)	3	5.1%	0		3	5.1%	2	3.4%
	L2 (English/Afrikaans)	3	5.1%	0		4	6.8%	15	25.4%
	Multilingualism	4	6.8%	3	5.1%	14	23.7%	0	
Coding subtotal 59									
Identity	Home Lang (isiXhosa/ Afrikaans)	5	12.5%	0		10	25.0%	0	
	English	0		5	12.5%	0		9	22.5%
	Multilingualism	2	5.0%	0		8	20.0%	1	2.5%
Coding subtotal 40									
Lang Ed Policy	Home Lang (isiXhosa/ Afrikaans)	1	5.9%			6	35.3%	0	
	L2 (English/Afrikaans)	0		2	11.8%	0		5	29.4%
	Multilingualism	1	5.9%	1	5.9%	0		1	5.9%
Coding subtotal 17									
Cultural Knowledge	Home Lang (isiXhosa/ Afrikaans/Arabic)	1	10%	0		9	90.0%	0	
Coding subtotal 10									

5 Translanguaging as a Pathway to Ethical Bilingual Education: An Exploratory Case Study from Kenya

Eowyn Crisfield, Isla Gordon and
Alexandra Holland

Introduction

The past decade has seen a sharp rise in English-medium international schools, with a concurrent increase in the number of students learning English as an additional language while also accessing the curriculum in English. The issues arising from learning in a second language are well documented (UNESCO, 2016), and acknowledged by some international curricula providers (Ballantyne & Rivera, 2014). In post-independence contexts in Africa, this focus on English-medium education increases the already present tension about which languages can or should be used in schools, and can lead to the exclusive use of English and the neglect of local languages. This chapter presents an exploratory case study of a private junior school (Grades 1–5) in Kenya which is engaged in prestige planning (Kamwangamalu, 2015) by transforming an international programme taught entirely in English into a programme using both national languages, Kiswahili and English.

This approach to language within the curriculum is based on the belief that a truly ethical educational model will attend to the linguistic needs of the students as a necessary element of their overall development. The school's vision is progressive and bold, but it faces significant practical challenges in terms of curriculum planning, pedagogical approach and resourcing, and greater ideological challenges, with language status being a key roadblock to successful implementation. A potential solution to overcoming these roadblocks is the considered use of classroom translanguaging (Lewis *et al.*, 2012b) which, rather than enforcing separation, brings languages together for learning and allows a local language to be presented in parity to English within educational settings.

An exploratory case study was chosen over other research methods for a number of reasons. Bilingualism and translanguaging in international education is a relatively new area of study and there is a limited research base to discuss. The case study is presented as an opportunity to engage in theoretical reflection on praxis. The study itself is not data-driven and is not intended to be replicated; rather, the goals are to help other schools contextualise translanguaging pedagogy and to document the process used in one school so that it can be used to support the development of similar programmes in other schools. Over the course of four years, curriculum developers and teachers in the case study school iterated and refined their programme; in documenting the process here, we further reflect on and refine what was learned.

This case study is grounded in three theoretical lenses. The first lens is the history and current situation of *language in education* in Africa, and specifically in Kenya, including the notion that indigenous languages are unsuited for educational purposes, particularly for complex and abstract subjects such as science and mathematics (Timammy & Oduor, 2016). The second is the tension between the rise in English-medium international education, alongside understandings of the importance of students' home languages in education. The third lens is theories of *bilingual education*, and how the development and implementation of bilingual models can be beneficial or detrimental to students' development: linguistically, academically and culturally.

Languages in Education in Africa

Since the beginning of the post-independence era (1957 onwards), issues relating to languages in education have been a topic of discussion, concern and research in many African countries, with a growing interest recently in bilingual education (e.g. Chimbutane, 2011; Kamwangamalu, 2015; see also Luckett & Hurst-Harosh, as well as Probyn, this volume). This does not mean, however, that the practice of *bilingualism in education* was unknown in the colonial era. For reasons ranging from religious to political, education in many countries was allowed or encouraged in the local languages, either exclusively or in tandem with the colonial languages. The lasting legacy of the relationship between local and colonial languages is the continued belief that access to a global language is the way of the future for Africa, in part to support relationships, trade and development within the continent, and in part as a need of the nation-state. This belief leads to a consistent undervaluing of the local languages, and the elevating of the former colonial languages (notably English,

French and Portuguese) as superior in terms of ability to deliver education (Chimbutane, 2011).

This chapter will not lend itself to a linguistic analysis of the capacity of African languages for teaching and learning, but does underpin itself with the belief that any language can become a vehicular language for all types of education if there is a will to make it so (Gacheche, 2010). This is not, however, a widespread belief in many countries, where the discourse tends to centre on the deficiencies of local languages for education. When local languages are used in education, it is often limited to short-term use of the local language as a support for learning the language of instruction (LoI), usually the former colonial language. The focus is not on the inherent value of the local language, which is innately connected to learning in the local context, or on the continued growth of the local language for cognition and learning (Ouane & Glanz, 2010; see also Luckett & Hurst-Harosh, this volume).

In the case of Kenya, these tensions have led to a fragmented history concerning language policy and language-in-education practice. Over the years there have been different attempts at implementation of a 'mother tongue' language policy, but attitudes in Kenya lean strongly towards the belief that English is the preferred LoI in schools, and that local or indigenous languages, including Kiswahili, are not adequate for the task of education (Nyarigoti & Ambiyo, 2014). Despite policy initiatives to provide for 'mother tongue-based education' in the early years, in practice these are usually limited to rural areas. This pattern is evident in local schools, but most particularly in schools that are deemed 'international', in that they are not delivering the Kenyan National Curriculum. In these schools, the co-national language is excluded from the LoI: at best, it is taught as an additional language, and sometimes it is not taught at all.

Current Issues in English-Medium International Education

The 2018 Global Opportunities Report estimated a worldwide total of 5.1 million students studying through the medium of English in international schools, of whom 80% are from their school's host country (ISC Research, 2018). English-medium international schools are generally not considered innovators in the area of languages in education. Despite frequently having multilingual student populations, they often maintain a monolingual habitus (Gogolin, 1997), either by design or by default (Carder, 2007). The term *monolingual habitus* is used to describe a situation in which a multilingual population functions in monolingual mode; in the case of schools, it describes multilingual schools in which languages other than the school language are rarely heard or used, either by explicit regulations or implicit conventions. Language attrition is a common occurrence in these schools, with the students gaining proficiency in English at the cost of their own languages (Carder, 2018). Excluding students' stronger languages in education is widely recognised as detrimental on many levels, and this includes students in prestigious international schools (Chalmers, 2019).

In addition to the undesirable linguistic outcomes, this reality is at odds with the stated aims of many international schools and curricula to develop global citizens and international-mindedness. Challenges to supporting other languages in customarily English-medium international education range from the practical to the ideological. In many cases, schools and parents see English-medium instruction (EMI) as a precious opportunity for students to learn English at a younger age, with the perception that this will open doors for them in later life (compare with Dalziel and Guarda's study of the tertiary context, this volume). This means that the issues connected to the stagnation or loss of their own languages are often minimised or ignored (Carder, 2018). Both parents and teachers/schools can be equally complacent about the development, or lack thereof, of students' home languages. Despite the complexity of languages and language learning in international schools, there is very little research done in these contexts. Research on language development and language attrition in international schools is almost non-existent, with the exception of small-scale action research projects carried out by teachers, which generally remain unpublished.

Linking Language Learning to the School's Mission and Vision

The case study school is the first in an integrated network of schools that aims to develop future leaders who will have the knowledge and skills to support the development of their communities. The school recruits young people who show potential for leadership, through their ability to think critically about challenges in their community and to take action to solve them. Students are recruited regardless of their background, and financial aid is provided to ensure that all students who are accepted can access the school. As a result, the student body is drawn from all parts of Kenyan society and has a high degree of socioeconomic diversity.

The mission of developing the future leaders for Kenya creates specific requirements for the school's curriculum where students need to be globally minded, but also deeply rooted in their local culture (Aga Khan Academies, 2018). To address this, the school uses the International Baccalaureate curriculum at all levels, implementing the Primary Years Programme (PYP), Middle Years Programme (MYP) and Diploma Programme (DP). The IB curricula provide a framework for an emphasis on a deep understanding of the students' own culture, which allows them to draw on the wisdom of their communities, to consider the relevance of external best practice to their own context and to adapt ideas so that they are tailored to the needs of their society. Additionally, in creating this deep link to and pride in their community and culture, the school seeks to avoid the danger of the 'brain drain' where students aspire to build their future lives in other places. As such, the school consciously works to create a curriculum that celebrates national language and culture, builds students' connections to their home and creates a deep-seated desire to use their education to improve the quality of life in their communities, not just for themselves and their immediate family, but also for the people around them. This rooting in their local culture serves the mission and vision of the school, and also creates the basis for intercultural understanding, where students are able to recognise and reflect on their own values and beliefs as well as understanding the perspectives of others (Skelton, 2007).

Several elements come together in building this deep connection to local context and culture. Firstly, 80% of the teaching staff are Kenyan, providing the students with strong positive role models from within their own communities. Secondly, the units of inquiry (UoI), around which the IB PYP and MYP are structured, are deliberately designed to equip students to access the wisdom of their communities, and the examples used are chosen to allow students to delve into issues relevant to their home country and community. These UoI present students with authentic local challenges to consider, and allow them to suggest their own ideas about practical action that can be taken.

Creating this grounding in local context and culture includes ensuring that students can access the language of their community and, for this reason, the school has gradually shifted from a traditional English-only programme to a bilingual programme. This model has been developed to provide students with the opportunity to build academic proficiency in both English and Kiswahili, as well as to combat the view that local languages are only languages of communication and emotion, while international languages are the languages of academic and technical knowledge (Efurosibina, 1994). This view implicitly emphasises the idea that academic knowledge is somehow 'alien' to the African context, or something that can only be accessed by throwing off one's own culture and taking on the culture of the 'West'. It is therefore desirable that students study not only art, music and literature through the medium of Kiswahili, but mathematics, science and technology as well, something that research suggests is often not the case (Alidou et al., 2006).

This focus on teaching students Kiswahili, so that they acquire both levels of fluency needed for academic purposes, i.e. Basic Interpersonal Communicative Skills (BICS) and Cognitive Academic Language Proficiency (CALP) (Cummins, 2005a, 2008a), is particularly important given the language profiles of the student body. Although BICS and CALP are now considered to be a simplistic representation of the bilingual continuum (Baker & Wright, 2017), they still provide a helpful framework for teachers in planning for language use across different contexts and for different purposes. The framework also highlights the issue of not confounding relative conversational fluency with the ability to do academic work, which requires more complex language and structures.

Some students admitted to the school in this case study at the age of six (Year 1) are fluent Kiswahili speakers, although this is far from the norm. The vast majority of students arrive with English as their dominant language, showing an imbalance between their learning of English and local languages that has become entrenched by the time that they start school. The use of Kiswahili alongside English as the LoI can help address this imbalance in their language skills and allow students to access a richer understanding of their local and national context than is available through English. Learning opportunities are designed for students to interview local people about their lives and jobs, and to interact within their community in ways that are more authentic – important preparation if they are to make change in their communities in the future. The use of Kiswahili also gives them access to primary sources about their context and to a wider range of resources relating to life in Kenya, rather than relying on views of their context written in English, often by outsiders. This, again, shows respect for indigenous knowledge and, for students, emphasises the necessity of understanding their local environment through the perspectives of people who live there.

Providing this linguistic connection is also vital if students are to use their education to enrich the lives of people in their communities. At present, too many students accessing an international education, even those being educated in their home country, are cut off from mastering their own languages to a high level and can end up culturally rootless (Carder, 2018). This lack also pushes them towards a future outside their society, as they may not have the linguistic skills to work effectively in a professional or managerial role in their community; their talents, knowledge and skills are lost to the country. The integration of both English and Kiswahili in student learning is therefore essential to the realisation of the school's mission and vision.

Building a Model for Ethical Bilingual Education

Every aspect of education and schooling is, in one way or another, involved in teaching values (Husu & Tirri, 2007). As Higgins and Jo (2016: 1) state, 'Thinkers throughout history have understood that education is an inherently ethical enterprise, and scholars have made this case both philosophically and empirically, demonstrating that education operates according to certain assumptions, implicitly or explicitly, about what is good and right, and, most importantly, about the good and right end of education'. Reflecting on the ethical considerations of decisions regarding children's languages is one aspect of ensuring that we are doing what is 'good and right' for them educationally and linguistically. Likewise, according to Hansen (2001: 826), 'the notion that teaching is a moral practice constitutes one of the world's most enduring understandings of the work .... the activity of teaching is itself saturated with moral significance, and it is so in ways that illuminate both the beneficial and the harmful influence teachers can have on students'. The language choices a school makes for its educational programmes, and whether these are beneficial or harmful to the students' identity, development and academic achievement, therefore have an ethical dimension. Whether we intend it or not, these choices also convey implicit messages to students about the values we hold with regard to the status of different languages and cultures.

While bilingual education may generally be seen as highly desirable, this is often linked to the desire for the acquisition of high-status global languages. Cummins (2005a: 586) describes this in some contexts as '... the bizarre scenario of schools successfully transforming fluent speakers of foreign languages into monolingual English speakers, at the same time as they struggle, largely unsuccessfully, to transform monolingual English speakers into foreign language speakers'. Where bilingual programmes do exist, in Africa or in other contexts, there is often little attention paid to how ethical these provisions may be in terms of their impact on students' connection with their identities, communities and local environment (Ouane & Glanz, 2010).

There is a clear need to recognise that any programme that creates a linguistic or cultural deficit for students, particularly in causing the attrition of languages relevant to their home context and culture, cannot be considered ethical in nature. Chumak-Horbatsch (2012) developed the idea of *linguistically appropriate practice* as a means of working with immigrant children in ways that support and enhance their language development. It can be argued that linguistically appropriate practice is necessary in all EMI programmes, as well as within bilingual programmes. In addition to considering the impact of education through English from a linguistic standpoint, the approach taken to language learning within a school needs also to be linked to the school aims. For international schools this means addressing students' home languages as a critical element of developing global citizenship.

There are two main aspects to consider when developing an ethical bilingual programme (Crisfield, 2018). The first aspect is the group perspective: the linguistic profile of the student population that will be served by the programme and if that programme meets their linguistic needs. Many bilingual programmes are transitional in nature, with the main goal being that students acquire another language, and the default position being that their own language will stagnate or be lost (Hornberger, 1991). These programmes do not adequately meet the linguistic needs of the students, who would be best served by maintaining and developing their own languages alongside the acquisition of a new language. The second aspect is the individual perspective: will the programme serve the needs of an individual student? In schools where the student body is heterogeneous in terms of language, a programme that meets the linguistic needs of one student may be detrimental to another. In both the group and individual perspective, there is a tendency to what Hélot (2011) calls *ignored bilingualism*, where the natural bilingual potential of students is suppressed or sublimated in the quest for a more desirable language profile.

In the instance of the case study school in this chapter, there was a clear mandate to move away from a traditional English-only model towards a model that would meet the linguistic needs of the students, as identified by the mission and vision of the school. This was in recognition of the fact that excluding one of the two Kenyan national languages was sending a powerful message about the value of local knowledge and local context as compared to English (Grimshaw, 2015). The school implemented an alternate days (2.5 days in English and 2.5 days in Kiswahili) bilingual model for students aged six to eight, in an attempt to promote equal development of both Kiswahili and English. While this worked fairly well in these grades, the school community was keen to find a more flexible model that would meet the developing needs of older students in the school.

The move to a pedagogical translanguaging approach was chosen for a variety of reasons. Firstly, the integration of the two languages seemed to provide an authentic representation of how Kenyans themselves use language on a day-to-day basis. It therefore seemed that a strict division between languages would not mirror the language use that was modelled for students in their local context. A decision was taken to trial a translanguaging approach in Grade 4 (nine to ten years old). In the context of this case study, the original definition for translanguaging of varying the language of input and output (Lewis *et al.*, 2012b) has been enhanced by the addition of *processing* as a stage within the translanguaging approach. Thus, the stages are referred to in a simple form using three parts: stages of *input*, *processing* and *output*. Using the translanguaging cycle would allow teachers to make decisions about which language would provide the best medium for learning within a UoI. For example, when considering methods of decision making in communities it would be appropriate for students to interview community members in Kiswahili to find out how consensus is reached in their context, while when looking at international models it would be more straightforward to access information in English. Translanguaging therefore presented a model which would allow students to engage with higher-order thinking, nurture their conceptual development and use the two languages in an academic context on a day-to-day basis.

From Theory to Practice: A Pedagogy of Translanguaging

The purpose of this exploratory case study was to track the implementation of translanguaging pedagogy, reflect on successes and challenges and use this information to continue to develop the programme. The case study is focused on the learning experience in one science and social studies based UoI with two Grade 4 classes (nine to ten years old), taught over three years consecutively. It involved a collaborative planning process between the school team and an external consultant, as well as work with parents to understand the rationale for introducing Kiswahili into the curriculum in Grades 4 and 5, and the nature and purpose of using translanguaging pedagogy. A final element of introducing the move away from English-only was working with the students themselves. Given that Kiswahili is perceived as having a lower status than English, it was important to work with the students to understand the changes in the programme, and the motivations for these changes. For students used to learning only or mainly in English, adding in a less developed language for teaching and learning requires not only support, but student buy-in as well. Working with both parents and students was key to being able to implement a new approach to languages in the school.

The unit chosen had a focus on ecosystems, and it offered opportunities to investigate a local ecosystem and to build scientific knowledge and language in Kiswahili and English. There were two planning systems put in place to oversee the translanguaging pedagogy. The first was the macro-plan (unit) and the second were the micro-plans (learning cycles). To develop the macro-plan, the teaching team and curriculum coordinators met two weeks before the start of the unit to decide upon the core elements for the unit. This included consideration of the following aspects: concepts; content; skills to introduce and enhance; opportunities and resources within the local environment; resources available to students; language structures; text genres; and vocabulary.

After the key learning outcomes had been outlined, the teaching team and curriculum coordinators addressed the aspect of language balance across the unit. One of the main challenges for the teachers was to find a balance of resources that involved both primary and secondary sources of information (people, places, books, online text) in Kiswahili and English, in order to provide the experiences necessary to build students' understanding of the concepts in both languages. It was also important to balance the use of the two languages across the four skills (reading, writing, speaking, listening) and to develop both languages intentionally at a concrete and conceptual level across the spectrum of academic language.

Given the challenge of finding authentic Kiswahili resources, where they were available, Kiswahili was given priority for that part of the unit, and a translanguaging cycle was built around these key resources. This was done to maximise the use of authentic Kiswahili resources for scientific inquiry. However, much of the planning focused around balancing the use of English input sources with the use of Kiswahili in the processing and output parts of the cycle, as English input sources outnumbered Kiswahili sources significantly. A final element of the macro-plan was to consider differentiation. To ensure that students used higher-order thinking skills in both of the languages across different learning engagements it was important that the tasks be differentiated and adapted to the language competencies of the individual students. Teachers planned for differentiation through the grouping of students, as well as the use of language support tools. The macro-plan was seen as the roadmap for the unit. It contained the main elements of the unit, the estimated language use across the unit, and differentiation for students with different levels of Kiswahili. The micro-planning was developed over the unit, for each lesson or set of lessons within a learning cycle. An example of one learning cycle from the unit follows in the next section.

The Translanguaging Cycle

One important **input** for this unit was a field trip to the game park where students carried out interviews with park rangers. This was a prime opportunity for students to use Kiswahili as the main language of **input** for learning about the selected ecosystem. In the micro-planning phase for this learning cycle, the teachers considered the language necessary for students to successfully complete the task of writing questions and interviewing the rangers in Kiswahili. Key vocabulary and sentence starters that would be needed for the field trip were introduced to the students in their Kiswahili language lesson. Students prepared questions ahead of the visit and interviews were meant to be carried out in Kiswahili.

Students were intentionally placed into mixed-ability Kiswahili language competency groups. Teachers then allocated roles to each group member, which involved one person asking the questions, another recording the interview and others taking notes. On return from the field trip, students were to use the film recordings to re-listen to the Kiswahili responses and write up a report in English with the information provided by the ranger, allowing them to **process** the information that they had been given, and transfer the knowledge from Kiswahili to English. During this part of the task cycle, the students were encouraged to use both languages dynamically, working together to ensure understanding and to create the written **output** in English. The information from the interviews was supplemented with reference materials found in books in the school library as well as on the internet, providing further **input**, but this time in English, as most of these resources were available in English only. As another **output**, the students then gave oral presentations in English to their peers, synthesising the information from the internet with the written report.

The learning engagement described above illustrates an *input-processing-output* learning process, where the intentional language for each step is chosen purposefully. As one of the final learning engagements, and the summative assessment for the unit, the students created a brochure with explanatory texts about the ecosystem and comments to encourage people to respect the natural balance of the ecosystem. The brochure was written in both English and Kiswahili and copies were published and given to the game parks for use with the local community. Rubrics were used to assess and evaluate the students' learning, in this case a rubric with learning outcomes for the students' language skills in English and Kiswahili and another rubric with learning outcomes for the conceptual understanding, knowledge and skills. This bilingual **output** allowed students' competency in both languages, as well as the subject matter – in this case scientific knowledge and skills – to be assessed.

Reflecting and Improving: Years 2 and 3

Implementing a translanguaging approach in any context adds a level of challenge to teaching and learning. In what is a relatively new pedagogical field, there is little in the way of teacher or curricular resources, and there are no Kiswahili-English models to draw upon. In the case study unit, the first year of teaching highlighted some areas that were addressed in subsequent years. In the first iteration, it seemed clear that a logical point of Kiswahili use was on the safari trip to learn about a Kenyan ecosystem. Kiswahili is widely spoken in the area, and it seemed to make sense to have the students inquiring about a Kenyan ecosystem in Kiswahili. Upon arrival, however, it became clear that the park rangers were not prepared to answer the students' questions in Kiswahili, simply because they are used to guiding tourists through the park in English. This error in presumption of language use could have been predicted if the normal work situation of the park rangers had been considered, but it was an excellent learning moment for the students, to see how easily one's own language can become marginalised even 'at home'. In subsequent years, the rangers were given the questions in advance so that they could prepare to discuss them in Kiswahili, thus reflecting the developmental nature of the approach.

Other refinements to the unit planning and teaching have included changes to assessment, to ensure balance in Kiswahili and English, as the teachers developed confidence in the ability of the students to inquire into scientific concepts in Kiswahili. The unit has now been taught over three consecutive years, and the resources created by previous classes were used to supply additional input sources in Kiswahili that were not otherwise available. In addition, in further iterations the unit expanded to allow students to explore other ecosystems, broadening the language development within the unit. This allowed the students to extend their use of Kiswahili outside the Kenyan context. A notable weakness is that input materials are largely unavailable in Kiswahili for this topic and they are therefore developed in-house or there is a preponderance of input in English, with processing and output happening in Kiswahili. Changes in the micro-plans for the unit, reacting to challenges and unexpected developments, guided changes in the macro-plan for the following year. The development of the unit macro-plan initially overestimated the possibilities for Kiswahili input, so subsequent macro-plans for the unit have been adjusted to account for this. This task cycle has been adapted and is now also being used in other areas of the curriculum, particularly in history and the arts.

One of the main challenges in a translanguaging approach is language balance. Especially in a bilingual programme, there is a need to ensure that students are engaged in learning in both languages, rather than defaulting to the stronger language. To investigate the issue of language balance, the school is now piloting methods of tracking the language use within the input-processing-output cycle in the units. Schools intending to use a translanguaging approach within a bilingual model need to consider how they will plan for and track language balance within the programme at all times. In a bilingual programme, it is often tempting to default to the language in which students have greater competency; students and adults need to be disciplined to use the planned language for the task as much as possible.

Reflections and Lessons Learnt: From Micro to Macro

The experiences described in this case study show that students can access the curriculum through two languages used dynamically, as demonstrated by the learning outcomes and products. It is also evident that implementing a translanguaging approach requires ongoing professional reflection and adjustment, to react to and adapt for unexpected challenges along the way. The case study has demonstrated that an international programme, which includes English as one of the languages of instruction, can still provide strong connections with local culture and language. This study has also provided support to counter parent and teacher concerns that moving away from English-only would impact student progress both in English and academically. Observations and standardised assessment data collected annually by the school suggest that the student competency levels in reading in English have not decreased since implementation of the translanguaging programme; if anything, the actual results showed an increase in comparison with previous cohorts who experienced a model that was closer to a monoglossic framework.

Here we present three key takeaways that could be useful to any school considering a translanguaging model in a bilingual programme.

Intentional planning in a translanguaging approach

Firstly, although it may initially seem that implementing a translanguaging approach is as simple as allowing or encouraging other language use in the classroom, to do so effectively requires time and commitment. Translanguaging pedagogy is not simply the presence of two or more languages in the classroom (Ganuza & Hedman, 2017), but the deliberate inclusion of two or more languages for the purpose of learning. This demands careful consideration of both curricular goals and language goals, and the alignment of the different phases of teaching and learning to ensure that both are achieved. The process takes time, and requires careful thought about which language will be used for each part of the unit in order to meet students' needs. In this case study, the teachers worked with planning templates to guide the language-related decisions through the input-processing-output cycles, both on a macro (unit) level and on a micro (lesson) level. This allowed for visual review of the planned language balance. The addition of tracking documents currently being piloted is to ensure that the language balance in the written curriculum is achieved in the taught curriculum.

Student engagement and agency

A second key reflection from this case study is the importance of students' understanding of the translanguaging model and why it is used. Engaging with complex ideas and abstract concepts in a language that is not their dominant language requires students to take linguistic risks and to demonstrate determination and resilience – and in doing so they need support from their teachers. Some students initially showed resistance to using Kiswahili in class. The teachers spent time discussing the benefits of bilingualism and the translanguaging model and provided opportunities for questioning, which helped to resolve this. Awareness of students' motivation and engagement became an important part of the teachers' professional observations. This type of learning experience also provided a key opportunity for the development of student metalinguistic and critical language awareness, and agency in the development of their own linguistic profile. Although this was not a key objective of the process of implementing a translanguaging pedagogy, the value of these side-effects became clear, and is now being built on in other areas of the curriculum as well.

Parental engagement

Finally, ongoing dialogues with parents, as well as workshops and parent education classes, have been key for supporting the translanguaging model. Indeed, the principles of bilingual education are often counterintuitive for a parent who is anxious about a child's academic performance across the curriculum and the child's mastery of English. In a broader context, language use in international schools is often influenced by parental expectations that the only language used at school should be the

LoI (in most international curricula this is English), regardless of the language of the community. Changing this mindset involves investing in building relationships with parents and providing opportunities for them to enhance their understanding of the nature of language and learning at school.

Limitations

This exploratory case study is a brief window into the complexity of teaching and learning in multicultural and multilingual environments. The focus was the process of implementing a translanguaging pedagogy, and the information presented is descriptive in nature. This method was chosen for the purpose of tracking the process of trialling a translanguaging model and improving it in context. The findings of this case study, in this context, may be very different when applied to learning situations with other language pairs, other teaching and learning styles and other models of education. Further experimental research would be needed to explore the impact on students' outcomes of a translanguaging approach as compared to an English-only approach in international schools.

Conclusion

This exploratory case study reveals some of the common challenges for international schools that are working to implement a programme where practices are chosen for their alignment with the school's values. In this project, the choices related to language policy, curriculum, and organisation of staffing and resourcing were closely informed by the school's vision and mission: to create students who can use their education to become ethical leaders in their communities. The school has been implementing a translanguaging programme for four years and discussions are ongoing about how students' bilingual proficiency can be maintained in the IB Middle Years Programme with the aim of having a majority of students graduating from the school with a bilingual IB Diploma in English and Kiswahili.

An interesting aspect of this case study is the school context and the situation of the two languages. As English is both the higher-status and stronger language of most of the students by the time they arrive in Grade 1, in this instance translanguaging is being used to leverage the higher-status language to promote the growth of the lower-status language. This unique application of translanguaging indicates its usefulness not only as a 'crutch' during the language acquisition phase, but also its potential to promote equal growth in high- and low-status languages, and to provide benefits to students on both sides of the language equation – bringing majority language speakers into a constructive language learning environment alongside minority language speakers. This may be of particular interest not only in multilingual communities, but also in international schools where the majority language speakers in the school can sometimes stay resolutely monolingual. Such students could benefit from the language sensitisation and the learning of other languages in the classroom that is provided by a translanguaging approach, particularly those languages widely spoken in the school's local context. This brings together the local and the global and gives students a deeper connection with the context in which they are growing up. Such an approach would also reinforce the value placed by the school on the host country language and culture, recognising the unique contribution that it can make to students' learning.

More significantly, the exponential growth of international education in the last decade seems set to continue, with one report predicting that the numbers of students in EMI international schools will double over the course of the next decade, from 5.1 million in 2018 to an expected 10 million in 2028 (ISC Research, 2018). Most of these students will be local nationals seeking an education in English for the perceived doors that it can open, rather than 'international' students studying outside their home country. All curricula make choices, and these choices inevitably have an ethical dimension through the implicit messages about what is valued and what is not. Given the importance of ideals such as international-mindedness and leadership in many international curricula, explicitly valuing and developing home languages and local languages as an integral part of the school experience, rather than as linguistic tokenism, becomes an imperative rather than an option. Making space for the use of languages other than English even in, or especially in, English-medium education allows students to build their identity, and explicitly shows the value that the school places on students developing their understanding of their own language and culture. Translanguaging presents a manageable way of integrating linguistically appropriate practice into the curriculum, and allows schools to support languages where access to suitable teaching resources may be limited. Translanguaging pedagogy has the potential to mitigate language attrition in English-medium schools, and to raise the status of other languages and their associated cultural capital, thus creating an ethical programme that meets the holistic needs of students.

6 Transcending Linguistic and Cultural Boundaries: A Case Study of Four Young Maldivians' Translanguaging Practices

Naashia Mohamed

Introduction

Growing up with two or more languages is the norm in many global contexts. Because of globalisation and increasing migration, schools around the world are becoming more multilingual and multicultural than ever before (Hornberger & Link, 2012). Due to the exposure not only to multiple languages but also to a range of multimodal and multisensory resources in everyday life, the linguistic capabilities and cultural experiences of children and young people across the world have become 'increasingly diverse and dynamic' (D'warte, 2018: 2). Young bilinguals and multilinguals possess translingual competencies that allow them to draw on multiple resources and deploy them with flexibility and purpose (Li Wei, 2014). This practice of translanguaging is increasingly recognised as the discursive norm for bilinguals and multilinguals and is largely accepted as a necessary process for the development of learners' linguistic repertoires (Palmer et al., 2014).

Schools play a significant role in children's linguistic development. Although the potential for one language to support and reinforce the other has long been established (Cummins, 1979), educators still struggle to find ways in which children's multiliteracy skills can be sustained and supported. By embracing children's linguistic repertoires and by viewing language as a resource, teachers can support multilingual learners to engage more fully in their learning (Flynn et al., 2019; García et al., 2011). When school policies regard children's home languages as problematic and discourage their use, there is a danger that the children may be deprived of the benefits of multilingualism. This could limit their language development (McMillan & Rivers, 2011), foster negative attitudes towards their home languages (Zúñiga, 2016), affect the formation of positive identities and can even lead to language loss (Rivers, 2014).

Studies that have examined practices of translanguaging have presented a range of geographical and linguistic contexts. However, there is a notable absence of studies that have explored translanguaging in South Asia, despite this being one of the most multilingual and multicultural regions of the world. Much of the research on translanguaging has also been conducted within educational institutions. Fewer studies have focused on children's languaging strategies outside the school context. Additionally, translanguaging studies have typically focused on bilinguals, with inadequate attention given to contexts incorporating more than two languages. This chapter seeks to address these gaps and to document the translanguaging practices of four children from the Maldives as they engaged in a series of storytelling tasks in the home context.

Children in the Maldives are exposed to three languages from a young age: Dhivehi, Arabic and English. However, due to a school system that has adopted English-medium instruction (EMI) as the norm, English has become increasingly dominant in young people's language practices (Mohamed, 2019). The following questions guided the study:

(1) How do children utilise their linguistic resources when creating and telling stories to each other?
(2) How are children's narrations affected by placing limitations on the languages they could use?

This study builds on the existing understandings of multilingual children's peer interactions outside school, and makes connections to how EMI school policies may affect their language use.

Translanguaging as a Natural Practice

The concept of translanguaging links to the notion of language as a social construct (Makoni & Pennycook, 2010) which recognises the way bilinguals and multilinguals make sense of their diverse linguistic worlds by moving between their languages spontaneously and flexibly during communication with others who share their languages (García, 2009a). As MacSwan (2017: 188) explains, a bilingual may select 'different social languages according to social and situational contexts ... sometimes making use of both languages simultaneously (codeswitching) and sometimes making use of just one'. Rather than being in possession of two distinct codes, bilinguals have one complex, dynamic, unitary linguistic repertoire which they draw from to suit their needs and purposes (Otheguy et al., 2015). This is why scholars such as Canagarajah (2011) and

Mazzaferro (2018) call for appropriate pedagogical strategies to meet the needs and practices of multilingual students.

The interest in translanguaging has burgeoned in recent years, and many studies have explored its role in educational contexts. One of the earliest studies that focused on the subject illustrated how children were active agents of their language construction, using a combination of Spanish and English to explain their language navigations (Zentella, 1997). Li Wei and Wu (2009) also draw on the agentive role children play when learning is viewed through a bilingual lens that values all the linguistic resources of the learner. They found that when bilinguals are allowed to deploy their language resources, children use translanguaging in creative and strategic ways. Canagarajah (2013a: 78) refers to this creative use of language as the reconstruction of 'third cultures or new spaces for the negotiation of meaning', adapting their language resources to the needs and demands of the context.

Li Wei (2018) claims that translanguaging is not only a practice among bilinguals and multilinguals, but that it reflects the way humans think and communicate in everyday life. Extending Pinker's (1994) language instinct metaphor, Li Wei refers to what he terms *translanguaging instinct* to describe the way human beings are naturally driven to go 'beyond narrowly defined linguistic cues and transcend culturally defined language boundaries to achieve effective communication' (Li Wei, 2018: 24–25). He goes on to explain that although this drive to combine all available cognitive, semiotic, sensory and modal resources in language use is innate, the availability and use of these resources are largely dependent on the context of language learning. Bilingual language learners who are exposed to cross-linguistic equivalents at a young age learn to associate a particular word or language with a particular context or addressee. If the addressee is not receptive to a particular language, the child will learn to code-switch to the other language to make meaning clear. With time, the child will learn to use different resources for different contexts and purposes.

Language and Education in the Maldives

The Maldives recognises Dhivehi as its only official language. Until relatively recently, this was the sole language used for everyday communication, both in and outside the home. Two other languages, however, play significant roles in Maldivian society. In the 1950s, during the period of British colonial influence, a formal system of schooling was developed, based on the British model. As a formal system of education was a new concept in the Maldives and few locals had been trained as teachers, schools were staffed by expatriate teachers and principals who did not speak Dhivehi. The English language was introduced into schools first as a foreign language, and then quickly became adopted as the main medium of instruction. It was heralded as the language of progress and modernity, and Dhivehi was relegated to a second-class status in the education system.

Promoting a monoglossic ideology, schools actively discouraged the use of Dhivehi within the school environment with the belief that it would limit children's proficiency in English and hinder their chances of academic progress. Due to the importance of English for academic and economic success, parents gradually began to introduce English in the home, with the hope of preparing their children for school (Mohamed, 2019). This pro-English practice spread across the country and soon became the norm. Simultaneously, the demand for English-medium schooling grew, and the value of education provided in Dhivehi diminished. As a result, no schools have offered education in the national language for at least the last two decades (compare with Crisfield *et al.*, this volume). The English language has become firmly entrenched both visually and verbally in Maldivian society (Mohamed, 2019).

In the current system of schooling, English is the medium of instruction for all school subjects except for two: Dhivehi and Islam. Although the majority of primary school teachers are Maldivians who share the same native language as the students, all instructional activities are expected to take place in English. Additionally, English is the language of communication in schools, with much of the interaction that happens within the school walls taking place in English. Visibly, too, English takes precedence over Dhivehi in the school environment, in the form of displays of student work, posters, notices and banners (Mohamed, 2016).

Being a Muslim country, religion is given a strong focus in education and society. Because Arabic is the language of the Qur'an and Islamic prayers, it is traditionally taught to children from a very young age. Typically, this would involve learning the alphabet, and reading the classical script to enable children to recite the Qur'an. Although Arabic is available in schools as an optional foreign language, the majority of Maldivians do not go on to achieve communicative competence in Arabic. However, Arabic greatly influences Dhivehi, with many of its words derived from Arabic roots.

Storytelling among Four Children

Following a case study approach, this study utilised storytelling tasks as the means through which to observe children's languaging practices. This approach was selected to allow the close observation of a small group of children in an environment where they felt comfortable to interact freely. Storytelling is a way to learn a language and make sense of the world (Miller & Pennycuff, 2008), is a natural way of interacting informally while building relationships and is linked with cultural practices. Storytelling is also a common part of school literacy practices, and four of the five selected tasks (i.e. all except Task 1) mirrored what children may need to do as part of their language learning in school.

Participants

The four participants were selected for three reasons. First, they formed a natural group as the children were known to each other. They had close friendships between them as they lived in the same apartment complex, and often played together. This allowed the opportunity to observe children who were comfortable with each other interacting naturally. Second, the children attended two well-established schools with similar English-dominant language policies. They had been identified by teachers as being academically strong with a high level of linguistic competence in both English and Dhivehi. Third, the children came from similar socioeconomic backgrounds and had at least one parent who had received university education overseas. It was expected that a similar family background and parental education levels would allow for parallels in access to literacy resources and language practices at home.

The participants in this study lived in Malé, the capital island. At the time of data collection, they were aged between six and 11 years. All four children identified themselves as Maldivians and had lived most of their lives in the Maldives, although they had all lived abroad for varying amounts of time. The parents reported that although Dhivehi was the predominant language of the home, both English and Dhivehi were used for communication within the family. All four children had learned sufficient Arabic to allow them to read the Qur'an and perform Islamic prayers. Pseudonyms used in this chapter were selected by the participants themselves.

Kamana, the oldest of the four children, was aged 11. As a young child, she had spent three years in Australia when her parents were at university and had memories of having attended kindergarten there. She had one younger sibling. Camilla, aged nine, had no other siblings but had close relationships with her similarly aged cousins. She too had spent time abroad, living in India for two years before she started school. Brian, aged seven, was the younger of two siblings. Brian was born in New Zealand but had lived in the Maldives since he was a year old, and thus had no recollection of his time overseas. The youngest of the four participants was Fred. His first two years were spent in Malaysia. He was six years old and was the elder of two siblings.

Brian was a participant in a previous study I conducted, and I first contacted his parents to recruit him for this study. The other children were suggested by Brian's mother. The parents of all the participating children were informed about the study and their consent obtained. In a short interview, they provided background information about the children, their access to and use of literacy resources such as books and multimedia and a general understanding of language usage at home. This information obtained from parents was used to get a better understanding of the children and their backgrounds.

All four children enjoyed reading and being read to. While Brian enjoyed reading informative books, the other three children preferred fiction. All four children had access to a range of literacy resources at home, including fiction and non-fiction books, dictionaries, word games, writing materials, and self-study workbooks to practice handwriting, develop reading and build vocabulary. The vast majority of these resources was in English. Each home included some material in Arabic and Dhivehi. According to their parents, the lack of Dhivehi literacy resources in their homes was due to the scarcity of available and appropriate materials in the context. In addition to print material, the children also had a range of DVDs for children in English and watched programmes on global television channels such as CBeebies, Disney and Nickelodeon.

The tasks

To study children's languaging strategies during storytelling, the participants were given five different storytelling tasks. Two of the tasks (Tasks 3 and 4) were designed to draw out a particular language. This was to examine whether children's language use was affected by being required to use a particular language. For the three remaining tasks, instructions were given in both languages to indicate that there was no limitation on the language they could use.

- **Task 1: StoryCubes.** The participants received a Rory's StoryCubes® set. This contained nine cubes with images on each side. The images were simple line drawings of objects (e.g. aeroplane), actions (e.g. dancing), places (e.g. palace) and people or animals. To begin the task, one child shook and rolled out the cubes. The child then had to narrate a story based on the nine images on the tops of the cubes. Once one child had narrated her story, the second child would re-roll the cubes and begin a different story.
- **Task 2: Illustrated story.** For the second task, the children received two illustrated stories from Heaton (1975), without any writing. One story showed two boys going fishing and the adventures they encountered. The second story showed a group of children going camping and experiencing an unexpected change of weather. The children had to select a story each and take turns in telling the stories.
- **Task 3: Picture description in Dhivehi.** The children received a selection of four photographs, all relevant to Maldivian culture and depicting the typical island life of its people. These included photographs of: a fishing boat with fishermen catching tuna; an elderly woman with her craft equipment for weaving the traditional embroidery on the *Dhivehi libaas* (traditional Maldivian dress); three men relaxing on a

joali (traditional outdoor seating made from wood and rope); and a *bashi* game (traditional team game played on the beach). The children were asked to use Dhivehi either to describe the photographs or to tell a story using one or more of the pictures as prompts.

- **Task 4: Picture description in English.** The children received a selection of four pictures. These included a drawing of a child's birthday party, a family's seaside holiday, a street scene and some children at a playground. The participants were asked to use English either to describe the pictures to each other or to tell a story using one or more of the pictures as prompts.

- **Task 5: Personal recount.** The children were invited to share a funny incident that had happened to them. They were asked first in Dhivehi, then immediately followed with the English question: *Can you think of a funny incident that happened to you recently? It must be a story your friend hasn't heard yet. Take a moment to think about what you could share, and when you are ready, tell each other your stories.*

The tasks were carried out in the home of one of the children and were audio-recorded. The children worked in self-selected pairs and performed the tasks independently, with the researcher simply observing in the background. The tasks were carried out over four different days, and they had as much time as they needed for each task. Each of the tasks was explained to the children in Dhivehi and English, and they had the opportunity to ask questions before they started. Once the children were ready to begin, they switched on the recording themselves.

Task completion time ranged from five to 15 minutes, resulting in about 140 minutes of recording in total. The data were first transcribed, then coded descriptively to identify the children's choice of language, shifts in language during an interaction, the possible purpose of such a shift and whether the shift resulted in communication breakdown or repair. The analysis then focused on instances where there appeared to be some breakdown of communication. These sections of the data were examined to focus on ways in which the children negotiated for meaning. The third round of coding focused on patterns of language use and how the children deviated from established language norms and used their creativity. The coding was done by both the researcher and a research assistant. Each worked individually on the coding, then compared their work to arrive at an agreed set of codes and categories, to ensure inter-rater reliability.

Patterns of Language Use

Four main findings emerged from the analysis of the data: the fluidity of language boundaries in the children's interactions; the creativity of language use; the underlying purpose of translanguaging; and the links to school practices.

Fluid language boundaries

It was clear that all four children had a preference for English over Dhivehi. Except when requested specifically to use Dhivehi, they opted to interact mainly in English, in a complex, multi-layered way that made use of their full linguistic repertoire. It was evident that this fluid translanguaging utilised not just individual words and expressions from their named languages, but also the application of grammatical rules interchangeably, without loss of comprehension. Consider the following excerpt from an interaction between Camilla and Fred as they prepared for Task 1:

Excerpt 6.1 *Camilla and Fred preparing for Task 1*

Speaker	Original (Dhivehi, English)	English translation
Camilla	Do you want to first **thalhuvaalafa** then throw them?	Do you want to first **shake** and then throw them?
Fred	**Aan.** OK.	Yes. OK.
Camilla	**Dhen hadhaabala.**	So do it.
Fred	So **mihaaru, hadhanvee gothakee–**	[shakes and throws the cubes] So **now what I have to do is–**
Camilla	**mihaaru hadhan vee gothakee,** you have to look at these pictures and make up a **vaahaka.** Just make it up as you **kiyaa** it to me.	**Now what you have to do is,** you have to look at these pictures and make up a **story.** Just make it up as you **tell** it to me.
Fred	**Aan.**	Yes.
Camilla	**Engijje tha?**	Have you understood?
Fred	Yes yes. I know **ey mihaaru.** Shall I start now?	Yes yes. I do know **now.** Shall I start now?

This excerpt shows the fused nature of the interaction between these children. Camilla's question in the first line is an example of how Dhivehi words are used smoothly in an otherwise English utterance. Similarly, as she interrupts Fred to explain what he has to do, she uses both Dhivehi and English phrases to form her instruction, interspersing both linguistic norms into a fused whole that appeared to make complete sense to one another.

Other examples of the fused nature of the language included instances where some words took on features of the norms of English and Dhivehi. For example, Camilla talked about *fummaning* and *lappaae.* Here, *fumman* means to jump. By adding the -ing suffix, she has applied the English grammatical rule of making a verb into its continuous form, meaning 'jumping'. Similarly, *lappaa* means to close. By adding the -ed suffix, Camilla indicates the past tense form of the verb. In this way, she was applying English grammatical rules to change the tense forms of Dhivehi words, creating new words in the process that were accepted and understood by her peers. In some instances, it was interesting to see that where confusions occurred, the repair took place in English. Consider Excerpt 6.2 from Fred and Camilla's telling of a story for Task 3, where Fred is using the fisherman as a prompt for his story.

Excerpt 6.2 *Task 3*

Speaker	Original (Dhivehi, English)	English translation
Fred	Dhen emeehun mas baanaa baanaa varubali vejje. Dhen Ali dhiyaee dhoneege dhirubaa kolhuga huri–	Then they got tired of fishing. Then Ali went to the bow of the sailing boat–
Camilla	Dhoneege what?	The what of the sailing boat?
Fred	Huh?	
Camilla	Dhoneege koachekey?	The what of the sailing boat did you say?
Fred	Dhoneege dhirubaa kolhu	The bow of the sailing boat
Camilla	Yes what's what?	
Fred	That's the front of the **dhoni**. You know, like the curvy part. At the front.	That's the front of the **sailing boat**. You know, like the curvy part. At the front.
Camilla	Oh ok. Ok. Ok. Sounds funny.	
Fred	Yes shall I **adhi kiyan vee tha**?	Yes shall I **continue telling the story**?
Camilla	Yes go on.	
Fred	Ok. Ehenveema, Ali hedhigothakee ...	Ok. So what Ali did was ...

Here we see Fred's use of the word *dhirunbaa kolhu*, to indicate the bow of the vessel, was not understood by Camilla. She interrupts his narration in English and Fred responds in English. Once meaning has been clarified, Fred reverts to Dhivehi to continue his story.

Creative language practices

The interactions between the children revealed that their language was highly creative. This involved the use of similar sounds and rhyming words to tell a story. Consider this excerpt from Brian's attempt at Task 1.

Excerpt 6.3 *Task 1*

Speaker	Original (Dhivehi, English)	English translation
Brian	Once upon a time there lived a fish a a a flounder fish called called once upon a time there lived a flounder fish called **Feekoai**. He was called **Feekoai** because he loved to flip and slip and zip through the forest of seaweed and hide from his friends. **Feekoai** was a was a **fai dhigu** fish, yes a **fai dhigu** fish with umm with fins of fff forest green. He imagined that he was a little fly and that he could fly fly fly up to see the sky. **Feekoai** was funny. He loved to float on his back, looking at the fumbling tumbling bumbling birds above, and singing fee fi fo fum. But, but but but he had to be careful to avoid the falcon, the fastest creature on earth, and so he would float quietly and carefully on his back flipping his fins this way and that. Flip flop flip flop.	Once upon a time there lived a fish, a a a flounder fish called called once upon a time there lived a flounder fish called **Feekoai**. [laughs]. He was called **Feekoai** because he loved to flip and slip and zip through the forest of seaweed and hide from his friends. **Feekoai** was a [laughs] was a **long-legged** fish, yes a **long-legged** fish with umm with fins of fff forest green. He imagined that he was a little fly and that he could fly fly fly up to see the sky. **Feekoai** was funny. He loved to float on his back, looking at the fumbling tumbling bumbling birds above, and singing fee fi fo fum. But, but but but he had to be careful to avoid the falcon, the fastest creature on earth, and so he would float quietly and carefully on his back flipping his fins this way and that. Flip flop flip flop.

As can be seen here, Brian opts to use a lot of words starting with the letter 'f' in his story. He names the fish *Feekoai*, the Dhivehi word for peekaboo, and describes the fish as *fai dhigu* fish – a fish with long legs. Although the story itself may not make much sense, he attempts to incorporate aspects from other stories (fee fi fo fum from *Jack and the Beanstalk*) and information he had learned from elsewhere (e.g. the falcon's speed) and use words starting with 'f' and rhyming words, showing his linguistic creativity.

Similarly, Fred's attempt to incorporate the formulaic language of stories from both English and Dhivehi in his telling of a story about a king, a parrot, an apple and a ring showed how he utilised his cultural capital from both his literary worlds to create a new understanding. Excerpt 6.4 shows how he started the story:

Excerpt 6.4 *Fred storytelling*

Speaker	Original (Dhivehi, English)	English translation
Fred	**Essaharegga ulhuvvi raskaleh.** Once upon a time there lived a powerful king. **E rasgefaanu** had a talking parrot that could see the future. **Komme dhuvahaku e rasgefaanu vidhaalhuvanee** the parrot, who is the most powerful of us all? And the parrot would say said O King of this land, you are not so powerful yet.	**Once upon a time there lived a king.** Once upon a time there lived a powerful king. **The king** had a talking parrot that could see the future. **Every day the king asked** the parrot, who is the most powerful of us all? And the parrot would say said O King of this land, you are not so powerful yet.
Camilla	He needed the ring	
Fred	Wait, it's my turn.	
Camilla	Ok go on	
Fred	The parrot would say O King of this land, you are not so powerful yet. You have to get the ring to become the **rasgefaanu** the all-powerful king of all the world.	The parrot would say O King of this land, you are not so powerful yet. You have to get the ring to become the **king** the all-powerful king of all the world.

Fred uses typical story starters from both Dhivehi ('*Essaharegga ulhuvvi raskaleh*') and English ('Once upon a time there lived a powerful king'). He borrows from both English fairy tales and Dhivehi folklore to create a new story of his own. He shifts between low and high registers in Dhivehi to signify the difference in the status of the king. Similarly, in completing Tasks 2 and 4, Kamana uses Dhivehi proverbs to apply Dhivehi cultural knowledge to stories told in English. In this way, these children fused together not just language, but also cultural practices.

Purposeful translanguaging

The data showed that there were six main purposes of shifting the language from one to the other: clarifying, elaborating, seeking agreement, using specific terminology, confirming and self-monitoring. The most common purpose for shifting from one language to the other was to clarify something that was being said.

Excerpt 6.5 *Fred storytelling*

Speaker	Original (Dhivehi, English)	English translation
Fred	Okay, so … **mithanun dho fashanvee?** Once a man went fishing. He caught so many fish that he became rich. So he got a lot of money. And he brought all the money home. **Mihiree thireega mihiree nun. Kihaa baivaru laari hifaigen eheree. Nuves hifey dho reethi koh?** He divided the money to all the houses and everyone became so rich that everyone that no one had to work anymore. Everyone got a lot of money and a lot of presents from this rich man. Some people got **dhoni** and some people got **libaas** that had a lot of gold in it and some people got **mee koacheh tha?**	Okay, so … **Should I start from here?** Once a man went fishing. He caught so many fish that he became rich. So he got a lot of money. And he brought all the money home. **He is here, see? See how much money he is carrying. Can't even carry properly, right?** He divided the money to all the houses and everyone became so rich that everyone that no one had to work anymore. Everyone got a lot of money and a lot of presents from this rich man. Some people got **sailing boat** and some people got **traditional Maldivian dress** that had a lot of gold in it and some people got **what is this?**

In Excerpt 6.5, Fred speaks primarily in English, but switches back to Dhivehi to ask for clarification regarding where to begin, to elaborate on the amount of money the rich man is carrying, to use specific Dhivehi words that have no English equivalent and, at the end, to seek clarification. He is focused on using English to complete the task, but switches to Dhivehi as a means of support in completing his task.

All four children used *dho* and *ingey* in their conversations, as a form of seeking agreement with what they were expressing or as a way of confirming a statement they had made (e.g. It's my turn now, *dho*? / The fish and the turtle told the man, this man *ingey*, to go to the pyramid.). They also switched between languages as a way of monitoring their language use and planning their task. For example, as Kamana prepared for Task 2, she planned out loud using mainly Dhivehi, considering her key vocabulary, the plot and her characters. She realised that she lacked the vocabulary in Dhivehi for *tent*, *campfire* or *firewood*, so she would tell the story in English.

Links to school practices

As previously noted, all four children predominantly used English. While the amount of English used varied, it was clear that they were comfortable using English in a range of different ways and for different purposes, switching to Dhivehi as a form of support. They interacted with each other informally and performed most of the tasks with ease. For Task 4, when the children were specifically asked to use English only, the stories contained almost no use of other linguistic resources, and the stories were told without much difficulty. However, the same degree of flexibility was not evident in their use of Dhivehi. Their use of Dhivehi was limited to formulaic expressions and simple everyday language. There was also a tendency to aim for more accuracy in their Dhivehi stories, which may explain the slower pace of these narrations. Their performance of Task 3, for which the children were asked to specifically use Dhivehi, showed this difficulty they experienced. In completing this task, there was an obvious hesitancy on the part of all children, with a lot more stops, slower speech, changes in language choice, self-corrections, lack of detail and more breakdowns in communication.

Of the four children, Brian appeared to use the least amount of Dhivehi and struggled to interact only in Dhivehi. Excerpt 6.6 shows his description of three men in a *joali* for Task 3.

Excerpt 6.6 *Brian storytelling*

Speaker	Original (Dhivehi, English, *Arabic*)	English translation
Brian	Ebaulheyo ebaulheyo thin meehun. Thin muskulhi meehun. Dhen ... dhen ... veegothakee ... edhdhuvahaku mi meehun dhiyaee hingaalan. Dhen veegothakee dhen veegothakee ... edhdhuvahaku thin meehun dhiyaee hingaalan along the beach and	There once lived three people. Three old people. Then ... then what happened was ... one day these three people went for a walk. Then what happened was what happened was one day three people went for a walk along the beach and
Kamana	Dhivehin ney kiyanvee	You have to say it in Dhivehi
Brian	Okay, so, mi meehun nah joali eh fenunee. Dhen meena bunee mihen hingaa and meena bunee no thihen nudhaanan and meena bunee I know, thihen ves nudhaanan thi hen ves nudhaanan, hingaa mithaa isheennan. Dhen dhen dhen emeehun isheenee and then no more talking. Because mi meehaa nidhee and e hisaabun vaahaka nimunee. *Wassalaam alaikum.* The end.	Okay, so these people saw a traditional woven seat. Then this person said let's go this way. And this person said no, I won't go that way. And this person said, I know we won't do that and we won't do that either. Let's sit here. Then then then the people sat down and then no more talking. Because this person fell asleep and [makes snoring sounds]. That is the end of the story. *Peace be unto you.* The end.

As can be seen in the excerpt, Brian had to be reminded by Kamana to interact in Dhivehi. During his telling of the story, he uses standard phrases from stories in Dhivehi such as *ebaulheyo ebaulheyo / edhdhuvahaku / e hisaabun vaahaka nimunee* which are common in children's stories. At the end, Brian also uses the Arabic farewell phrase (*Wassalaam alaikum*), to signify the end.

Kamana used the most Dhivehi. Her descriptions in Dhivehi, however, were of a written style rather than an oral narration. Excerpt 6.7 shows part of Kamana's description of the *bashi* game.

Excerpt 6.7 *The bashi game*

Speaker	Original (Dhivehi, English)	English translation
Kamana	Mi thasveerun dhakkaidhenee rashegge beach ga rashegge gondudhoshugaa anhenun thakeh bashi kulhey thaneve. Bashi e ee anhenunnah khaassa kurevifaivaa kulhumekeve. Miee haveeru ge hiygaimu manzarekeve. Iru dhanee ossen ossumaa dhimaalah .... ossumaa dhimaalah... iru dhanee ossumaa dhimaalah ... iru dhanee ossumaa dhathuru kuramun neve. Kulhivaru balan gina guna meehun ais eba thibi eve. Kulhibalaa meehun thibee deck chair thakeh gaa insheendhe laigen araamu kollaigen neve.	This picture shows some women playing bashi on the beach of an island, on the beach of an island. Bashi is a game that is special to women. This (picture shows) the pleasant time of the late afternoon. The sun is going to set ... is going to set ... is going to set ... the sun is going to se ... the sun is travelling towards its setting point. Many people have arrived to watch the game. The spectators are seated and relaxing in deck chairs.
Brian	And what about the telephone towers?	
Kamana	That's nothing to do with the story. **Iru ge dhoadhithah –**	That has got nothing to do with the story. **The sun's rays –**
Brian	What's that?	
Kamana	**Iru ge dhoadhi?**	**The sun's ray?**
Brian	Yes	
Kamana	The sun's rays	
Brian	Ok fine. But it's boring. Your story is boring. Make it interesting.	
Kamana	Bashi e ee Dhivehi anhenunge medhugaa emme aanmmu koh kulhevey kulhivareve. Bashi kulhenee boalha akaa reketakaa	This is a game that is typically played among Maldivian women. This game is played with a ball and a racquet.

| Brian | That's like a **Dhivehi filaavalhu.** Make it interesting. MONSTER! A monster comes in the game. | That's like a **Dhivehi lesson.** Make it interesting. MONSTER! A monster comes in the game. [growls, pretending to be a monster] |
| Kamana | **Dhen,** don't ruin my turn. Now I have to start again! | **Hey** don't ruin my turn. Now I have to start again! |

Written Dhivehi requires each sentence to end in 'eve' to indicate a complete thought, primarily because older forms of written Dhivehi did not use punctuation marks and this practice of using 'eve' suggested that it served the purpose of a full stop. This style, however, is never applied in oral usage. Kamana's adoption of the written style in her oral descriptions (and notably never in her actual speaking in Dhivehi to the other children) suggests that she was attempting to be formal. She also does this by incorporating some Dhivehi words of a higher register reserved for formal occasions or for addressing people of higher status (e.g. *isheendhevadaigen thibbevee*/were sitting down; *ballavamun gendhavanee*/were watching). However, as Brian points out, it sounds 'like a Dhivehi lesson' rather than a story. Brian does not understand the phrase *iru ge dhoadhithah* and interrupts Kamana to ask. It is interesting to see how this exchange takes place in English when Kamana explains what it means.

In addition to Kamana trying to use Dhivehi correctly, she repeatedly reminded others about language use. For example, she corrected Brian's use of both English and Dhivehi (e.g. 'you don't say *I wanna.* You must say *I want to.*'), and reminded Fred to refrain from mixing his languages. To a lesser extent, this link to school practices and norms was evident in Camilla's language too. For example, as Fred was struggling to tell a story in Dhivehi, she told him (in English) to 'use describing words' to expand his story. She also commented on how characters with Dhivehi names like Ali must talk in Dhivehi and that characters with Western names like Mr Rodgers must speak in English. These comments suggest that the children are enacting the norms of language use at school.

Discussion

This study set out to understand how young multilinguals used their linguistic repertoire to create and tell stories to each other, and how placing limitations on which languages they could use affected their storytelling. The findings demonstrate that the participants actively made use of their full linguistic knowledge and skills to engage in storytelling. Overall, they favoured English but used Dhivehi in different ways and to varying degrees to perform the tasks and make meaning. The languaging strategies evidenced here show that these children made purposeful, sophisticated and intuitive shifts in language, fusing their named languages and different registers together in creative ways. The translanguaging practices also show that these children not only drew on their linguistic resources but also bridged their cultures by fusing elements from their distinct cultural worlds into one meaningful whole – what Canagarajah (2013a) refers to as a third culture. In this way, they are seen to transcend local boundaries and cultural borders. The hybrid nature of their languaging processes appeared effortless and normal, supporting existing evidence of translanguaging practices and the agentive role children play in using language strategically and creatively (Li Wei & Wu, 2009).

The way in which the children engaged with Task 3 was markedly different from their performance in the other four tasks. Being required to use only Dhivehi restricted their ability to create a meaningful story and narrate it with ease, as they did for the other four tasks. Tellingly, this difficulty was not evident in their stories for Task 4, where they were asked to use only English, suggesting that their competence in English was higher than their competence in Dhivehi. In fact, the majority of content words used by all participants were in English, and the bulk of the Dhivehi formed function words. Where longer stretches of Dhivehi were used, much of this was in the form of formulaic expressions. Dhivehi formed a type of scaffold for their predominantly English stories – a vehicle through which they established and negotiated meaning and self-monitored their languaging.

This difference in their ability to communicate in English and Dhivehi links to the difference between the conversational/playground language and the academic/classroom language (Cummins, 1979). The features of Dhivehi used by the children in this study linked to the limitations of the conversational language used in everyday life. Although Dhivehi is the national language, when children are exposed to mainly English and are actively discouraged to use Dhivehi in school, this is hardly surprising. When their language is constantly rejected in that context, they learn to adapt and adjust their idiolects accordingly (Li Wei, 2018). When the children's language is devalued in the school and the wider society, they develop their second language at the expense of the first language and culture. Given the central role that language and culture play in the establishment of positive identities (Evans, 2014), suppressing the use of one language over the other may affect not just the children's linguistic abilities, but their sense of who they are and where they belong.

Conclusion

Despite the small-scale nature of this study, it has several implications for educational policy and practice. These findings point to the need for transformative educational practices that recognise and harness translanguaging as a tool for learning (see also Goodman *et al.*, this volume). The English-first ideology promoted by schools is out of sync with the sociolinguistic reality of the everyday languaging in which young people in the 21st century engage. Requiring students to limit their language use to one language not only has detrimental effects on the children's ability to perform, but could have lasting effects on their linguistic development. When the majority of students and teachers share the same language, and are second language users of English, it makes little practical or pedagogical sense to impose such language policies. As Canagarajah (2011: 415) reminds us, 'it is important that we develop our pedagogies ground up, from practices we see multilingual students adopting'.

In addition to validating multilingual children's multilingualism within the school, it is clear that strenuous efforts need to be made at a broader societal level to ensure that children and young people are equipped with age-appropriate resources that would strengthen their native language and instil a sense of pride for the culture.

7 Translanguaging in Partial EMI Secondary Science Classrooms in Hong Kong

Jack Pun

Introduction

The role of translanguaging in second language (L2) learning has been under-researched. However, there is considerable evidence that translanguaging processes are present in English as a medium of instruction (EMI) classrooms (Toth, 2018b; Toth & Paulsrud, 2017). There is also evidence from bilingual classrooms that translanguaging can serve as a pedagogical technique that creates a space in which all learners can draw on their entire linguistic repertoires in acquiring, understanding and demonstrating subject knowledge (García *et al.*, 2017). For example, EMI teachers providing first language (L1) information within an L2 lexis benefits vocabulary retention, and allowing learners to use their L1 in tasks also promotes L2 production (Camó & Ballester, 2015). Many teachers also consider the use of the L1 indispensable for effectively explaining content knowledge in the L2. However, arguments for L1 use in L2 learning run counter to the immersion pedagogy (Lasagabaster, 2013), which posits that using the L1 robs learners of opportunities to infer the meaning of L2 expressions. Given that EMI classrooms are predicated on the benefits of extensive exposure to English, there is a need for a detailed understanding of how translanguaging is used in EMI classroom interactions in Hong Kong.

Using the L1 in L2 learning

Research into second language acquisition (SLA) suggests that meaningful negotiation plays an important role in the L2 acquisition process. Such negotiation can be conducted successfully using the target language with guided feedback. According to the interaction hypothesis (Long,

1983), when learners are exposed to more comprehensible input, they make greater use of the L2 through meaningful interactions with teachers. This provides more opportunities for teachers to provide corrective feedback on the learners' use of the L2, which ultimately contributes to L2 learning. The interaction hypothesis is supported by previous research into learning in EMI classrooms in Hong Kong (Lo & Macaro, 2012). This research shows that in order for students to learn subject knowledge in the L2 effectively, they need to develop the necessary L2 proficiency and capacity for L2 learning by filling in their current language gaps (Yip *et al.*, 2003).

Studies have shown that teachers and students in EMI science classrooms encounter many linguistic challenges (Chan, 2014; Lin, 2006; Lo & Macaro, 2012, 2015; Wannagat, 2007; Yip *et al.*, 2007). A particularly common issue is that their limited L2 skills discourage students from responding to their teachers' questions. Lo and Macaro (2012) found that both the number and the sophistication of student exchanges with teachers were reduced in EMI lessons, with much simpler forms of exchange sequences (e.g. yes/no responses). Teachers also paid less attention to form-focused instruction in the L2, and students in turn had limited opportunities for L2 learning. In general, students had difficulties in communicating their ideas in the L2 and the sequences of questions and answers were constrained as a result (Lo & Macaro, 2012).

In another study, to account for how a bilingual science teacher interacts with students through their everyday language in the L1 to develop their disciplinary language in the L2, Lin and Wu (2015) analysed an EMI junior secondary science classroom in Hong Kong. In their analysis, EMI students with a low English proficiency were able to develop their disciplinary language in the L2 if teachers and students used translanguaging in their classroom exchanges (Lin & Wu, 2015). Through the partial use of the L1, students were able to understand the content knowledge and thus contribute to class discussions in the L1, and gradually develop knowledge of the equivalent meanings in the L2. Lin and Wu (2015) argue that the teacher's pedagogical expertise is important for creating a space for translanguaging and thus helping students to develop knowledge of the content.

In light of the fact that an increasing number of studies have reported the benefits of translanguaging in EMI teaching (Lin & He, 2017; Lin & Wu, 2015), translanguaging can perhaps be beneficial in EMI contexts where the teacher and students share the L1 and L2. Translanguaging – bilinguals' act of accessing different linguistic features (from both L1 and all L2s) to maximise their communicative potential – may allow students in an EMI classroom to interact with teachers and peers, drawing on their full range of linguistic repertoires in learning. Nonetheless, research on translanguaging in the EMI setting has been limited and few practical pedagogical suggestions for supporting students' language choice in EMI classrooms are available (Lin & Lo, 2017), although see Crisfield *et al.*, this volume. An interesting question is whether L2 language gaps can be filled by translanguaging in an EMI classroom in Hong Kong.

Translanguaging, code-switching and the EMI classroom

Translanguaging describes how bilinguals or multilinguals discursively utilise their linguistic repertoire in the meaning-making process (García, 2009c). Generally, it is a natural occurrence in this process, during which people draw on multiple linguistic resources that are eventually codified and labelled as different language systems (Lin & He, 2017).

Both code-switching and translanguaging have positive pedagogical implications for language learning by raising bilingual learners' communicative competence to achieve a pedagogical aim in a classroom (García *et al.*, 2017). When interpreting these findings, caution must be taken not to confuse code-switching and translanguaging. Code-switching is the process of shifting between two language codes, whereas translanguaging refers to learners utilising their complete existing language repertoires (García & Li Wei, 2014). Translanguaging is a discursive practice in which bilinguals access their different language features in their existing controlled cognition in order to make sense of their bilingual worlds (Coronel-Molina & Samuelson, 2017; García, 2009c).

Other previous research has explored how learners use their L1 in addition to English in EMI classrooms for content learning using code-switching patterns (Lin, 2006; Lo, 2014; Lo & Macaro, 2012). In one recent study, Lo and Macaro (2012) examined the quality of teacher–student interaction in EMI junior secondary classrooms. Their results showed that teachers and students tended to switch between Cantonese (L1) and English (L2). They interacted socially about non-academic topics by inserting English technical terms into Cantonese grammar and discourse.

Despite the potential pedagogical benefits of both code-switching and translanguaging, the impact of code-switching on language learning is not clearly known in cases where students cannot comprehend the content knowledge of a lesson (Arthur & Martin, 2006). That is to say, the value of code-switching lies not in bilingualism per se, but in teaching. Translanguaging makes a far deeper contribution: 'it refers to reinforcing communication through L1 to comprehend and discuss content during the learning activity in both languages' (Lewis *et al.*, 2012b). Thus, the pedagogical objective of translanguaging should be for the subject knowledge to be fully understood by the learner in both languages.

A growing body of evidence supports the role of translanguaging in teaching and learning a language (Adamson & Fujimoto-Adamson, this volume; Cummins *et al.*, 2015; García & Li Wei, 2014; Lin & Lo, 2017), with a specific focus on how teachers and students operate between home language and target language and utilise other linguistic resources to communicate and construct their learning experience in bilingual classrooms (García & Li Wei, 2014; Lin & Lo, 2017). These studies have emphasised the importance of recognising learners' diverse language backgrounds and their fully or partially utilised linguistic repertoire for meaning-making, learning and demonstrating their knowledge in the classroom. Studies of EMI practices have moved away from monolingualism to explore how bilingual or multilingual learners can utilise their multilingual resources, particularly in classrooms where teachers and students share the same L1.

For example, Lin and He (2017) examined the role of translanguaging in the context of moving away from the traditional concept of code-switching, arguing for a dynamic view of language over a clearly bounded language code for learners' linguistic resources. They explored the valuable pedagogical and identity-affirming functions of translanguaging in content-based classrooms comprising multilingual students (see also Reilly, this volume). Their observations were that South Asian ethnic minority students needed to operate in their home or community language (e.g. Urdu or Cantonese) but needed to fulfil their learning activities in a classroom language (e.g. English), with teachers in Hong Kong deliberately translanguaging when engaging in meaning-making processes in science classes.

Nonetheless, limited research is available on the translanguaging process in EMI settings, and evidence supporting practical suggestions for overcoming students' language challenges appears to be inadequate. This chapter aims to address research gaps by exploring how translanguaging facilitates meaning-making and learning in the context of Hong Kong secondary EMI science classrooms.

Case Studies in Hong Kong

In this chapter, the research question is how science teachers and students in Hong Kong construct their science-learning experience in lab classes using translanguaging as a pedagogical scaffolding for meaning-making and understanding abstract scientific knowledge. I also examine the role of translanguaging in these lessons with reference to the recent literature on how translanguaging operates as a dynamic activity (Lemke, 2016) in content-based classrooms and on how teachers and students make use of their developing scientific language, home language and other linguistic repertoires during teaching and learning.

EMI science classrooms in a secondary school context

For the study in this chapter, the data were collected from a large-scale study exploring the quality of EMI classroom interaction in eight EMI secondary schools in Hong Kong. Nineteen teachers and 545 students from Grade 10 and 11 EMI science classes were recruited from eight EMI secondary schools in Hong Kong. Since the government's fine-tuning of the language policy in 2010, schools have been allowed to adopt EMI at senior levels provided that the students' English proficiency has improved to the threshold level for learning in an English environment (Hong Kong Education Bureau, 2009).

The students in this study were from Grade 10 and 11 EMI science classrooms (physics, chemistry and biology) and from two types of EMI secondary schools in Hong Kong: early full EMI (i.e. full EMI instruction from Grades 7 to 12) and late partial EMI schools (i.e. Chinese-medium instruction from Grades 7 to 9 and partial EMI instruction from Grades 10 to 12). They had completed six years of primary and three years of junior secondary compulsory education. The students were in the first and second years of senior science.

Regardless of their medium of instruction (MOI) at the junior levels, the students in both groups had studied integrated science from Grades 7 to 9. Students had used Cantonese as the MOI from Grades 7 to 9, and later switched to EMI in Grades 10–12, with nearly all subjects and public examinations conducted in English. The students gradually improved their English proficiency at the junior levels, as assessed by examinations held at every grade. During the data collection, the students were studying the Hong Kong Diploma of Secondary Education science curriculum in Grades 10–11. The students had already received three to four years of integrated science training, covering topics including scientific investigation, life and living, the material world, energy and change, the Earth, and the relationship between science, technology and society (CDC & HKEAA, 2007a, 2007b, 2007c).

The teachers in the study had graduated from a university in Hong Kong and obtained a bachelor of science degree in their relevant teaching disciplines and a postgraduate diploma in education. These academic qualifications are a common requirement for teaching science in local secondary schools. At present, there is no standardised English assessment for content-subject teachers in Hong Kong to teach at an EMI school. The teachers had no formal qualifications in teaching science in English and had not participated in any EMI teacher training. The inability to formally measure teachers' English proficiency could constitute a potential limitation of the study. Nevertheless, the level of these teachers' English proficiency was not related to the study's objectives. Under an MOI school policy, teachers and students are expected to fulfil teaching and learning tasks in English. Although English is only the instructional language, during lab sessions the teachers and their students tended to translanguage using the students' existing linguistic resources such as scientific English and everyday dialogue in Cantonese, suggesting that EMI teachers and students tend to insert English technical terms into Cantonese grammar and discourse.

Detailed observation of the biology classrooms

Thirty-four video-taped classroom observations were collected during the first and second years of the senior science curriculum (Grades 10 and 11) in these EMI schools. The researcher took notes during the observations and conducted interviews with the teachers and students in order to understand the teaching objectives and learning outcomes of the observed lessons. All the participants received a verbal explanation about the aims and objectives of the research project, as well as their right to withdraw at any time and an assurance of confidentiality. Written informed consent was obtained from all participants during each phase of the project. All of the recorded classroom data were transcribed and translated into English and then analysed using NVivo software. The author double-checked the translations and transcriptions against the original audio-recordings. The quality of the interaction sequences of teachers talking to students, teacher-to-student exchanges and student-to-student interactions was analysed. A more detailed micro-analysis of the discourse was then carried out to examine how the different types of speech perform different interactional and pedagogical functions in EMI classrooms depending on their operational settings (Seedhouse, 2004).

The biology lessons in this study are examples of a teacher and learners sharing the same L1 and using different linguistic features or various modes of what are described as autonomous languages to construct science experiences and explore science concepts in an EMI classroom. This process was conceptualised by Lemke (2016) as a dynamic activity flow connecting speech and activity in a science classroom.

Lin and He (2017) reported on how ethnic minority students in science classrooms utilised translanguaging between their developing academic language and multilingual repertoire as a pedagogical tool, moving away from the traditional understanding of languages as monolingual entities in language teaching. They identified three scenarios for translanguaging: (1) in pedagogical scaffolding, (2) in identity affirmation and (3) as dynamic activity flow in content learning activities. In my analysis of EMI science lab classes, I observed similar learning episodes of students deliberately translanguaging between L1 (Cantonese) and L2 (English), and developing scientific English and other linguistic repertoires (e.g. gestures, diagrams and songs) as a pedagogical tool. In addition, I observed the pedagogical functions of translanguaging in developing students' higher-order thinking about abstract science phenomena.

Developing students' higher-order thinking

In a Grade 10 biology lesson, the teacher introduced the concept of photosynthesis and explored factors that affect the rate of photosynthesis with the students. As Excerpt 7.1 shows, the teacher (T) and his students (S) engaged in lively but systematically structured interactions. The interactions are described in the form of initiation-response-feedback (IRF) sequences. Excerpt 7.1 reports on five IRF sequences in 20 turns, two of which are extended IRF sequences. The teacher initiated the interaction by asking the students to suggest possible factors that affect the rate of photosynthesis. Students gave their answers and the teacher evaluated their responses. If the answer was correct, the teacher acknowledged the student's answer and moved on to the next factor. If the answer was inconsistent with the teacher's view, the teacher provided extensive feedback. The IRF sequence was then repeated as the teacher moved on to further explore how certain factors (light intensity, carbon dioxide concentration, oxygen, amount of chlorophyll, water source) affect the rate of photosynthesis.

In Excerpt 7.1, the teacher used a number of teacher interventions (Mortimer & Scott, 2003) in the form of extended IRF sequences. His interventions included focusing on a student's idea by honing in on a particular student's response, expanding on what a student said, further exploring the ideas, asking for clarification and reviewing a student's response with the whole class. For example, in Turn 19, the teacher asked the students to elaborate on why carbon dioxide is a limiting factor for photosynthesis. Then, from Turns 20 to 25, he built on the students' answers to discuss the role of stomata in the process of gas exchange. In this period of interaction, the teacher intervention involved developing the students' understanding of the scientific story.

The teacher focused on a particular student's response ('stomata' in Turn 20), marking the key idea by enacting a confirmatory exchange with the student ('because it comes from the stomata' in Turn 23). The teacher then checked the students' understanding by asking for clarification about the role of the stomata in plants (in Turn 23). Finally, he returned to and revised the idea (in Turn 25) by summarising the function of the stomata in gas exchange. The teacher made several interventions from Turns 20 to 25, including sharpening ideas, selecting ideas, marking key ideas, sharing ideas, checking the students' understanding and reviewing. These efforts appear to have been designed to help the students develop their scientific reasoning, by making it explicit and clear that stomata are a controlling factor in the amount of carbon dioxide intake during gas exchange. This may help the students to understand why carbon dioxide can affect the rate of photosynthesis.

Excerpt 7.1 *Grade 10 partial EMI biology lesson (T = Teacher; S1 = Student 1)*

Turn	Speaker	Original (Cantonese, English)	English translation	Initiation-response-feedback (IRF) sequence
17	T	還有嗎?很簡單, we have mentioned chlorophyll, we have mentioned water. And the last one should be …?	**Anymore? Very straightforward,** we have mentioned chlorophyll, we have mentioned water. And the last one should be …?	Initiation (open Q)
18	S1	CO_2.	CO_2.	Response
19	T	為什麼 CO_2 a limiting factor?	**Why is** CO_2 a limiting factor?	Feedback (expand)
20	S1	Stomata.	Stomata.	R′
21	T	Limited by stomata. 為什麼會 limited by stomata? 你能回答我嗎?	Limited by stomata. **Why will it be** limited by stomata? **Can you tell me?**	F′ (acknowledge + expand)
22	S1	Because it comes from the stomata.		R″
23	T	Because it comes from the stomata. 什麼是 role of the stomata in plants?	Because it comes from the stomata. **What is the** role of the stomata in plants?	F″ (acknowledge + expand)
24	S1	Gas exchange.		R‴
25	T	Yes, 它被用於 of gas exchange. They allow the CO_2 from outside to go into the leaves. So the number of stomata will have an effect. 這可能是原因之一.	Yes, **it is the site** of gas exchange. They allow the CO_2 from outside to go into the leaves. So the number of stomata will have an effect. **It will be one of the possible reasons.**	F‴ (acknowledge + expand)

The last column in Excerpt 7.1 highlights the topics discussed in the interaction. It shows that the teacher made attempts to elicit further responses on the possible factors of photosynthesis by asking questions in his feedback moves. After the students answered questions on topics like chlorophyll, stomata and gas exchange, the teacher worked with them to explore different views by responding to and providing feedback on each student's response to generate new meaning and co-structure understandings of different views about the scientific phenomenon. Students produced incomplete utterances (e.g. in Turn 22) consisting of noun phrases referring to scientific items when responding to their teacher.

In these exchanges, the teacher did not encourage them to produce complete sentences nor did the teacher make any attempt to correct a student's language mistakes or provide any feedback on how to acquire the language of science in the L2 context. During the process of the lab experiment above, the dialogues between the teacher and students proceeded mostly in the L1, which was used for matters of experimental operation or instruction. For example, the teacher tried to ask a range of questions to develop the students' understanding of the factors that affect photosynthesis. In Excerpt 7.1, the teacher took account of his students' observations of the science phenomenon. He also explored different views with his students, to co-construct understanding about how carbon dioxide is a limiting factor for photosynthesis.

Excerpt 7.2 is from a Grade 11 biology classroom. The teacher introduced the concept of chromosomes. The teacher asked the students to guess the number of pairs of chromosomes in humans and the number of chromosomes in each pair from the father and mother. She used the analogy of counting postage stamps to help the students understand sets and the number of chromosomes in a set. She then helped the students to distinguish between diploid (two sets of chromosomes, 2n) and haploid (one set of chromosomes, 1n) cells in sexual reproduction. There was a large amount of interaction between this teacher and the students in the form of IRF sequences, exploring the students' understanding of how to count the number of chromosomes in human cells. The teacher used several technical terms throughout the interaction, e.g. *homologous chromosomes, diploid and haploid cells, paternal chromosome* and *maternal chromosome.*

On numerous occasions, the teacher used Cantonese to explain these abstract technical terms and to offer hints to help the students understand them (e.g. in Turn 195). Excerpt 7.2 shows how the teacher used the L1 primarily to help the students understand abstract and difficult science concepts by asking higher-order questions, and used the L2 to repeat scientific noun phrases to facilitate the students' retention of content in the L2. The teacher made several efforts through a sequence of initiations to explain the concept of immunity and to describe different types of immunity.

Excerpt 7.2 *Grade 11 partial EMI biology lesson (T = Teacher; S1 = Student 1)*

Turn	Speaker	Original (Cantonese, English)	English translation	Initiation-response-feedback (IRF) sequence
164	T	How many 染色體 [father's sperm]?	How many **chromosomes** [father's sperm]?	Initiation (open Q)
165	S1	Twenty-three.		Response
166	T	幾個 [mother's]?	**How many** [mother's]?	I (open Q)
167	S1	Twenty-three.		R
168	T	Twenty-three. 那麼 對於 each pair, 為 什麼一個來自 father一個來自 mother?	Twenty-three. **So for** each pair, **why does one come from** the father **and one come from the** mother?	F (expand)
172	T	這裡, 有幾多對? 有幾多對 homologous chromosomes?	**Here, how many pairs are there? How many pairs of** homologous chromosomes **are there?**	I (open Q)
173	S1	Two.		R
174	T	Two pairs.		F (acknowledge)
176	T	幾多對 are there?	**How many** sets **are there?**	I (open Q)
177	S1	Two.		R
178	T	Two. 我地說細胞有 兩對? 每個精子和 卵子有幾多對?	Two. **Our** cells have two sets? **How many sets do** sperm **and** eggs have?	F (expand)
179	S1	一對.	One set.	R'
183	T	Diploid cells, haploid cells. 人體 中有多少個 haploid cells?	Diploid cells, haploid cells. **How many** haploid cells **are there in** humans?	I (open Q)

184	S1	只有兩種.	Only two kinds.	R
185	T	哪種 haploid cells?	Which kind of haploid cells?	F (expand)
186	S1	Sperm and egg.		R′
187	T	其他細胞, 皮膚, 骨骼, 頭髮都係兩倍體細胞。	Other cells, skin, bones, hair, are all diploid cells.	F′ (ignore)
189	T	為什麼叫它們為 diploid cells?	Why are they called diploid cells?	I (open Q)
190	T	因為當你發現一個 chromosome, 它總是有一個夥伴. 它們總是成對出現. 所以它們被稱為 diploid cells.	Because when you find a chromosome, it always has a partner. Always in a pair. They are called diploid cells.	I (statement)
195	T	Okay, 對於配對在一起的相同大小的 chromosomes, 它們叫什麼?	Okay, for the same size chromosomes paired together, what are they called?	F′ (expand)
198	S1	Homologous chromosomes.		R‴
199	T	這意味住 chromosomes have the same shape and size, 或者有時可以說相同的結構和大小.	That means the chromosomes have the same shape and size, or sometimes you say the same structure and size.	F‴ (ignore)

The example shown in Excerpt 7.2 illustrates how the teacher asked higher-order questions using the L1 (Cantonese) to investigate the students' understanding of highly cognitive demanding concepts around the human defence system (immunity). The teacher taught the students about immunity in the human body. She used a number of higher-order questions in the L1 (e.g. 'why' and 'what') to make the abstract science content more explicit. By using higher-order questioning in the L1, the teacher could use extended IRF patterns to elicit the students' understanding of abstract scientific terms, such as 'non-specific', 'pathogens', 'antigens' and 'leukocytes', and make their semantic relations in biology explicit to the students.

In Excerpt 7.2, the teacher began an introduction with an extensive explanation at the beginning of the lesson drawing on the students' understanding of organisms such as bacteria and viruses which attack human defence systems. This explanation was offered to help the students understand the primary function of our human defence system, and the teacher further elicited the students' understanding of different types of defences using a number of higher-order questions in the L1, such as '*Which kind of* haploid cells?' and '*Why are they called* diploid cells?'

From Turns 164–199 we can see the teacher asking higher-order questions in the L1 to facilitate the students' understanding of scientific terms and their semantic relations. These questions were used in an interactive way, which had the potential to facilitate higher-order thinking, through a considerable amount of input, and expanded on the students' answers using follow-up feedback in a number of interactive sequences. The IRF sequences allowed the teacher to draw on the students' responses (e.g. by repeating the responses) in the initiations (follow-up questions). The students' responses can be viewed as a translanguaging practice, and through building on others' utterances, teacher and students were co-constructing scientific knowledge.

A summary of the students' language use shows that they used nouns or noun phrases to refer to scientific items. One noticeable difference in this example compared to Excerpt 7.1 is that the students produced technical English terms when responding to their teacher in Cantonese (L1). In the examples presented above, the teachers predominantly used English for instruction. In these exchanges, the teacher again did not encourage the students to produce a complete sentence, or make any attempt to correct the students' language mistakes or provide any feedback about how to acquire the language of science in the L2 context. After the students gave different answers in topics A, B and C, the teacher decided which was consistent with her planned scientific explanation and used it as the source for further questions.

Teacher–Student Interaction through Translanguaging

As seen in the analyses above, translanguaging can provide a meaningful space for English learners to draw on their full linguistic repertoires when learning science in an EMI context. In particular, translanguaging can offer a space for students to develop higher-order thinking and understanding of scientific concepts. In the two examples of biology lessons, when exploring abstract science concepts such as photosynthesis (in Excerpt 7.1) and chromosomes (in Excerpt 7.2), the use of translanguaging in teacher–student interaction enabled extended teacher's talk, followed by expanded student responses and follow-up by the teacher.

In the process of translanguaging, the teacher was able to draw on the students' full linguistic repertoires to help them acquire, understand and demonstrate their understanding of photosynthesis. The teacher initiated the interaction using the L1 as the classroom language, asking students in the L1 about the possible factors that affect the rate of photosynthesis. Although the students gave their answers in English, they were short and not elaborated. The teacher then provided another follow-up question by translanguaging the students' scientific terms in English, everyday language in Cantonese, which allowed the students to utilise their existing linguistic resources.

According to Cummins (2000: 35), 'the most successful in teaching English LEP [limited English proficient] students, oral proficiency [measured by formal tests] takes three to five years to develop, and academic English proficiency can take four to seven years'. Students need to attain sufficient English proficiency to allow for effective spoken interactions in the classroom. The results of this study might show how the use of translanguaging in EMI science classrooms, particularly among students with a low English proficiency, can facilitate all levels of English learners to draw upon their full linguistic repertoires to acquire science knowledge. The examples shown in this paper strengthen García and Li Wei's (2014) argument supporting a holistic view of meaning-making repertoire, in which bilingual learners are able to use their linguistic system for meaning-making in a content-based classroom context. The examples also suggest that science experiments have great potential for bilingual learners to engage in translanguaging and provide a great deal of social space for bilingual users to bring together different dimensions of their 'experience and language resources' into one coordinated meaning-making performance.

Research has also advocated that science teachers explore how different linguistic resources can develop students' scientific knowledge. For example, they may draw on bilingual students' different linguistic features and the various modes of their autonomous languages to explain abstract science concepts and facilitate the deconstruction of science knowledge (García, 2009c; Lemke, 1990; Lo, 2014). Multimodal resources might include symbols, graphs and diagrams, mind maps, tree diagrams, flow charts, crossword puzzles, whiteboards and video games. It is important to note that many of the multimodal resources have already been adopted in EMI science classrooms, and teachers are trying hard to broaden and develop the resources needed to easily convey science knowledge to students in Hong Kong.

Due to the scope of this study, it was not possible to conduct a detailed analysis of the relationship between language and multimodal resources in explaining scientific ideas, nor to examine the ways in which science teachers use multimodal resources to explain abstract scientific concepts to students. In future research, it would be worth exploring the use of these language resources to identify whether and how they help L2 learners unpack the highly technical, dense and abstract discourse patterns characteristic of scientific discourse.

The Role of Translanguaging in the Science Classroom

The role of translanguaging in the observed EMI science classrooms reveals its substantial pedagogical benefits for language and meaning construction in science classrooms. Students can draw upon their full linguistic repertoires to acquire science knowledge. The use of translanguaging opens up a space for the students to build on others' responses when presenting their own views. Compared with early full EMI classrooms in Hong Kong, these late partial EMI classrooms contain more (but shorter) student initiations and responses and more use of higher-order questions by teachers, but less direct feedback to students. In addition, students in these partial EMI science classrooms use their linguistic repertoires to perform translanguaging by switching between registers (e.g. everyday language versus academic language) and drawing on their peers' responses to construct further utterances. Both the teachers and students tend to use their L1 to leverage the students' linguistic diversity, allowing for flexible language practices to develop the students' English and scientific knowledge.

This study sought to answer its research question by analysing the role of translanguaging in classroom interactions in EMI science classrooms. Science teachers focus more on content instruction than they do on the ability of students to offer elaborate responses in the L2 (English). Thus, science teachers should be encouraged to pay more attention to form-focused instruction in order to provide students with more opportunities for L2 learning alongside the development of scientific knowledge. This study suggests that a detailed analysis of interactions can be of great assistance in developing teachers' understanding of the complexity of teaching science and language. Since translanguaging is still an emerging paradigm in the field of EMI research, more work should be done by EMI science educators in Hong Kong to effectively fulfil the intended pedagogy. Recognising the role of translanguaging is valuable for future EMI pedagogy and EMI teacher training.

8 Translanguaging in a Graduate Education Programme at a Cambodian University

Sovicheth Boun and Wayne E. Wright

Introduction

In countries where English is a second or foreign language, many universities have opted to use English-medium instruction (EMI) in an effort to respond to the global educational trend, characterised by internationalisation and student mobility (Dearden, 2014). This is especially true in developing countries (see Fenton-Smith *et al.*, 2017). The rationale is often related to issues reflecting the dominance and global spread of English: textbooks and materials available only in English; courses often taught by native professors who obtained their training through English-medium universities; courses sometimes taught by visiting international faculty; and students' need to access and contribute to the predominantly English academic literature.

Cambodia, where this study takes place, has especially had its struggles over the language of instruction issue. French was a prominent language of instruction in universities during Cambodia's 90 years as a French protectorate (T. Clayton, 1995). Following independence in 1954, a Khmerisation effort took place that put more emphasis on Khmer as a medium of university instruction. However, the formal education system was abolished by the Khmer Rouge from 1975 to 1979; teachers and other educated Cambodians were targeted for execution (Chandler, 1993). Support to rebuild the education system following the genocide came primarily from Vietnam and Russia; hence, Vietnamese and Russian became the languages of instruction along with Khmer in some universities (T. Clayton, 2006). Western aid returned to Cambodia in the early 1990s, and French and English became prominent mediums of instruction in higher education. However, French has lost its prominence, and English now dominates in higher education programmes, particularly at the graduate level (S. Clayton, 2008; T. Clayton, 2002).

With the national language of Khmer being used as the medium of instruction in public schools, the lack of sufficient English proficiency among many students has made the implementation of EMI in higher education particularly challenging. At one of the country's flagship public universities, the official language of instruction in the master of education (MEd) degree programme, along with other graduate programmes, is English. However, the level of English proficiency among the students varies widely, and many instructors who are bilingual in Khmer and English often find it necessary to use Khmer to make the course content accessible. This results in patterns of language use best described as translanguaging (García, 2009a). The purpose of this study is to understand the nature of the use of English/Khmer translanguaging practices in the MEd programme, in particular exploring the multifaceted language practices and views of bilingual Cambodian faculty and students in the programme and how these practices make course content more accessible.

Translanguaging in Higher Education

Some language experts express concern about the global spread of English and its impact on local languages, referring to such practices as linguistic imperialism or even linguistic genocide (Phillipson, 1988; Skutnabb-Kangas, 2000; Skutnabb-Kangas & Phillipson, 1999). Nonetheless, using English as a medium of instruction in classrooms does not necessarily have to mean English-only instruction with a devaluing of local languages. Of particular concern is the degree to which students have sufficient proficiency in English to fully comprehend instruction in English. Research among language minority students in the United States has found that instruction in English can be made more comprehensible through effective use of students' native language (Echevarria *et al.*, 2017; Wright, 2019; Wright & Li, 2006). Research has also shown that classroom code-switching during formal instruction is common in bilingual settings, but tensions exist in finding the proper balance for both academic and political purposes (Li Wei & Martin, 2009).

García (2009a) has expanded and popularised the concept of translanguaging, first coined by Welsh educator Cen Williams (1994), which provides a new lens for understanding how bilinguals use their languages in ways that go beyond traditional notions of codeswitching. While *languaging* refers to the language practices of people (Shohamy, 2006), *translanguaging* refers to communicative practices that ensue when bilingual people language bilingually. García (2009a: 45) defined translanguaging as 'multiple discursive practices in which bilinguals engage in order to make sense of their bilingual worlds'. Although the complexities of bilingualism and the resulting translanguaging are seldom acknowledged in educational settings, García and Li Wei (2015: 226–227) contend that 'translanguaging in schools not only creates the possibility that bilingual students could use their full linguistic and semiotic repertoire to make meaning, but also that teachers would "take it up" as a legitimate pedagogical practice'. (For more on *legitimacy*, see Luckett & Hurst-Harosh, this volume.)

Although much of the early literature on translanguaging focused on primary and occasionally secondary educational settings, more recent research has explored these multiple discursive practices of bilingual students in higher education (Barnard & McLellan, 2014; Doiz *et al.*, 2013; Fenton-Smith *et al.*, 2017; Mazak & Carroll, 2016; Palfreyman & van der Walt, 2017; see also Goodman *et al.* and Dalziel & Guarda, this volume). With higher education increasingly being characterised by global movements of people and ideas, translanguaging has the potential to challenge the dominance and privileging of English that still dominates university language policies and practices (Mazak & Carroll, 2016). In fact, as Palfreyman and van der Walt (2017: 3) point out, the promotion and use of English by policy makers, students and academics have 'paradoxically resulted in increased multilingualism on campuses, as increasing numbers of students from diverse backgrounds use the lingua franca to access and develop knowledge and competencies in a variety of languages'. In line with Mazak and Carroll (2016) and Palfreyman and van der Walt (2017), in this chapter we argue for the promotion of the languages that the students bring to their higher education studies as resources for learning, and for the need to support multiple languages and literacies, irrespective of the status and spread of such languages.

The Master of Education (MEd) Programme

Cambodia has made tremendous progress in rebuilding its entire education system over the past four decades following the genocide. However, many challenges remain. Recognising the need for advanced academic training for Cambodian professionals working to further develop the nation's education system, one of Cambodia's oldest flagship universities established the MEd programme in 2006. The university itself was only 15 years old at the time it was shut down by the Khmer Rouge in 1975 (i.e. the onset of the genocide period in Cambodia). Most faculty and students perished during the genocide or fled to other countries. However, the university has been making a substantial comeback since its re-opening following the genocide in the 1980s. Despite significant challenges, by the time of this study in 2009 the university had over 10,000 students with about 400 faculty and staff members, offering bachelor's and master's degrees in the sciences and social sciences. It also offered the top foreign language programmes in the country. Only about 15 faculty members held PhD degrees, which they were able to earn with the support of government and international assistance through doctoral programmes in countries such as the United States, Australia and Japan (Boun, 2014). Today, the university is one of the leading public universities in Cambodia.

With financial support from the European Union (EU), the MEd programme was able to provide scholarships for education officials and staff from the Ministry of Education, Youth and Sport (MoEYS). Fee-paying students included Cambodian staff of local and international non-governmental organisations (NGOs) working in the education sector, public and private school administrators and teachers, instructors from other universities and recent graduates from bachelor degree programmes. At the time of this study in 2009, the first cohort of about 43 students had finished their coursework and were gradually completing their theses. The second cohort of about 17 students were completing their second year of coursework, and the third cohort of about 60 students were finishing their first year.

Officially, the medium of instruction for the MEd programme was English. The rationale for this decision provided by the programme's founders included several factors: (a) lack of relevant Khmer textbooks; (b) most education research and reports in Cambodia are published in English; (c) native faculty members received their graduate training through English-medium programmes outside Cambodia; (d) a general lack of standardisation for educational terms in Khmer; (e) some courses were taught by non-Khmer speaking international visiting faculty; (f) a large number of international NGOs work in Cambodia's education sector; (g) English is the lingua franca of the Association of Southeast Asian Nations (ASEAN); (h) regional educational meetings sponsored by ASEAN, UNESCO and UNICEF are conducted in English; and (i) students were expected to write their theses in English to make them accessible to the broader education and research community.

Nonetheless, Khmer is the national language of Cambodia, the medium of instruction in public K-12 schools and many undergraduate programmes, and is the operating language of MoEYS and the Cambodian government as a whole. Despite the official policy of English as the medium of instruction for the MEd programme, the reality was that admitted students had a wide range of proficiency in English. While the programme's entrance exam tested students' Khmer and English writing abilities on education topics and English reading comprehension, English ability was only weighted at 60%, and students only needed to score 50% or higher to be admitted into the programme.

It quickly became apparent that the English proficiency of many of the students was too low to handle the academic coursework. A general pattern was that officials from MoEYS tended to be older with strong knowledge of the education system, but had the lowest English proficiency skills, while the opposite was true for other students who tended to be younger, stronger in English, but less experienced in the education field. Thus, the faculty found the need to be more flexible in terms of the medium of instruction by allowing and engaging in translanguaging practices to ensure students' success in the programme.

Participants and Research Questions

The participants include the six core faculty members of the MEd programme (see Table 8.1), and students from Cohorts II and III. Five of the faculty were native Cambodians, all of whom earned graduate degrees from universities in Japan or the United States. Instructors A, B and C were the founders of the MEd programme, and Instructor B is the current Programme Director. Instructor F was a non-Khmer speaking international faculty member from Germany. Appropriate informed consent, in both verbal and written forms, was obtained from all the participants.

At the time of this study, the first author (Boun) was one of the core Cambodian faculty members. The second author (Wright) speaks Khmer, and was a visiting Fulbright Scholar from the United States. He also taught courses in the programme, advised students, worked closely with the core faculty and served on the advisory board to further develop the programme.

This study addresses the following research questions:

(1) What are the views of the faculty members regarding the use of Khmer and English in the programme?
(2) What are the attitudes of students regarding the use of Khmer and English in the programme?
(3) What is the nature of the Khmer/English translanguaging practices within the graduate programme? And how do they address the language and academic needs of the students?

Context of the Study

To answer these research questions, we conducted a mixed-methods case study consisting of semi-structured interviews, participant

Table 8.1 Faculty participants

Faculty member	Nationality	Highest degree, country earned
Instructor A (Programme Founder)	Cambodian	PhD, Japan
Instructor B (Programme Founder and Director)	Cambodian	PhD, Japan
Instructor C (Programme Founder and Former Director)	Cambodian	PhD, Japan
Instructor D	Cambodian	PhD, Japan
Instructor E	Cambodian	MA, United States
Instructor F	German	MA equivalent, Germany

observations, analyses of programme documents and a student questionnaire. Each faculty member was interviewed for one to two hours, predominantly in English with some translanguaging. Participant
observations were conducted in three courses taught by the second author
(Wright) or co-taught with a core Cambodian faculty member:

(1) Educational Policy (17 students – Cohort II)
(2) Research Seminar I (17 students – Cohort II)
(3) Research in Education (30 students – Cohort III)

We also conducted three observations in courses taught by other
instructors, as well as participant observations in programme meetings
and activities. Forty-seven students from Cohorts II and III completed a
questionnaire with selected response and open-ended items at the end of
the term. The questionnaire asked students about their views on the use
of Khmer and English and which uses of Khmer they found to be most
effective in helping them access and comprehend course content. We digi-
tally audio-recorded each interview and most classroom observations and
made digital copies of programme documents. Additionally, we kept field
notes of classroom observations, programme meetings and activities.
Each interview and selected portions of classroom recordings were fully
transcribed. NVivo was used to assist with organising, coding and analysing our data from the interviews, observations and programme documents. Descriptive statistics for the quantitative questionnaire data were
calculated using Excel. Interview excerpts included here preserve the
actual words and authentic phrasings of the participants, and thus are not
edited to conform with the grammar of a standard variety of English.

Striking a Balance between English and Khmer

The interviews with faculty members and the participant observations
revealed a range of views and practices in terms of the use of English and
Khmer in the classrooms. The five native Cambodian instructors reported
teaching predominantly in English, given that this was the expectation of
the programme. Although they agreed that English should be the predominant language of instruction, all acknowledged the need to incorporate Khmer in their instruction. The use of Khmer was guided by the
objectives and nature of the course content, and the needs of the students
(compare with Pun, this volume). For example, Instructor A stated, 'These
people [students] come here, they need the knowledge and skill. They need
to know about education, and if any language can help them understand,
why you put that language away?'. Instructor E commented, 'If you focus
too much on English, then you go away from the content of the course'.

Instructor B, who also serves as the Programme Director, stressed that
incorporating Khmer in the courses was essential to include all students.
He argued '[our] target is not only for the people work[ing] in the

education-related NGOs' (i.e. students with typically stronger English proficiency), but also for Ministry officials and teachers (i.e. students with typically lower English proficiency). Instructor A further emphasised the need to remove the language barrier.

Excerpt 8.1 *Interview with instructor*

Instructor A: If we stick to medium of instruction only in English, that's going to be difficult for some of them. And what is the point of this programme? Our objective is to provide knowledge and skill in education policy, education-related issues to those people to go back and apply. And if we use the language as a barrier to that, some of them may quit.

Some instructors felt more needed to be done to accommodate students with lower English proficiency. They suggested a dual-track programme in which some courses are taught primarily in Khmer while others are taught primarily in English. For example, Instructor E suggested:

Excerpt 8.2 *Interview with instructor*

Instructor E: We [should] have that English-only MEd programme and the bilingual one that should cater to only Ministry people. That would help because it's probably too late for those people who try to master English to come to study.

Self-Reported Translanguaging Practices

In this section, we describe how the instructors and the students engaged with each other and among themselves in 'the process of making meaning, shaping experiences, understandings and knowledge through the use of two languages' (Baker & Wright, 2017: 280). Through the interviews and observations, we identified a number of translanguaging practices used by both faculty and students, the most common of which included the following:

(1) Using Khmer to summarise or explain the main points after presenting in English.
(2) Using Khmer to provide new information or examples.
(3) Using Khmer in small-group discussions before sharing to the whole class in English.
(4) Using Khmer to draw the students' attention and make them feel comfortable in class.

While all instructors acknowledged the need to use the native language, the strategies they used varied. Many described using Khmer to summarise or explain the main points after lecturing in English. Instructor A, for example, reported that:

Excerpt 8.3 *Interview with instructor*

Instructor A: When I start, I normally speak English. Later on when I move to a complex part, and then I need to check in, you know, because that is a core of my lecture, so after I speak it, I repeat in Khmer. I say it again in Khmer. This is one strategy.

Instructor A also stressed the need for instructors to simplify their use of English. He said most instruction should be in English, but suggested Khmer be used at the end to review: 'You can do the discussion in the classroom for two hours and a half or something [in English] and then half an hour you can speak Khmer to sum up.'

Instructor C reported that many of his students wanted him to use English in his instruction, but he would try to give explanations in Khmer when students worked in groups and 'when the concept is getting more and more difficult'. He acknowledged that sometimes he is not sure if students' lack of understanding is due to the medium of instruction or the heavy content of the lesson. However, he noted 'a big increase in the students' understanding' when he used Khmer (see also Adamson & Fujimoto-Adamson, this volume). Instructors A, D and E, who insisted that they mostly used English in class, reported that they provide an explanation or summary in Khmer when requested by the students or when they felt the need based on the students' reactions. They found that their students were 'very happy' when they used some Khmer in class. Wright's (Author 2) students told him they were extremely nervous when they learned they would have a Fulbright scholar from the United States as their instructor, but were greatly relieved when they heard him speak Khmer.

A few instructors used Khmer to provide new information or examples or to clarify the concepts presented. Instructor C stated that, 'When I give examples, I tend to say in Khmer'. Similarly, Instructor D mentioned that it is good to give the examples in Khmer, even for his own benefit: 'Sometimes I might have difficulties also to use English. In that case, I feel it's hard for me to get the right words, the right concepts. So that's one thing that also I try to use Khmer.'

Khmer was also used by both students and the instructors when giving presentations or during group discussions. Instructor A stated that:

Excerpt 8.4 *Interview with instructor*

Instructor A: Normally I use English material, but when I do presentation, I do in Khmer. Sometimes I do only in English, but when they have to answer my question, when they have to do presentation about their topic, they can do it in Khmer.

Instructor E mentioned that at the beginning of the semester he did not allow the students to use Khmer when presenting. However, he later allowed them more flexibility:

Excerpt 8.5 *Interview with instructor*

Instructor E: I realized that those students who were from the Ministry could not really do it well, so I allowed the option to use Khmer or English. So, some of them did both, and some did only in English, and some did only in Khmer.

Instructor F, from Germany, was the only non-Khmer speaking instructor in the programme. He expressed his initial shock at the students' low level of English proficiency and described having to make many modifications to the readings, assignments and tests. Even then, he found it was a real struggle for both himself and the students. While he required students to present in English, he made exceptions for a few students because he did not believe they could do their presentations otherwise.

Our classroom observations revealed that across all instructors, regardless of what language was used during the presentations, the PowerPoints and the materials were all in English. In the courses taught by Khmer speaking instructors, the two languages were used fluidly to present, explain, give examples, summarise or check for understanding. Khmer was used during small-group discussions and sometimes when students reported their group ideas to the class. Instructor B explained, 'We want them to participate [in the group discussion]. If it's in English, it's impossible'. He observed that students with limited English tended to be disadvantaged during group discussions; thus, he divided students into groups based on their English ability so they could help each other: 'When they are in the team, they express the idea of what happened [in Khmer], and then the reporter of the team will report [in English to the class].' Instructor F also made sure the weakest English speakers were in groups with stronger English speakers so they could provide assistance in Khmer.

Some instructors reported using the native language to make the students feel comfortable or less bored in class. Instructor A used Khmer to 'make [students] relax in order to attract attention'. He added that if he spoke in English all the time for three hours, some people might fall asleep: 'When I look around [and] I see some people feel bored, because it is an afternoon session, I switch into Khmer, telling a little bit to make them awake.' Instructor B noted that his students felt 'more comfortable' and could present their ideas more clearly when they were allowed to speak in Khmer. He added that when he spoke in Khmer, he always included something funny to 'relax' the students and help them understand:

Excerpt 8.6 *Interview with instructor*

Instructor B: Sometimes I feel like, okay let's speak Khmer and then make jokes, make fun. Because I notice that when I speak Khmer, I always include something kind of amusing. And something to make them understand, and at the same time they feel a little bit amused with the language.

As reported by the instructors and confirmed through observations, the two languages were used flexibly and dynamically as the instructors engaged in the meaning-making processes, shaped their students' experiences in class and promoted their understanding and knowledge of course concepts. As Instructor C pointed out, 'If they read in English and then they try to write in Khmer, I think they have the internalisation of their understanding much better'.

Translanguaging Practices in Action

In this section, we present two snippets of classroom interactions that exemplify the translanguaging practices between the instructor and students. The interactions were based on an Educational Policy course taught by the second author (Wright).

Using L1 to provide new information

San (pseudonym) is presenting an article written by the instructor (Wright & Li, 2006) about two newcomer Cambodian students in a middle school in the United States struggling with math instruction in English. His PowerPoint is in English.

Excerpt 8.7 *Student's presentation*

Speaker	Original (Khmer, English)	English translation
San	As we know, they 'come from the country which lacking of running water.' និយាយអោយច្បាស់ ប្រទេសក្រីក្រ អញ្ចឹងគាត់មិន អាចចេះបានទេ។ អញ្ចឹងធ្វើ អោយគាត់មិនអាចជាប់រៀង test ហ្នឹង បានទេ។	As we know, they 'come from the country which lacking of running water.' In short, a poor country. Thus, they cannot learn. Thus, it made it so they could not pass the test.
Instructor	តាមពិតពីរនាក់ហ្នឹងចេះ, គេឆ្លាត។ គេរៀនអស់នៅ កំពង់ស្ពឺ, OK? ··· គេចេះ បូកលេខ, គេចេះ, you know, រូបមន្ត អ៊ីខ្លះ។ ប៉ុន្តែចេះដល់ កំរិតរបស់ស្រុកខ្មែរ។ ដល់ពេល ទៅស្រុកអាមេរិក បញ្ហាកំពូល គឺអត់ចេះភាសាយើង។ អញ្ចឹង ពេលខ្ញុំជួប គេ, ទៅជួយពន្យល់ ភាសាខ្មែរ គេនាប់ចេះ គេនាប់ ចេះមែនទែន! ពេលប្រលង all in English.	Actually, the two students knew a lot, they were smart. They learned everything in Kompong Speu, OK? ... They knew how to add, they knew, you know, some math formulas. But their knowledge was at the limit of Cambodia. In America, their biggest problem was they didn't know the language. So when I met them, and helped explain in Khmer, they learned very quickly! When they were tested, it was all in English.

In this excerpt, both languages were used fluidly and effectively by both the student and the instructor. Having read from the PowerPoint presentation in English, the student then provided additional information in Khmer to elaborate the point. The instructor interjected to clarify and add new information about the two children, mostly in Khmer, to provide additional context to help the class understand the reading.

Using L1 to repeat information and provide further explanations

In this excerpt, the instructor was presenting about conflict of interests in policy implementation and was giving an example from the United States in the context of the aftermath of Hurricane Katrina.

Excerpt 8.8 *Instructor's presentation*

Speaker	Original (**Khmer,** English)	English translation
Instructor	So let me give you one example. In the United States, President Bush … after New Orleans … they have a big flood, remember? In New Orleans គេមានទឹកជំនន់យ៉ាងធំនៅក្នុង New Orleans ហើយមានមនុស្សច្រើន គេបាក់ផ្ទះបាក់អ្វីៗ។	So let me give you one example. In the United States, President Bush … after New Orleans … they have a big flood, remember? In New Orleans, **there was a big flood** in New Orleans **and many people lost their houses and stuff.**
Students	Yeah!	
Instructor	And then George W. Bush says I will help the school in New Orleans. I will give the money to buy software for the computers, but they must buy software from my brother [laughing].	
Students	Wow!	
Instructor	អញ្ចឹង Bush ថានេះលុយជួយ សាលា … ទៅទិញ computers … ទៅទិញសំការ: computer, ប៉ុន្តែ ទៅទិញពីប្រូនប្រុសរបស់ខ្ញុំពី ក្រុមហ៊ុនភាគ់។	So Bush said here is the money for the school … to buy computers … buy computer **software,** but go and buy from my brother's company.
Students	Oh!	
Instructor	So, good policy, right? Money helps schools. Who benefits economically? Another Bush. [laughing]	
Students	[laughing]	

As the instructor was giving this example, he first spoke in English, and then he switched to Khmer to repeat what he had just said to make sure they understood about the flooding in New Orleans. He then explained in English how President Bush gave the money to the school in New Orleans to buy computers and software, with the requirement to buy them from his brother's company. Then, he paraphrased in Khmer to ensure that the students understood. Finally, the instructor switched back to English to check the students' understanding of the concept of conflict of interests in policy implementation.

Students' Attitudes towards Translanguaging

A questionnaire was administered to 47 students from Cohorts II and III. Student responses revealed that nearly all wanted courses taught primarily in English. This appears to be aligned with the instructors' pattern of language use in instruction. As shown in Table 8.2, many students (67%) used both Khmer and English to talk to their instructors in person before or after class or during the break, although more Khmer was used during such bilingual interactions. Only a few (9%) used only English to talk to their instructors. When talking to other students before or after class or during the break, a majority used either only Khmer (50%) or both languages with more Khmer (40%). A large number of the students took notes in either only English (60%) or both languages with more English (26%).

Table 8.3 shows the students' views about the helpfulness of the use of Khmer in instruction. All students reported that they found it somewhat helpful (47%) or very helpful (53%) when the instructors provided quick explanations in Khmer. Also, a majority found instructors' presentations in Khmer somewhat helpful (60%) or very helpful (24%). Interestingly, nearly all reported that instructors' presentations, which included a mix of Khmer and English, were somewhat or very helpful in ensuring their comprehension of course content, and hence a strong preference for translanguaging.

A majority of students also reported other allowances for the use of Khmer in the programme to be somewhat or very helpful, such as using Khmer to ask questions or make comments (92%), and being allowed to

Table 8.2 Students' language use pattern

	Only English	More English than Khmer	More Khmer than English	Only Khmer
Talking to the instructor in person before or after class, or during the break	9%	27%	40%	24%
Talking to other students before or after class, or during the break	6%	3%	40%	51%
Taking notes in class	60%	26%	11%	3%

Table 8.3 Helpfulness of the use of Khmer

	Not very helpful	Somewhat helpful	Very helpful
Instructors providing quick explanations in Khmer	0%	47%	53%
Instructors' presentations in Khmer	16%	60%	24%
Instructors' presentations which included a mix of Khmer and English	3%	21%	76%
Being allowed to ask questions or make comments in Khmer	8%	50%	42%
Being allowed to use Khmer in our presentations	26%	69%	5%
Being allowed to use Khmer in small-group discussion	5%	58%	37%
Being allowed to use Khmer in our written work	47%	40%	13%

use Khmer in their own presentations (74%) and in small-group discussions (95%). However, the students' opinions were split regarding the use of Khmer in their written work: 47% found it not very helpful and 53% found it somewhat or very helpful. In courses taught by the second author (Wright), English was used about 80% of the time and Khmer was used about 20%, and nearly all students reported that they felt this was a good balance. The majority of students reported they predominantly used Khmer when speaking to the instructors and to each other outside formal instruction. However, all students reported using only English when emailing their professors. This preference likely reflected the challenges at the time of using Khmer fonts on a computer. English was also predominantly used by students when taking notes while studying and during class.

Discussion

The findings revealed that under the official EMI policy of the MEd programme, many students struggled with the English language demands of the programme. Students with the lowest English proficiency participated in the classroom the least, with several indicating a lack of full understanding of the English text they read. At the same time, the faculty expressed deep concerns about the low levels of English of many of their students, and reported making changes or adjustments to ease the language demands of the coursework. Students appear to have struggled most in the courses taught by the non-Khmer speaking international instructor. Given the fact that the other faculty and students were bilingual Khmer-English speakers, that there was a range in English proficiency among the students and that Khmer was the dominant language of Cambodia, a number of translanguaging practices ensued inside and outside the classrooms. Such practices are commonly evidenced in other EMI university programmes in multilingual contexts (Barnard & McLellan, 2014; Fenton-Smith *et al.*, 2017; Mazak & Carroll, 2016; Paulsrud *et al.*, 2017a). Translanguaging as a pedagogical practice is increasingly being used to enable bilingual students to engage with rigorous content, to access difficult texts and to produce new language practices and new knowledge (Kagwesage, 2013; Stroupe, 2014).

The medium of instruction issue was never fully discussed or resolved by programme faculty, at least at the time of the study. While some official documents indicated that English was the language of instruction, others indicated that both Khmer and English were used. The findings showed that the instruction was predominantly in English, and all course texts and materials were in English. However, Khmer played an important role in the classroom and across the programme. Khmer was often used by the instructors to accommodate the students, usually in the form of quick explanations, summaries or examples, as well as to draw the students' attention and make them feel comfortable in class (Mazak *et al.*, 2016; Tayjasanant & Robinson, 2014). Also, when faculty met one-on-one with students for advising, such as with a thesis student, the conversation was predominantly in Khmer. The majority of the students did class presentations in English, but the students with the lowest English skills presented in Khmer. Khmer was typically the dominant language during small-group discussions and cooperative learning group tasks. Students mainly spoke Khmer to each other and to their instructors, before and after class and during the break. The instructors also tended to use Khmer when interacting one-on-one with students during group or individual work. Khmer played an important role in terms of humorous comments. The students' attitudes towards translanguaging, reported in the questionnaire, were also aligned with the observed practices in that they shuttled 'between acts of language that are socially and educationally constructed as being separate' (García & Li Wei, 2014: 80). The attitudes of the students towards translanguaging were overwhelmingly positive (Daryai-Hansen *et al.*, 2016; Moody *et al.*, 2019; Rivera & Mazak, 2017). Despite some individual differences, the majority of the students found translanguaging to be helpful and beneficial to their learning.

From a more critical perspective, translanguaging practices observed at the university addressed the educational and linguistic inequality experienced by the students. Through dynamic and multiple discursive practices, the instructors were able to help the students overcome the linguistic barriers to their learning outcomes. Hurst and Mona (2017) viewed these translanguaging practices as a multilingual pedagogical approach which is grounded in a social justice framework (see also Luckett & Hurst-Harosh, this volume). According to Cumming-Potvin (2009: 84), students within a socially just pedagogical framework should not be affected negatively by 'discrimination through sex, language, culture, ethnicity, religion or disability (or socio-economic status and geographic location)'. In the context of Cambodia, with its complex social history and linguistic ecology, this pedagogy disrupts the EMI classroom environments prevalent in graduate education while at the same time benefiting those students who have the least access to opportunities for English language development. The act of translanguaging, Li Wei (2011: 24) has argued, creates a social space for the students by 'bringing together different dimensions of their personal history, experience, and environment ... into one coordinated and meaningful performance'. Translanguaging as pedagogy thus has a potential to challenge the somewhat unquestioned dominance of English and create culturally and linguistically sustaining classrooms (Robinson *et al.*, 2018) and, as maintained by Daryai-Hansen *et al.* (2016), must be explicitly encouraged and conceptualised as legitimate language use.

Notwithstanding, similar to the findings by Doiz and Lasagabaster (2016), translanguaging was not habitually employed in classroom practices by the instructors because it was not generally accepted in all learning and assessment tasks. In other words, contrary to the primary goal of translanguaging pedagogy, the instructors in our study did not seek to consistently leverage the students' primary language to enhance their access to the course content. Although the majority of the students found translanguaging practices helpful and favourable, the instructors made sure that English remained the primary medium of instruction. None of the instructors made explicit efforts to help the students improve their English in class, nor did they make such a comment in the interviews. In fact, Instructor C stated in the interview that the university's Vice Rector always mentioned the 'concept of globalization', and he suggested that 'our graduates from our university should be able to communicate in English'. However, in a study by Kim (2011), it was found that some students are opposed to EMI because classes may help improve their English ability but hinder their learning of the subject matter. Doiz and Lasagabaster (2016: 174) suggested that the EMI instructors should be made aware of this counterbalanced approach – focusing on both content and language – because 'this approach will help students make the most of EMI' (see also Lyster, 2007). Kym and Kym (2014: 57) argue that the ultimate goal of an EMI programme is to enable students to acquire both the content and language, 'not sacrificing one for the other'.

Conclusion

This chapter reports the findings of a study conducted at a Cambodian university which aims to explore the multifaceted language practices and views of bilingual Cambodian faculty and students in the master of education programme. The results reveal that students struggle with the demands for English within the programme, and desire and benefit from the use of Khmer, along with English, which makes course content more accessible and comprehensible. These results also show that while English is dominant, it is relegated to mainly formal instruction in the classroom, while Khmer remains an important language for one-on-one and group interactions during less formal meeting times. The Khmer/English translanguaging practices within the classroom and across the programme make the academic content more accessible to the students and provide greater opportunities for success than if the programme is conducted entirely in Khmer or English. The study provides insights and guidance to other educators grappling with EMI issues, and a better understanding of translanguaging practices in academic settings where the use of a single language may be insufficient.

9 Student Translanguaging Practices in the EMI Classroom: A Study of Italian Higher Education

Fiona Dalziel and Marta Guarda

Introduction

This chapter explores student translanguaging practices in English-medium instruction (EMI) at the University of Padova in northern Italy. EMI can be described as: 'The use of the English language to teach academic subjects (other than English itself) in countries or jurisdictions where the first language of the majority of the population is not English' (Macaro *et al.*, 2018: 37). In line with developments on a national level, EMI has increased rapidly at the University of Padova in recent years, and it now offers 57 English taught programmes (ETPs). In this EMI setting, the relationship between English, the local language (Italian) and other languages is not specified; in fact, no guidelines are provided for lecturers regarding classroom language use. Yet despite the common belief in the benefits of an English-only approach (Chellin, 2018), studies have revealed that in many EMI classes both lecturers and students activate translanguaging practices (Guarda, 2018). Translanguaging, as explained below, is intended here as the strategic use that multilingual speakers make of their entire linguistic repertoire so as to facilitate the effective learning of content (Canagarajah, 2011).

The study presented in this chapter involved the observation and audio-recording of six two-hour EMI lessons from different disciplines. The authors chose classes in which they had been informed by lecturers that students would be invited to actively engage in group work or oral presentations, so as to unveil the possible use of spontaneous translanguaging practices. This chapter will focus on the following research questions:

(1) Which translanguaging patterns emerge in student language practices?

(2) Which functions do these instances of translanguaging perform?

After illustrating the communicative purposes of translanguaging in the observed lessons, the chapter will conclude with reflections on the extent to which these practices might be determined by the local Italian higher education (HE) context and whether there should be greater attempts to legitimise and foster translanguaging in EMI.

An Ecology of EMI

A brief overview of the implementation of EMI at a national and local level in Italy is required here as a basis for reflection on translanguaging. In line with an ecology of language approach, we take the view that the context is 'not just something that surrounds language, but that in fact defines language, while at the same time being defined *by* it' (van Lier, 2004: 5). Although its history is not as long as in northern European countries (see, for example, Hultgren *et al.*, 2015; Wilkinson, 2013), EMI has fast been gaining ground in Italy in recent years. In 2018, a total of 397 bachelor's and master's degree programmes taught in English were offered at 59 Italian universities (Universitaly, 2019), as opposed to 245 programmes in 52 universities in 2015. These figures provide an indication of the powerful drive towards internationalisation characterising higher education in Italy.

The linguistic implications of EMI have been the subject of intense debate in Italy. For example, objections to the decision taken by Milan Polytechnic to deliver all its graduate courses in English reached the Constitutional Court in 2017. One of the fears driving this action concerned the future health of the Italian language, tied to the belief that its exclusion from university courses could ultimately result in severe domain loss. Another concern was the quality of EMI courses and a fall in academic standards (see, for example, Motta, 2017). Related to this are the findings of Costa and Coleman's (2013) survey of the state of the art of EMI in Italy: for example, both lecturers' and students' levels of English were considered to be a potential problem by 30% of respondents. This issue should be viewed against the backdrop of language competence in Italy, which has still not reached the level of some of its European neighbours. A 2016 EU survey showed that 66.1% of the population of Italy aged between 25 and 64 could speak at least one foreign language; despite being above the average for Europe (64.6%), this figure is well below that of other countries such as Sweden (96.6%) where EMI has a longer tradition (Kuteeva, 2018). The role of Italian and language competence in English are both issues that impact on attitudes to EMI and translanguaging in the Italian context.

EMI was first introduced at the University of Padova during the 2009/2010 academic year. In the academic year 2018/2019 it offered 57 ETPs across all of its eight schools and over 700 individual courses taught in English in Italian-language degree programmes. Despite the intent to attract a greater number of international students, the vast majority of students on EMI courses at Padova are Italian. The university thus provides an opportunity for them to have the benefits of 'internationalisation at home', defined by Beelen and Jones (2015: 69) as 'the purposeful integration of international and intercultural dimensions into the formal and informal curriculum for all students within domestic learning environments'. For international students, English is a medium enabling them to study a content subject in a country whose native language they most probably do not know; local students instead choose to study on EMI courses to gain better career prospects in today's globalised world by improving their competence in English (Ackerley et al., 2017). If learning English is thus valued by students, one might expect their practices to be linked to commonly held (albeit not necessarily well-founded) beliefs about language learning, such as the avoidance of the students' first language (L1) so as to ensure as much target language input as possible (McMillan & Rivers, 2011).

The issues of domain loss and language competence mentioned above are indicative of one erroneous equation lying at the heart of many EMI discussions. It is often assumed that the only way to reach the objectives of internationalisation is by imposing 'English-only' education (Daryai-Hansen et al., 2016; Phillipson, 2003). Yet, as Wilkinson (2017: 41) reminds us: 'Internationalization does not mean that education has to be offered in a single language.' In northern European countries with a longer tradition of bi/multilingual education, the threat of English has often been mitigated by what Phillipson (2015) calls 'additive' ways – in other words by preserving the vitality of the local languages and by seeing English as an additional, prevalent yet not dominant, option. One could thus argue that in an Italian HE context, translanguaging could represent a means to reduce the risk of domain loss for the Italian language and at the same time facilitate the acquisition of content knowledge in cases of low English language competence. At this point it is necessary to unpack the concept of translanguaging and reflect on its role in EMI.

Translanguaging in EMI

In line with García (2009b), the term translanguaging is intended here as encompassing any practice or 'set of practices' (Mazak, 2016: 5) in which multilingual participants engage in 'flexible bilingualism' (Creese & Blackledge, 2010: 112). In other words, speakers 'shuttle between languages, treating the diverse forms that form their repertoire as an integrated system' (Canagarajah, 2011: 401) extending beyond the 'socially and politically defined boundaries' of the languages involved (Otheguy *et al.*, 2015: 281). In education, translanguaging has been described as encompassing a variety of practices such as transliteracy (Baker, 2011), code-meshing (Canagarajah, 2011) and translation. When there is an underlying 'principle that deliberately draws on students' plurilingual competences' (Daryai-Hansen *et al.*, 2016: 30), one can, as Ganuza and Hedman (2017) suggest, talk about 'pedagogical translanguaging'. In the case in question, the ultimate goal is indeed knowledge construction, but there are no pedagogical guidelines favouring and encouraging the use of multiple languages. Instead, we could say that when translanguaging occurs it does so spontaneously, and despite a prevailing belief in the merits of an 'English-only' approach, as mentioned above. Creese and Blackledge (2010: 113) mention 'the burden of guilt associated with trans-languaging in educational contexts': while it would perhaps be going too far to call the use of translanguaging 'stigmatized' as in Carroll and van den Hoven's (2016) study, it is certainly neither acknowledged formally nor encouraged in our context.

Yet, spontaneous translanguaging does occur, and it is this that our study seeks to describe. As the prescribed language of instruction is English and the context is that of an Italian university, our examples of translanguaging almost exclusively involve the use of the Italian language. It is important to clarify that in our investigation we do not simply take into consideration examples of what is also referred to as 'code-switching', in other words, utterances containing a mix of two or more languages. As the language of instruction is English, we consider any use of Italian or other languages to be instances of translanguaging, including where bottom-up student practices, such as reading a text in English and discussing it with peers in Italian, are reminiscent of pedagogical translanguaging. More specifically, in our study translanguaging encompasses practices such as: requesting or providing the translation/explanation of an unknown English term; using Italian and English in what Ljosland (2010: 104) calls 'fringe situations', in other words for matters regarding classroom management, socialisation and task organisation; asking questions in Italian after listening to a lecture in English; commenting on course content in a language other than the source language; or using Italian to discuss a collaborative writing or oral task.

Up until now research on translanguaging in English-medium HE settings has been scarce. Part of the existing literature has looked at translanguaging as activated or perceived by EMI lecturers (see, for example, Adamson & Fujimoto-Adamson, this volume; Boun & Wright, this volume; Chang, 2019; Doiz & Lasagabaster, 2016; Luckett & Hurst-Harosh, this volume; Mazak & Herbas-Donoso, 2014; McMillan & Rivers, 2011), while a limited number of studies have been devoted to the translanguaging strategies adopted by EMI students (e.g. Andersson *et al.*, 2013; Boun & Wright, this volume; Goodman *et al.*, this volume; Kagwesage, 2013). Research conducted at a Ukrainian university (Goodman, 2016) unveiled a variety of examples of translanguaging involving English, Russian and Ukrainian. Interestingly, in EMI lessons students tended to use Russian rather than Ukrainian to support their learning, for example in seeking lexical clarifications. As in our own context, translanguaging here was not part of a pedagogical approach, with both teachers and students attempting to adhere to an English-only approach: 'These multilingual repertoires, intertwined with the students' multilingual identities, emerged despite explicit efforts to keep the task in English' (Goodman, 2016: 63). A study undertaken at Roskilde University in Denmark, instead, investigated the translanguaging strategies of students on a foreign language course in German, which adopted a content and language integrated learning (CLIL) approach (Daryai-Hansen *et al.*, 2016). Although not strictly speaking an EMI course, as language was not solely used as a means to deliver course content, the authors' findings are of relevance here. With reference to Ferguson's (2003) categorisation (Daryai-Hansen *et al.*, 2016: 34), they found examples of practices related to 'curriculum access', but very few of 'classroom management discourse' or 'interpersonal relations'. The difference in the Danish context was that translanguaging was not only welcomed but actively encouraged as part of the educational approach adopted.

From English-Only to Translanguaging at the University of Padova

This section will delve into the research already carried out into EMI at the University of Padova in order to provide some background to the present study. For example, a recent survey administered to 42 Italian EMI lecturers (Chellin, 2018) revealed the prevalence of an English-only approach, with 76% never using their first language in lessons. As regards students' language use, 83% of the respondents had observed students' choice of other languages in class, mostly to speak about topics not directly related to lesson content, to provide peer assistance or in the context of group discussions. Most (69%) believed such practices to be beneficial as 'students feel more comfortable to use both languages' (Chellin, 2018: 88), but only one made a comment that indicated that such use represented in some way an intended pedagogical approach: 'I try to make the best use of polilinguism in class' (Chellin, 2018: 89). Those firmly opposed to students translanguaging in class consider it important for students to 'force' themselves to use English at all times, mostly so as to involve the international students, whose competence in Italian might be low, and to prepare students for their future in 'an English speaking (scientific) society'.

In another small-scale study (Dalziel, 2020), classroom language practices in EMI were explored by administering a questionnaire to

34 students studying on a BA course in psychological science. A total of 26 of the students involved were native speakers of Italian, three were English-Italian bilinguals, and of the remaining students there was one native speaker each of Hungarian, Polish, Serbian/Croatian, Spanish and Turkish. Focusing on the language(s) spoken while conducting pair or group work, only four students (11.8%), of whom three were international students, answered 'Always English'; the most common answer was 'sometimes only English and sometimes only Italian, depending on the task or situation' (52.9%), followed by 'A mix of English and Italian' (29.4 %). Yet despite their actual practices, it is curious that most of the students (58.8%) felt that they should use English all the time. In other words, they do not acknowledge their own language practices as being the right ones, mirroring the idea of 'guilt' mentioned above.

Italian students are concerned about excluding international students from the dialogue, yet when asked about the reasons for speaking Italian, one international student referred to the chance to improve her language competence. In fact, as will be discussed below, the total prohibition on translanguaging in the EMI classroom denies international students a valuable language learning opportunity. Overall the students' replies appear to confirm that the adoption of translanguaging practices helps in verbalising content knowledge and thus enhances the learning process. It is worth mentioning that one Italian student noted that translanguaging is more demanding than holding a monolingual conversation: 'when I'm really tired, I have difficulties alternating between languages, so the language in which we started the conversation will come more naturally' (Dalziel, 2020). This would seem to contradict the idea of speakers of two or more languages moving effortlessly between them. If we take translanguaging as a useful skill, one could argue that rather than discouraging its use students should be given adequate opportunities to develop this skill. For, as van der Walt (2013: 92) observes, the use of the local language alongside English offers students the 'possibility of quality teaching and learning opportunities as well as increased employability'.

Exploring Student Translanguaging in the EMI Classroom

The data discussed in this chapter have been collected as part of a wider project currently in progress at the University of Padova with the aim of gaining a deeper understanding of student language practices and perspectives of EMI. Part of this project is an ethnographic study which includes the administration of a questionnaire on perspectives of EMI to 367 students and semi-structured interviews conducted with 40 of these participants. One finding is that local language use on the part of the lecturers generates mixed feelings among the students as it is often viewed as indicating a lack of competence. On the other hand, in group work or in questions after class, adopting translanguaging strategies is common among students and seen as a way of ensuring the understanding of content and negotiation of meanings (for preliminary findings, see Guarda, 2018). In the following section, these strategies are explored in greater depth in relation to their communicative functions.

As mentioned above, the data analysed for the present study were collected through the observation and audio-recordings of six two-hour EMI lectures from various disciplines. More specifically, while audio-recordings aimed at documenting student oral production and interaction, classroom observation with field notes sought to capture any visual aids (e.g. notes, slide presentations or videos projected, etc.) as well as the environment in which the oral production and interaction took place. All the students observed were informed about the aims of the research project and were asked to sign a consent form in order to participate in the study. They were also assured that their anonymity would be guaranteed. Table 9.1 gives an overview of the classes observed.

Table 9.1 EMI classes observed and audio-recorded

Degree course	Students	Activity type
Master's degree (MA) in cognitive neuroscience and clinical neuropsychology	16 students, of which half had L1 Italian; other L1s were English, Danish, Spanish and French	Oral presentation: four students deliver a lesson on a topic they have previously chosen, using slideshows and videos.
MA in medical biotechnologies	23 students, of which 20 had L1 Italian and two had L1 German	Oral presentation: two groups present a scientific paper to the rest of the class.
MA in pharmaceutical biotechnologies	30 students, of which 29 had L1 Italian and one had L1 Moldavian	Group work: divided into groups, students collaborate to extract the most relevant pieces of information out of a scientific paper and then report to the whole class.
MA in local development	21 students, of which eight had L1 Italian; other L1s were Persian, English, Arabic, Russian, French, English and Uzbek	Group work: five students lead a discussion and group work on a topic they had presented in a previous lesson.
MA in animal care	25 students, of which 24 had L1 Italian and one had L1 Russian	Group work: in groups, students discuss a given case study and come up with solutions that they later report to the rest of the class.
MA in business administration	35 students, of which 30 had L1 Italian; other L1s were Chinese, German, French, Ukrainian and Russian	Group work: in groups, students prepare so as to perform a role-play.

Data from the audio-recordings were analysed and triangulated with the field notes originating from classroom observation so as to identify and make sense of translanguaging patterns activated by students to engage 'cognitively and socially' (García, 2009b: 158) in the EMI classroom. In order to make translanguaging episodes available for categorisation, all lessons were transcribed using an adapted version of the ELFA Transcription Guide (2004). This was deemed to best illustrate language use in contexts, such as EMI, where English is the official academic lingua franca (ELFA). The methodology used for the analysis is qualitative, with thematic analysis (Braun & Clarke, 2006) adopted so as to pinpoint translanguaging patterns in the data and to categorise them according to their main function. The analysis was inspired by Gotti's (2015) taxonomy of code-switching in EMI contexts. Drawing on Klimpfinger's (2007) and Cogo's (2009) research on English as a lingua franca communication, Gotti's (2015) study investigated the use of code-switching by EMI lecturers to fulfil their communicative efforts, namely to ask for assistance, signal cultural identity, show engagement in conversation and ensure comprehension. The fact that Gotti's study focused on an Italian setting where English is the academic lingua franca made it a good starting point for analysing the emergence and function of multilingual strategies as activated by EMI students. Yet, Gotti's taxonomy showed some limitations, in that it seems to regard code-switching as a one-dimensional shift between two autonomous codes. Thus, his taxonomy was adapted to the specific context under scrutiny. This was done at two levels: at an ideological level, which meant moving away from a view of language separation so as to embrace a more fluid and heteroglossic view of multilingual practices that extend beyond code-switching; and at an operational level, with the identification of new categories to best capture the practices emerging in the context under investigation.

Functions of EMI Student Translanguaging Practices

One observation is that translanguaging practices were activated much more frequently when students were conducting group work than when they were performing oral presentations. This may be linked to the very nature of the activities involved. On the one hand, oral presentations required a higher degree of preliminary preparation and were delivered in front of an audience which also included the lecturer. In this type of situation, students may have been more inclined to adhere to the shared language 'policy' of their course, especially since their performance was taken into account for their final evaluation. By contrast, group work as observed in the four lessons illustrated in Table 9.1 was conducted more freely, without the constant presence of the lecturer and with a lower degree of formality. Despite still perceiving group work as a 'core teaching and learning' task (Ljosland, 2010: 104), the students seemed to feel more free to draw from their linguistic repertoire in flexible ways so as to better achieve their communicative aims, even more so in groups where they all shared the same mother tongue. In the lessons observed, translanguaging was activated to perform a variety of functions, some of which resonate with Gotti's (2015) study: appealing for assistance; ensuring comprehension; verbalising content knowledge; task management; signalling cultural identity; and strengthening cooperation. To present these functions, we draw on Daryai-Hansen *et al.* (2016) who, inspired by Ferguson's (2003) categorisation, distinguish between three broad functional areas of translanguaging, namely translanguaging for 'curriculum access, 'classroom management discourse' and 'interpersonal relations'.

Appealing for assistance

One of the functions of the translanguaging practices adopted to foster curriculum access consists of asking for help so as to overcome or avoid communication breakdowns due to lexical gaps. According to Gotti (2015: 86), these practices are activated by students who 'rely on the cooperation of other students and even lecturers from their own linguistic background'. The observed lessons unveiled several episodes in which students asked for assistance. In Excerpt 9.1, one of the students, S5 – for ethical reasons, students' names have been substituted with identifying tags – does not know the English equivalent for *lampadina* (light bulb) and explicitly asks for help ('how do you say light bulb'). A member of the same group tries to offer a creative translation, 'the lighter'. A second student promptly intervenes by providing the right equivalent. The episode ends with a joke on the part of the first speaker ('I can't speak English') aimed at reinforcing engagement in the conversation.

Excerpt 9.1 *Pharmaceutical biotechnologies*

Speaker	Original (Italian, English)	English translation
S5	come si dice lampadina	how do you say light bulb
SU	the lighter	
S7	light bulb	
S5	io non so parlare in inglese	I can't speak English

In Excerpt 9.2, one of the students (S2) struggles to find the English word for *mostra* (exhibition). Instead of performing a direct speech act to ask for assistance, she uses a rising pitch while uttering the Italian word *mostra*. This is enough for her classmate (S1) to provide the right translation. The first speaker thus repeats the English equivalent and is able to continue her report.

Excerpt 9.2 *Local development*

Speaker	Original (English, **Italian**)	English translation
S2	in in Gurna there is a project in 2001 that aims to preserve and foster local erm art and tradition so they made a kind of erm **mostra?**	in in Gurna there is a project in 2001 that aims to preserve and foster local erm art and tradition so they made a kind of erm **exhibition?**
S1	exhibition	
S2	exhibition that regards the local tradition	

Ensuring comprehension

In Gotti's (2015) study, the category of ensuring comprehension indicated the activation of code-switching on the part of the lecturer with the aim of checking whether students had understood a certain concept or lexical term. In the present study, instead, it was found that students used other practices so as to guarantee full comprehension of the texts (both oral and written) that they were using in class and thus favour curriculum access. In the pharmaceutical biotechnologies lesson, for instance, the members of one of the groups were observed reading the assigned scientific paper in English but discussing its main points in Italian only. By activating transliteracy practices whereby literacy input and output are in different languages (Baker, 2011), the students aimed at making sure that all the members of the group could understand the information contained in the assigned paper. This strategy resonates with Williams' early definition of translanguaging (Williams, 1994, in Baker, 2011) as the pedagogical practice of students' switching the language of input and output 'to maximize understanding and performance' (Baker, 2011: 288).

Another example of this category was detected in the cognitive neuroscience lesson, in which one of the students showed the class a video related to the topic she had to present. Since the video was in Spanish and had no subtitles, the student was observed pausing it several times to sum up its contents in English and share them with the class, so as to ensure that all her peers could access the information contained in the video. This episode seems to suggest that students are indeed capable of drawing on all the linguistic resources that are available to them to enhance their communicative potential (García, 2009b).

Verbalising content knowledge

Gotti's (2015) study revealed that lecturers occasionally resorted to another language so as to provide more detailed explanations of a concept. It seems, however, that this practice only occurred at the level of single words, to avoid misunderstanding and convey greater nuances of expression. In the context under investigation, it was observed that the students who used their mother tongue to give more specific explanations primarily aimed at achieving a deeper understanding of a specific concept before conveying it to their peers through English. In these situations, therefore, translanguaging was activated because it had a potential cognitive advantage for the speakers themselves, thus promoting a 'deeper and fuller understanding of the subject matter' (Baker, 2011: 289) and guaranteeing better access to course content. By verbalising content knowledge in their mother tongue first, students were then able to reformulate it in English with more precision.

Excerpt 9.3 *Animal care*

Speaker	Original (English, **Italian**)	English translation
S12	I mean maybe veterinarian and the teacher are not are not being the same … the teacher gave the information and the veterinarian doesn't want to give the information	
S9	**il veterinario non voleva dare le informazioni** mentre **il, il** pathologist **sì** … I would say just the teacher and not the veterinarian	the veterinarian **did not want to share the information** while the pathologist **did want to** … I would say just the teacher and not the veterinarian

Excerpt 9.3 above originates from a lesson in bioethics in which students were discussing a controversial case study with several stakeholders involved. While negotiating the role of each stakeholder, S9 first addresses the issue in Italian ('the veterinarian did not want to share the information while the pathologist did want to'). It may be noted that S9's opinion of the role of both veterinarian and teacher (the pathologist) is in line with what S12, an international student, has just said. Yet S9 feels the need to articulate the concept in Italian. Only after doing this is she ready to share her ideas with the rest of the group in English. This example suggests how translanguaging is linked to the speaker's ability to 'break boundaries' between languages (Li Wei, 2018: 25) in order to articulate views and participate in meaning negotiations with deeper awareness of the subject matter.

Task management

Belonging to the functional area of translanguaging for classroom management (Daryai-Hansen *et al.*, 2016), the task management function characterises translanguaging practices that are activated to give suggestions or instructions to other students in order to effectively perform a given task. In our study, this function occurred mostly when students were collaborating in groups, as in the following example.

Excerpt 9.4 *Pharmaceutical biotechnologies*

Speaker	Original (English, Italian)	English translation
S4	low bio-availability [dictating]	
S6	sì okay	[writing on the blackboard] **yeah** okay
S5	**io aggiungerei mhm … LOW** oral bio-availability	**I would add mhm … LOW** oral bio-availability

In Excerpt 9.4, the students have to agree on the most salient points of a paper. While speakers S4 and S6 are negotiating which points are worth writing on the blackboard and then reporting to the class, speaker S5 intervenes by suggesting an improvement to the text ('I would add mhm … LOW oral bio-availability'). In this case Italian is used to perform the pragmatic speech act of advice, in order to better achieve the final aim of the performed task. The noun phrase in English in the same utterance, on the contrary, marks the speakers' return to the contents of the task, and thus to the language associated with it.

Task management strategies also emerge from Excerpt 9.5, in which one of the students leading the group discussion intervenes to encourage his peers to ask for support if they have doubts about the task they have to perform ('if you have any questions please ask'). His invitation is welcomed positively by a fellow student, who thanks him using the same linguistic code.

Excerpt 9.5 *Local development*

Speaker	Original (Italian)	English translation
S14	**se avete domande potete chiedere**	**if you have any questions please ask**
S13	grazie	thanks

Signalling cultural identity

The use of unplanned exclamations, tags, conjunctions and pause fillers in another language while speaking English reveals the speaker's complex and fluctuating cultural identity. According to Klimpfinger (2007), the occurrence of these episodes represents unintentional code-switching which, as Gotti (2015) also specifies, is often linked to speaker anxiety. In the lessons observed, only a few episodes of such translanguaging practices were found. They all occurred in the medical biotechnologies class, in which the students were being evaluated on their performance in an oral presentation. The following excerpt exemplifies them.

Excerpt 9.6 *Medical biotechnologies*

Speaker	Original (English, **Italian**)	English translation
L	okay what is the function of this in the medium	
S3	well they use this amount of insulin with transferee to differentiate this immortal line of mouse myoblast into myotype myotube myotypes erm **boh**	well they use this amount of insulin with transferee to differentiate this immortal line of mouse myoblast into myotype myotube myotypes erm **I don't know**

In Excerpt 9.6, the lecturer (L) asks the student (S3) a question about the amount of insulin used in the study presented in class. The student seems unsure of her answer and does not know whether to use the word 'myotube' or 'myotype'. After some repetition and hesitation, she unintentionally uses a typical Italian exclamation ('*boh*'), normally associated with uncertainty, thus revealing her cultural identity. Unlike in Gotti's (2015) study, in which the occurrence of this type of translanguaging episode was commonly activated by students with a lower degree of competence in the language, the instances we observed seemed to be linked more to the students' emotional state than to their language knowledge.

Strengthening cooperation

This refers to episodes in which interactants make use of translanguaging to maintain interpersonal relations (Daryai-Hansen *et al.*, 2016) and reinforce the sense of solidarity within the group. Several instances of this function were observed in the lessons in which students were asked to collaborate to achieve a common goal.

Excerpt 9.7 *Pharmaceutical biotechnologies*

Speaker	Original (**Italian**, English)	English translation
S5	**fai la L strana comunque**	by the way you have a funny way to write L
S6	**la L?**	the L?
S5	**sì**	yes
Ss	[laugh]	

In Excerpt 9.7, S5 uses the group's mother tongue to comment on her peer's handwriting ('by the way you have a funny way to write L'). Her comment does not contribute to the task carried out by the students, yet it plays a social function by shifting the focus of the interaction from the academic activity itself to the interpersonal relationships at play. The fact that her comment is welcomed with laughter from all the interactants seems to suggest that S5's communicative and social purposes have been met.

In the group discussions we observed, the reinforcement of positive social relationships was also sometimes promoted by the use of humour through translanguaging. The example reported in Excerpt 9.8 below is taken from the business administration class in which the students had to discuss the best strategy to ask for a salary increase.

Excerpt 9.8 *Business administration*

Speaker	Original (English, Italian)	English translation
S19	we love you **mettiti a piangere** [laugh]	we love you **start crying** [laugh]
S17	**che bei divani che c'ha**	**what lovely sofas he has**
S16	**dì che noi siamo il sindacato degli ingegneri iniziamo a fargli paura** [laugh]	**tell him we belong to the union of engineers let's start scaring him** [laugh]

As can be noticed, the interactants embrace humour by suggesting exaggerated strategies their fictional persona should activate in order to ingratiate himself with the human resources manager. As in Excerpt 9.7, these turns do not contribute to the task and the students are well aware of the inappropriateness of using such exaggerated tones in a formal negotiation. Their use of humour, instead, plays a social role in the group discussion.

Discussion

This study reveals common threads in translanguaging practices in EMI. Students adopt translanguaging for a variety of functions, for instance to ask for assistance and thus avoid potential communication breakdowns due to language gaps. In this light, translanguaging has the potential to activate student–student cooperation and, as Li Wei (2018) puts it, to facilitate meaning-making. This is particularly relevant in contexts such as EMI, in which negotiation of knowledge and co-construction of meanings among speakers from different linguistic and cultural backgrounds are the key to enhanced learning of both content and language.

Translanguaging is also adopted to ensure full comprehension of the resources that the students use in class, for example through the activation of transliteracy practices whereby the students' linguistic repertoire is used flexibly and interchangeably for literacy input and output. As described above, students juggle between languages, pushing and breaking boundaries between them (Li Wei, 2018), for instance by reading written texts in one language and discussing their contents in another language. Judicious use of the linguistic repertoire that multilingual students have at their disposal, therefore, may allow them to successfully navigate the complex waters of cognitively demanding academic tasks, thus giving them better access to course content. This seems to confirm findings from previous research in HE settings (e.g. Andersson *et al.*, 2013; Chang, 2019; Daryai-Hansen *et al.*, 2016; Doiz & Lasagabaster, 2016; Kagwesage, 2013), which show that translanguaging practices have great potential to drive forward the learning process and lead to fuller acquisition of content.

Deeper understanding of subject-related concepts (Baker, 2011) is also promoted by translanguaging practices in which students verbalise content knowledge in one language – typically their first language – before reformulating it in another language, English in the case of EMI. This practice can have two main advantages: firstly, processing concepts in both (or all) the multilingual speaker's languages might help the speaker to grasp them in greater depth; at the same time, it may serve as reinforcement and scaffolding for other interactants.

The study revealed that translanguaging was also used as a means of signalling cultural identity through the insertion of exclamations, conjunctions and pause fillers taken from another language. In our data, such use was triggered by the speaker's emotional state and generally went unnoticed by interactants. Yet, it helps reveal the fluidity with which multilingual speakers shuttle across both fuzzy language boundaries (García, 2009b) and fluctuating multicultural identities (Celic & Seltzer, 2011).

Two further functions of translanguaging were identified, namely managing tasks and strengthening cooperation among students. Both refer to the flexible use of a multilingual speaker's repertoire in 'fringe situations' (Ljosland, 2010: 104), in other words, for matters that are not strictly related to the core teaching and learning activity. As in Ljosland's (2010) study, in which multilingual patterns were observed when students were performing collaborative tasks, our data revealed that speakers were able to select features from their full linguistic repertoire in giving suggestions or instructions to other students so as to achieve a given task and communicate appropriately. In Excerpt 9.4 reported above, for instance, the speaker shows that she can flexibly move from one language to another, using her L1 for task management related communication and English for content-related utterances. This seems to be in line with Creese and Blackledge's (2010: 112) recognition that 'languages do not fit clear bounded entities' and that, for multilingual speakers, all languages are useful and 'needed' to communicate and negotiate meanings.

In so-called fringe situations, the 'social side of translanguaging' (Chang, 2019: 33) emerges as a way to enhance the affective atmosphere among speakers and thus create a safe place for everyone to express their ideas. As illustrated above, the use of translanguaging in expressions that do not apparently contribute to the academic task being performed, as well as in humour and jokes, helps shift the focus to the interpersonal relationships among interactants. As such, translanguaging offers multilingual speakers a fluid space to perform their identities (Li Wei, 2018) and achieve interactional and social aims (Daryai-Hansen *et al.*, 2016), which in turn reinforce cooperation. This seems to confirm García's (2009b) claim that translanguaging can be a powerful resource for multilingual speakers to engage both cognitively and socially in an increasingly complex society.

Some Final Reflections

Overall, the findings presented here reveal that students on EMI courses adopt translanguaging not only to ensure understanding and avoid possible misunderstanding by filling possible lexical gaps, but also in the co-creation of communicative events in which two languages complement each other. This seems to resonate with the comment of one psychological science student (Dalziel, 2020), according to whom language choice may depend on: 'the effectiveness of some linguistic structures themselves: some words, to me, represent their meaning more effectively in English, some others in Italian'. There are also signs of positive interdependence, with translanguaging used to make sure that one's peers have fully understood elements of a lesson.

However, as mentioned above, these practices occur despite the belief on the part of both lecturers and students that English should be the sole language of the EMI classroom. Returning to the van Lier quote about context defining language (see Section 2), it should not be forgotten that the Italian students studying on this degree programme have specifically chosen an EMI course rather than one taught through Italian. Against the background of national levels of language competence lagging behind other European countries, these students wish to be immersed in the English language, which might not have been the case in their school careers, in order to improve their proficiency. Another determining factor in English-only choice in our context is the presence of international students, with English deemed to be the language of inclusion. This points to a conception of English as an academic lingua franca, fostering collaboration and the co-construction of meaning in an international context, and belonging to its users rather than to its native speakers. Such a view could in part allay the fears of EMI sceptics who see the use of English as an imposition, rather than a tool for international collaboration.

Yet as this study suggests, in spite of potential contextual constraints on translanguaging practices, the phenomenon is clearly present in this EMI environment. What appears to be absent is any conception of the pedagogical and communicative advantages of parallel language use (see, for example, Källkvist & Hult, 2016). As Cummins (2005b: 22) observes, 'bilingual instructional strategies can usefully complement monolingual strategies to promote more cognitively engaged learning'. Instead, the ideology of parallel monolingualisms is prevalent, with a view to the fact that in their future lives, students will most likely need to be able to communicate in English proficiently. This, however, overlooks the possible advantages in a plurilingual society of being able to switch effectively between languages and to participate in 'dynamic and creative linguistic practices' (Li Wei, 2018: 15). As regards international students, although they may initially have limited language skills in the local language, by means of translanguaging and negotiation of meaning with their peers, they could be helped in their attempts to become part of the host society, albeit for a limited period of time. Paulsrud *et al.* (2017b: 16) talk of 'processes of transformations through the creation of spaces in which multilinguals can use and expand their linguistic repertoires'. Perhaps the judicious and systematic adoption of translanguaging practices in EMI could itself reshape the context, turning the English-only bubble in an Italian university into a truly multilingual learning space.

10 Translanguaging and Transfer of Academic Skills: Views of Kazakhstani Students in an English-Medium University

Bridget A. Goodman, Sulushash I. Kerimkulova and D. Philip Montgomery

Introduction

Translanguaging in academic settings can be understood both as the process of using one's multilingual repertoire for learning academic skills, and as students' ability to transfer academic language practices across languages and contexts. The phenomenon has been described both as 'complex discursive practices that enable bilingual students to also develop and enact standard academic ways of languaging' (García & Sylvan, 2011: 389) and as 'the ability of multilingual speakers to shuttle between languages, treating the diverse languages that form their repertoire as an integrated system' (Canagarajah, 2011: 401). In other words, translanguaging is both an approach to teaching and learning, and the application of that learning. If students are engaged in learning in an English-only space, their development and application of both English and additional languages may be hindered (Allard, 2017).

Translanguaging pedagogies are increasingly documented and promoted not only in primary and secondary education contexts where multilingual students are minoritised and their rights to multilingual development need to be advocated for (e.g. Menken & García, 2010; Probyn, this volume; Tian & Link, 2019), but also in higher education in contexts worldwide where multilingualism is the norm (Mazak & Carroll, 2016). However, it remains unclear whether translanguaging practices are seen as necessary or useful in an educational context where (1) English is a foreign, non-dominant language, (2) students choose to enrol in English-medium instruction (EMI) programmes, and (3) those students come with high general proficiency in English (as a second or third language after Russian and Kazakh) for studying at the postgraduate level. At the same time, these students may find it necessary or useful to engage in translanguaging as they apply skills across languages and contexts during or after their studies.

This study aims to make three contributions to the understanding of translanguaging and EMI. On a practical level, the study reflects on the capacity of the focal university to meet its goal of producing 'fluent and nuanced communicators across languages' (Nazarbayev University, 2018: 24). On a theoretical level, the study sheds light on the interplay of the concepts of translanguaging and transfer (DePalma & Ringer, 2011; Haim, 2015). On an empirical level, the study explores the practices of translanguaging and transfer in an under-investigated multilingual context, thus contributing to the body of existing literature on translanguaging and EMI.

To that end, based on survey and focus group/interview data from students and alumni at a university using EMI in the city of Nur-Sultan, Kazakhstan, we investigate whether translanguaging is a valued or recognised strategy for developing academic skills in English. We also show the extent to which these translanguaging practices are viewed by students and alumni as successful or unsuccessful across languages and contexts.

National Language Policy and Practices in Kazakhstan

Kazakhstan became an independent nation after the collapse of the Soviet Union in 1991. The state language of Kazakhstan is Kazakh, a Turkic language. Russian, the former Soviet supranational language and language of power, continues to be an official language, an interethnic language and a language of wider communication. The country also boasts 130 ethnic groups, many of which have schools or cultural centres to maintain their mother tongue. Within this context, the Kazakhstani government over nearly 10 years has been actively developing a trilingual education policy of teaching different subjects in Kazakh, Russian and English in secondary schools and higher education institutions. This policy outlines the roles of each of the three languages in the following way: 'Kazakh as the national language, Russian as the language of interethnic communication, and English as the language of successful integration in the global economy' (Nazarbayev, 2007: 38). The goal of this educational policy is to see at least 15% of the population proficient in three languages by 2020 (MEXT, 2011: 8).

In practice, language proficiency is varied and language use is fluid. Russian language use predominates in large cities and the northern and eastern areas of the country that are geographically closer to Russia. The

Kazakh language is more prevalent in rural areas and in southern and western cities. Minority language use tends to be concentrated in communities located in the southern areas closer to China and Uzbekistan. Across cities and villages, English language use depends on individuals and educational institutions where English is a medium of instruction. More commonly, people speak in a mix of Russian and Kazakh, a practice referred to locally as 'shala Kazakh'. The prevalence of multiple languages, and the frequency of mixing of languages to the point of having a named mixed variety, suggest that translanguaging is a common practice in society, and likely in educational settings as well.

The Focal Institution and Programmes

The focal site, Nazarbayev University Graduate School of Education (NUGSE), was established in 2012. With strategic support from the partner institutions, the University of Pennsylvania and the University of Cambridge, and a diverse team of local and international faculty, NUGSE offers two-year master's degree programmes in four concentrations (school education, higher education, inclusive education and multilingual education) and a four-year PhD in education. Each programme is competitive; only 20% of applicants are admitted. Candidates are screened on the basis of the Cambridge International English Language Testing System (IELTS)/Test of English as a Foreign Language (TOEFL) scores, an essay or research proposal which demonstrates relevance and leadership for their intended programme, and an interview. Admitted students take courses on education theory, research methods and thesis development. Each programme culminates in a thesis or dissertation written in English – nearly always an empirical study of varying topics and research designs – of up to 20,000 words for master's students and 80,000 words for PhD students. To support academic skills development, master's students take two years of academic English (EAP) face-to-face and online; PhD students take one semester.

While this programme structure indicates that English is the sole dominant language at NUGSE, other policies and practices index a more dynamic trilingual or multilingual environment. In addition to English, NUGSE students take one semester of Kazakh language based on proficiency level, ranging from basic to academic. To conduct research for their studies, students must prepare informed consent forms in all languages participants are likely to be fluent and comfortable in (e.g. Kazakh, Russian, Mandarin or Uzbek). Students collect data in these languages and English, but must write and present their results in English. Within the larger university setting, official events are generally conducted with PowerPoint slides in three languages. Presenters speak in English, Russian or Kazakh, while two simultaneous interpreters translate into the other languages through headsets and translate comments and questions

Figure 10.1 Library sign in English, Kazakh and Russian (photo by first author)

between the audience and presenter(s). Faculty members of both local and international origin are often bilingual (high proficiency in one mother tongue, e.g. French, plus English), multilingual (high proficiency in two mother tongues, or one mother tongue and one national language, plus English) or plurilingual (knowledge of an array of languages at varying levels of ability and use). In many cases, faculty include Russian, Kazakh or related languages (e.g. Ukrainian, Kyrgyz, Turkish) in their repertoire. Signs around campus do not indicate a consistent policy but are often in three languages, although English dominates (see Figure 10.1).

Moreover, it is normative in the institution and the workplace that students inhabit a multilingual space after graduation. Many NUGSE students and alumni find themselves working at one of the Nazarbayev Intellectual Schools, a network that is tasked with implementing the teaching of different subjects in three languages. Other students are teachers at international schools where the language of instruction is English but the student body is multilingual, or work for international companies where they are expected to help translate and interpret across languages. Thus, the sociolinguistic, pedagogical and ideological environment of NUGSE affords the potential for both the development of international-level academic skills in English and the use of multiple language varieties in multiple modalities as a resource. The environment outside NUGSE provides potential for the application of knowledge of multiple languages and modalities for performing work duties.

Linking Transfer and Translanguaging

As described elsewhere in this volume, translanguaging is defined as both an array of pedagogical resources (see, for example, Sahan & Rose, this volume) and an array of language practices by individuals with multilingual repertoires (see, for example, Mohamed, this volume). As a pedagogy, it involves teachers and students using all of the named languages or language varieties in their repertoires to support comprehension and communication of content. Translanguaging is also a practice that allows for the alternation of languages in different modalities, i.e. listening in one language and writing in another, or reading in one language and translating the text into another (Hornberger & Link, 2012; Lewis *et al.*, 2012b; Williams, 1994, 2000). As an everyday practice, translanguaging can best be understood as the fluid use of multiple semiotic resources from different named language groups, or the seamless movement among language varieties in communication.

Transfer can refer to the application of specific linguistic resources from one language to another, or the application of more broadly learned strategies across contexts. While the term *transfer* was previously used in second language acquisition and contrastive analysis research to mean 'negative influence' or 'interference' of a language student's first language (L1) on their second language (L2) (usually English), this meaning has lost currency (Cenoz & Gorter, 2011; DePalma & Ringer, 2011). Researchers have since acknowledged that linguistic transfer is not unidirectional (L1 influencing L2), but rather multidirectional (Cenoz & Gorter, 2011) and positive (Haim, 2015).

As a term to describe the ability to apply knowledge and skills to new contexts, *transfer* has been used to describe the ways in which students apply writing strategies from their first-year writing and EAP courses to other subjects and how recent graduates adapt to the workplace (DePalma & Ringer, 2011; Green, 2015). This notion, best described as *transfer of learning*, has also been criticised for being too narrow. DePalma and Ringer (2011) take issue with previous definitions that see this transfer as 'consistent reuse' of previous learning; newer conceptualisations, they argue, should acknowledge 'the moves students re*shape* and re*form* learned writing skills to fit new tasks' (DePalma & Ringer, 2011: 137, emphasis in original). Therefore, they suggest the term *adaptive transfer* to mean 'the conscious or intuitive process of applying or reshaping learned writing knowledge in new and potentially unfamiliar writing situations' (DePalma & Ringer, 2011: 141), adding that the process is: (1) dynamic, (2) idiosyncratic, (3) cross-contextual, (4) rhetorical, (5) multilingual and (6) transformative. This last characteristic of adaptive transfer – transformative – is particularly aligned with Li Wei's (2018) argument that translanguaging is a cycle of transformative resemiotisation which, through development of creative language forms, also transforms power relations and the human mind itself.

Bridging the concepts of adaptive transfer and translanguaging more broadly, we can define academic skills development in EMI as the development of diverse writing and speaking styles and structures through dynamic, multilingual processes. These processes are idiosyncratic as they are dependent on students' and teachers' repertoires, practices, abilities, needs and wishes. As students develop these skills, they transform their understanding of academic languaging and apply that transformed understanding for new audiences using an array of new and prior languaging practices. Based on these theoretical grounds, we show that students' views of translanguaging in an educational context, and reflections on their own communicative practices, index the power of English as well as the use of Russian and Kazakh, at times, but not always in transformative ways.

Study Design

In contrast to recent studies of translanguaging in EMI which have taken a case study or ethnographic approach (e.g. Goodman, 2016; Groff, 2016; Toth & Paulsrud, 2017), the data presented in this chapter come from a mixed-methods study employing surveys, focus groups and interviews. The authors have been serving as faculty members in this institution for six years, and have been conducting annual reflections on their teaching practices. The purpose of focusing on students and alumni was to systematically understand and document their awareness of pedagogical and communicative practices that fall under the umbrella of translanguaging, and their perceptions of the utility of such practices for learning and for communication. This focus on learners and their views is consistent with the stated importance of the 'reports of the lived linguistic experience' (Otheguy *et al.*, 2018: 18) of individuals who engage in translanguaging.

First, the research team submitted a study protocol with data collection instruments to the Nazarbayev University Institutional Research Ethics Committee (IREC); IREC approved the research in May 2017. Next, the survey was distributed in English – perceived by the research team to be a language in which participants could easily respond based on the admission requirements of the programmes and performance in English in classes – to all students and alumni from the master's and PhD programmes in education at NUGSE ($n = 364$) as of May 2017. Respondents ($n = 127$) rated themselves on a 5-point scale according to can-do statements related to reading and research, speaking, writing and evaluation skills for each of three languages: Kazakh, Russian and English. Students also evaluated the usefulness of different pedagogical approaches to academic skills development. To explore trends identified in the quantitative data and the dynamics of language and academic skills development, focus groups were conducted with two to nine students and alumni from each degree concentration ($n = 24$) from June to November 2017. Individual interviews were conducted with alumni from one master's programme ($n = 20$) in January–February 2018. Care was taken to ensure that facilitators of student focus groups were not, at the time of the focus group or in the future, in a position to assess students' work. In focus groups and interviews, participants were invited to speak in any language they felt comfortable with, but, as predicted, nearly all communication was in English. Responses in focus groups and interviews are reported in the original, unedited language. As an additional member check, the results of the data analysis were presented to current students and alumni at a research seminar at NUGSE, and again at an international conference on translanguaging, in April 2019. The attendees did not dispute but rather affirmed that the findings were consistent with their lived experiences.

Views of Translanguaging for Learning

Of the 32 activities that students were asked to rate on a 5-point Likert scale from 'extremely useful' (5) to 'not useful at all' (1), four focused on the dynamic use of different languages for meaning-making and communication:

(1) 'receiving instructor explanations or feedback in Kazakh or Russian' ($M = 3.35$, $SD = 1.082$);
(2) 'using Kazakh or Russian with my peers to complete group tasks' ($M = 3.32$, $SD = 1.033$);
(3) 'translating new words' ($M = 3.26$, $SD = 0.983$); and
(4) 'using non-English language sources in English research writing' ($M = 3.03$, $SD = 1.042$).

These mean scores indicate that students generally perceive these activities as 'moderately useful'. However, these four items had the lowest average scores on the list. Specific educational practices in multiple languages were not perceived to be as useful as more general feedback and assessment activities (Montgomery *et al.*, 2019).

Focus group discussions suggest three interrelated reasons why translanguaging is not viewed by students as a strongly supportive pedagogical practice:

(1) the presence of both monoglossic and heteroglossic teacher beliefs;
(2) idiosyncratic behaviour stemming from individual student repertoires and conscious choices; and
(3) the view of translanguaging as a natural behaviour rather than a strategy.

According to the students, teachers in the same institution have a range of practices which do or do not support translanguaging in this context. One multilingual education programme student simply did not recall any use of Kazakh or Russian in classes for the purpose of raising the awareness of academic skills. A secondary education programme student said that some of their teachers make jokes in Russian, but others 'even stop us when we are speaking or discussing in Russian. They prefer us to speak English'. In contrast, a multilingual education programme student noted that 'in Foundation of Multilingualism, because it is the name of the course [laugh] we were encouraged to use the language that we were the most comfortable in discuss[ing] different ideas and academic assignments in groups'. Another multilingual education programme student recalled a teacher who invited guest speakers to discuss policy in Russian. Only one student, from the higher education programme, recalled an instance when a teacher required output in multiple languages; the students were instructed to draft material for a website not only in English but also in Russian and Kazakh.

Two multilingual education programme students suggested that they did not have sufficient academic skills in their mother tongues to shuttle among languages for academic purposes (Excerpt 10.1; this student's name and all names hereafter are pseudonyms).

Excerpt 10.1 *Interview with student Anna*

Speaker	Original (English)
Anna	I think the reason why we do not use Russian or Kazakh, while talking to classmates during peer review is that teachers never taught us what is a topic statement or thesis statement in Russian or Kazakh language, so that is why it's more comfortable for us to explain it in English. Because we know what is it, but I can't explain it in Russian or Kazakh.

Similarly, the second student reported that, occasionally, when students speak Russian or Kazakh, they switch to English to express ideas that they cannot explain without English language terminology.

The convergence of teacher beliefs and idiosyncratic, multimodal choices regarding the use of languages can be seen in the following exchange between Anna and another multilingual education programme student, Assel. In Excerpt 10.2, Assel and Anna initially describe a difference in practice regarding the use of Russian or English, respectively, in peer feedback.

Excerpt 10.2 *Focus group*

Speaker	Original (English)
Assel	For example, for peer reviewing I think I use only Russian to explain. If I review someone's work and I want to explain what I would like to do better, to improve I use Russian. Because it is the most effective way to explain what I want.

Anna   On the contrary, I use only English. Because my peer reviewers do only in English. Because I am used to it. Sometimes I can't remember the right equivalent in Russian, and it doesn't sound natural when I am giving feedback in Russian.

However, it is soon revealed that the difference in language choice is actually dependent on the modality of the feedback. That is, Assel gives oral feedback in Russian, but aligns with Anna's choice to give written feedback in English (Excerpt 10.3).

Excerpt 10.3 *Focus group*

Speaker	Original (English)
Assel	Is it for oral or for written language?
Anna	It is for written.
Assel	Because I was talking about oral. In writing, yes, probably English.
Facilitator	Assel, why?
Assel	Because it is easier. If I am writing I am writing specific, very short sentences like where we consider, or maybe I got used to get feedback from professors in English and I can do the same. But in oral speech it is totally different.

Assel's explanation is that she is now 'used to' giving and receiving feedback in English because English is the language her professors use for this purpose. This explanation might also account for why Anna feels that giving written feedback in Russian 'doesn't sound natural'.

In contrast to Anna, who avoided the use of multiple languages if it did not feel natural or useful, other students' responses suggested that they engage in translanguaging practices without thinking of them as a formal or conscious meaning-making strategy. In Excerpt 10.4, an alumna of the inclusive education programme, Sara, reflected on this natural practice for academic skills development.

Excerpt 10.4 *Interview with Sara*

Speaker	Original (English)
Sara	It is like changing the language so quickly that you even don't think about it … even on the paper when we were writing ideas, probably again both here is an English word, here is a Russian word and just not paying attention to it. But then when we put it all together into a real report for the final draft of course it was all in English.

In this case, Sara (and her writing partner) used both English and Russian seamlessly and instinctively to formulate ideas before finalising a paper in the sole target language of the task, English.

To sum up, students and alumni have engaged in translanguaging practices or encountered translanguaging pedagogies in the course of their studies at NUGSE. However, they do not rely on translanguaging for meaning-making or for producing academic language. It will be shown in the next section that these same students and alumni value the academic and language skills learned in English for communicating in Kazakh and/or Russian for different purposes in workplace settings.

Transfer of Academic Skills as (Un)successful Translanguaging Practice

Although all interviewed alumni highly valued the academic skills that they had acquired in English while studying at NUGSE and expressed willingness to apply them in their workplaces, they reported varying degrees of success in doing so. Some alumni reported on their ability to successfully apply these skills when doing their job tasks either by (1) reusing and directly applying prior knowledge or (2) reshaping/transforming such prior knowledge to fit new contexts and situations. However, others faced challenges in their efforts to transfer skills, including not being able to utilise these skills either because of the specifics of the work they did or because those skills were not demanded or accepted by the employers.

Reusing and directly applying prior knowledge and skills to new contexts

Those respondents who reported that they directly used English knowledge or skills when fulfilling tasks in Kazakh or Russian talked about English as a more 'concise language, being to the point' in comparison with Kazakh or Russian. At the same time, some of them emphasised not the importance of the English language per se, but the skills that they have learned in English. 'I think here is not the language itself, but the skills that I transfer from English to Kazakh, Russian', was the way one alumna, Masha, expressed it. As an example, she pointed out the application of the writing style, specifically in structuring the writing, outlining the main idea and being clear, all of which is considered 'very important and highly used' at work. Interestingly, this alumna used the word 'transfer' when describing the phenomenon of applying her knowledge of English into Russian and Kazakh. There were similar cases of using the English word 'transfer' in the survey data by two alumni: (1) 'I just could transfer my knowledge from [NUGSE] in daily life, where I mostly use Russian'; and (2) 'We had no courses related to academic Russian skills. However, I think that I transferred some skills from academic English.' These uses of the term 'transfer' suggest these alumni are aware of the concept of transfer, and consciously apply their knowledge and skills in new contexts.

The direct application of skills was reported not only in structuring written articles and reports, but also in the way alumni did presentations in other languages. As Masha noted: 'English language presentation skills helped me to structure the presentation, I think it is the most important when you know how to say, how to begin, how to develop and actually this system I use in Kazakh and Russian languages.' A similar application was echoed in the answer of another alumna, Fariza: 'I can make it [presentation] in any language as I have learnt in English language.' Fariza explains further that for presentations and for writing articles, she uses the same skills and 'style' she has learned in English for communicating in Kazakh or Russian.

It is important to note the perceived impact of transferring English language structures on transformations in thinking and writing in Kazakh or Russian. Excerpt 10.5 demonstrates how one alumna, Yana, expressed this impact.

Excerpt 10.5 *Interview with Yana*

Overall, alumni like what they produce as a result of the application of

Speaker	Original (English)
Yana	I started to apply this strategy to have all very structured on Russian and on Kazakh as well. Now I am trying to write in Kazakh and that's why I try to, first in the intro I try to write like a mindmap and then to dedicate every paragraph to a particular point that I mentioned in the intro. And then I see that my reports and my writing became different in Russian and Kazakh after I studied here.

their skills to new contexts. Sara, for example, spoke with pride about her choice of report writing style: 'it is difficult for me and probably for those who read my reports, because it might seem it harshly written sometimes: too short, too to the point, without any dressing it up, short recording, but I like it. I like it, it is easier for me.' Surprisingly, this choice indicates a privileging of preferred structures learned in English over the forms their Kazakh or Russian language audience might prefer, although alumni do accommodate to their audiences' preferences as regards language choice. The data above speak in favour of the abilities of alumni and the opportunities they have at their workplaces to strategically transfer the English language and academic skills to Kazakh and Russian language contexts.

Reshaping/transforming prior knowledge to fit new contexts

While the alumni in the previous section offered explanations of their successful direct transfer and use of their English language skills among different languages and contexts, other alumni reported experiences when they had to reshape or reform their prior knowledge to fit new contexts and situations. The need for such transfer was caused either by their employers' requirements or their own understanding of such needs as they noticed differences between languages. There were a number of cases when alumni were somehow forced by their employers to adapt their skills and reshape them by developing new skills in writing in Russian or Kazakh. Alima describes in Excerpt 10.6 her experience of writing a research proposal in Russian, although she felt she only had the necessary skills in English.

Excerpt 10.6 *Interview with Alima*

Speaker	Original (English)
Alima	We wrote proposal in English and then we suddenly decided to have everything in Russian and I said I can't do this in Russian, but I had to, so they forced me to do everything in Russian, because there were some people from Tajikistan, who didn't speak English.

Alima does not identify any specific strategies she used to complete the proposal in Russian, but she does reflect that 'we have to develop those skills' to write in Russian as well as in English.

Some of the interviewees reported on differences between what they learned from academic writing in English and the way they are required to write academically in Kazakh or Russian. Most of the transformations in writing that they mentioned were connected either with the style of writing or with formatting. For example, one alumna, Gulnara, said: 'it [writing] is difficult, because in English we cannot say, or write as "we", but in Kazakh and Russian it is important to say "we"'. Gulnara added that she was taught in English to write clearly and concisely and to avoid the so-called 'throat-clearing phrases', i.e. unnecessary word-wasting expressions in writing that add little or no substance to the sentence. She notices the use of these forms in Russian and Kazakh and thus has to take these differences into account when reading or writing in these languages.

It is worth mentioning that some of the interviewed alumni also started to expect clarity in verbal and written communication and academic integrity from other people. Although they do not try to make other people speak in the way they speak now, there is occasional evidence that alumni try to share their knowledge either with their colleagues or even in a wider societal context outside their workplace. A vivid example of this would be the case when one alumna, having observed plagiarism in articles on the internet written in Kazakh and Russian, wrote feedback to one of the authors. Although she did not get a response, the act of writing and pointing out plagiarism deserves appreciation and can serve as an example of adaptive transfer. That is, the student is bringing practices of academic integrity from NUGSE, where it is highly valued, to Kazakhstani contexts where it is not yet recognised and practised. In this instance, adaptive transfer can be redefined to include attempts to change the environment around oneself, i.e. to adapt the environment to one's own experience, along with adapting or transforming one's own practice.

Challenges with utilising English language academic skills

In a number of cases, alumni reported that they were able neither to directly transfer nor to adapt and transform their skills. While trying to apply English language skills to completing a task in Russian or in Kazakh in their workplaces, they faced resistance, failure and demotivation. Their challenges are mostly connected with: (1) lack or absence of knowledge and skills in writing in Kazakh and/or Russian; (2) differences in style of writing and communication across three languages; and (3) inability to utilise their skills because of the specifics of the work they did or because those skills were not demanded or accepted by the employers.

Many alumni found it difficult to produce different types of texts in Russian such as emails, reports, research papers or articles for publication. They saw the major reasons for this as an absence of experience and training in writing and doing research in the language, unawareness of terminology and unfamiliarity with structure. Excerpt 10.7 illustrates how Sara describes her lack of experience and knowledge of forms of writing in Russian.

Excerpt 10.7 *Interview with Sara*

Speaker	Original (English)
Sara	For me it is difficult to write in Russian because [of] the structure, the format, everything and I never specially learned how to write some formal letters and everything in Russian ... but I tend to translate [from English] into Russian. I understand it should be different but I cannot get what, and it takes me so much time about it and focus in Russian. ... I have to use the format and style that [employers] require.

Sara acknowledges that there is a difference in expectations in writing in Russian, and therefore she should reshape or transform her writing in some way. In the end, however, she is only able to translate from English into Russian. While translation is identifiable as a translanguaging practice (Jones, 2017), for Sara the direct transfer of English skills to Russian writing does not constitute translanguaging as a resource but rather a 'recourse, i.e. a last resort' (Tastanbek, 2019: 10). Another alumna, Moldir, frames her challenges not in terms of language forms but in the broader practices: 'I have the idea, okay, what if I publish in Russian, and I don't have confidence, I don't have skills to do this ... I think that's another culture, another system of evaluation of those.'

A comparison of English academic skills transfer to other languages revealed that alumni are more prepared to transfer to Kazakh than to Russian. While some alumni recognised that they cannot write in Kazakh in spite of their high Kazakh language proficiency in general, still those who are proficient seem to be more successful in doing it. Zukhra obtained a job that required research skills such as writing consent forms in three languages, and she praised the academic Kazakh course at the university for preparing her to do such tasks in Kazakh: 'Academic course of Kazakh was very helpful, because we knew specific words that to use in this kind of consent forms, I mean academic language.' These differences in application between the Russian and Kazakh languages may be explained by the fact that students took academic Kazakh language courses at GSE, while there was no similar Russian language course.

Another challenge that alumni reported is an inability to utilise their academic skills, either because they are not required in their workplaces or because their attempts to use new styles of writing, new styles of thinking and new styles of presenting are not accepted by their employers. Such situations turn some of them into passive followers of the employers' demands which contradicts their willingness to bring some positive changes into their workplaces. Zukhra describes her employer's rejection of language forms learned in English and translated into Russian for the Ministry of Education of the Republic of Kazakhstan (Excerpt 10.8).

Excerpt 10.8 *Interview with Zukhra in English and Russian*

Speaker	Original (English, **Russian**)	English translation
Zukhra	You know we had very different challenges when writing these reports in Russian language … we learned to be cautious in our writing, to use more hedging language 'it might possibly affect that' or something like that, we wrote all the report using this language, I mean where it is needed. However, it was not accepted at all—	
Sulushash	by employer	
Zukhra	by employer.	
Sulushash	Why?	
Zukhra	They say, 'What is that? **Это возможно повлияет на вот это. Это повлияет на вот это**', and that's all. They don't want to see 'it might possibly affect', they want to see 'it WILL affect', so it is stronger, they say 'we need strong arguments'.	They say, 'What is that? **This might possibly affect that. This will affect that**', and that's all. They don't want to see 'it might possibly affect', they want to see 'it WILL affect', so it is stronger, they say 'we need strong arguments'.

Zukhra's employer rejects her transfer of the English practice of hedging into Russian. He questions the sentence written with the phrase 'в о з м о ж н о   п о в л и я е т' (might possibly affect), and tells her to change this phrase into 'п о в л и я е т' (will affect) to make the statement stronger. Zukhra reported a similar negative response to her style of making presentations. Other respondents find it challenging to bring some changes into their workplaces, as such attempts lie beyond what 'they [Ministerial people and their employers are] used to' and what 'they want to see'. As Excerpt 10.9 shows, Moldir suggested that the problem is not one of language forms, but of Ministry employees' negative ideologies about graduates from Nazarbayev University and English-medium education in general.

Excerpt 10.9 *Interview with Moldir*

Speaker	Original (English)
Moldir	People of Ministry say: 'Here you come with the English education to us and try to teach us something' … They think that English language of instruction teaches something different from their … from local education.

Some alumni reported feelings of dissatisfaction and even depression due to an inability to utilise English language skills in their workplaces. They highly value the knowledge and skills that they have acquired, and are willing to apply them when fulfilling their job tasks. However, if they are deprived of opportunities to use them, they are demotivated and concerned about losing these skills. Nazgul expressed her concern in this way: 'I teach basic English. I don't really use all those skills, I actually am thinking that I am losing them at the moment and I am getting depressed because of thinking of it.'

When reporting different experiences with the transfer of their English academic skills, alumni speak, on the one hand, in favour of their readiness and potential to apply them strategically and successfully to new contexts and new languages (Kazakh and Russian) and even use them transformatively by adapting and reshaping these skills to fit the demands of new situations and tasks. On the other hand, they reveal the presence of different cultural norms best described as an unwillingness or resistance by employers to accept new styles of thinking and writing. This, along with graduates' inexperience in writing and doing research in languages other than English, causes challenges with adaptive transfer.

Discussion and Conclusion

The data presented in this chapter indicate that students in this Kazakhstani EMI institution perceive only limited utility of translanguaging in the classrooms. This is likely due to the fact that students come with strong proficiency levels in English for learning in English, and do not need or expect teachers or peers to use Russian, Kazakh or other languages to contribute to meaning-making. When students do engage in translanguaging in the school setting, it is part of their natural communicative repertoire.

Outside the classroom, the perspective changes dramatically. As alumni, participants describe an active ability to translanguage in work contexts. They engage in strategies such as communicating with different languages according to the preferences of their audience, writing in Russian and Kazakh using English genre structures, borrowing English terms directly into Kazakh and Russian texts and even translating directly from English to Kazakh or Russian. At the same time, alumni are strategic in their employment of translanguaging. They notice differences in language styles and although they find it challenging to meet them, they make moves to adapt their prior knowledge to meet the new requirements of their employers. By doing so they reveal their ability not only to reuse but also to 'reshape practices that they have learned' (DePalma & Ringer, 2011: 140). In other words, alumni of this school do not only appear to 'copy, borrow, imitate, [and] import' various aspects from one community to another (Wenger, 1998: 129), but they can be viewed as agents who can shuttle and 'shuffle' (Deumert, 2018) among languages, thereby '[shaping] the texts and the contexts that they share with readers as they move from one writing situation to the next' (DePalma & Ringer, 2011: 144). These findings also seem to reflect Wenger's (1998) concept of brokering, during which individuals translate and coordinate elements from one community of practice into another. Good brokers, like alumni who attempt to transfer academic learning to the workplace, 'open new possibilities for meaning' (DePalma & Ringer, 2011: 109) when they must 'adapt and reinterpret ways of behaving' (DePalma & Ringer, 2011: 129) in new environments.

The challenges presented in this chapter of applying English language knowledge and academic skills into Russian or Kazakh suggest that employers are reluctant to accept new styles of thinking, writing and presenting information. This means that adaptive transfer may be less *dynamic* than DePalma and Ringer suggest, when alumni find themselves in environments that may resist efforts to be *transformative*, because not all contexts are so receptive to communicative tools wielded by learners exercising agency. This further suggests that in addition to the six criteria of adaptive transfer that DePalma and Ringer suggest, we might add a seventh criterion: *daunting*. Carving paths to adaptive transfer can be frustrating and require great effort.

Moreover, while students at times demonstrate awareness of transfer strategies which help them cope with challenges, the challenges themselves suggest a necessity to increase the linguistic repertoire of Kazakhstani students in EMI programmes by equipping them with academic knowledge and skills in all three languages. This includes encouraging EMI professors and institutions to acknowledge the utility of multiple languages in teaching and learning and offering professors pedagogical approaches that encourage student output in three languages. Such approaches would provide students with more opportunities for successful application of their knowledge and develop them into 'writers who are capable of shaping the knowledge to suit their own needs' (De Palma & Ringer, 2011: 138).

Acknowledgments

The data presented in this chapter were collected for the research study, 'Building Academic Genre Knowledge in Multilingual Contexts: The Case of a Kazakhstani University', conducted by the Nazarbayev University Graduate School of Education Academic Writing Research Group. The authors thank group members Jason Sparks and Dilrabo Jonbekova for their contributions to this study.

11 Translanguaging for Learning in EMI Classrooms in South Africa: An Overview of Selected Research

Margie Probyn

English-Medium Instruction in the South African Context

As a whole, this volume sets out to provide global perspectives on translanguaging in English-medium instruction (EMI) classrooms. This raises questions as to what translanguaging might mean in EMI classrooms in a post-colonial country such as South Africa: how it might be experienced and in what ways these experiences and perceptions might be found to be in common with or differ from those in other contexts. As suggested by Kerfoot and Hyltenstam (2017: 2), '… dialogue across contexts opens up opportunities for reconstituting and expanding dominant theory so that it may become more productive in analysing both northern and southern social realities'. They further state that conditions and experiences with multilingualism and education in South Africa and other post-colonial countries often prefigure the challenges that the Global North has been facing more recently (see also Heugh, 2014).

The practice of EMI, defined as 'The use of the English language to teach academic subjects in countries or jurisdictions where the first language (L1) of the majority of the population is not English' (Dearden, 2014: 1), applies to education in South Africa. English is the home language of less than 10% of the population and yet the majority of children learn through the medium of English from the fourth grade or earlier. However, this is not an example of the recent 'growing global phenomenon' of EMI (Dearden, 2014: 2), but is in fact one of very many examples of post-colonial education systems where a colonial language has long been entrenched as the medium of instruction. Although there is frequent reference to English as the language of learning and teaching (LoLT) in South African schools, the term EMI is seldom if ever applied and this perhaps reflects the normative, unmarked position of English in education.

This chapter describes the linguistic ecologies of schools across the shifting South African linguistic landscape which still bears the imprint of colonial and apartheid-era ideologies, fragmentation and inequalities. South African research on language and learning in EMI contexts that prefigures current interest in translanguaging research is briefly outlined and discussed. This is then followed by an overview of a selection of more recent research studies in multilingual classrooms that adopt translanguaging lenses and challenge prevailing monolingual ideologies and practices. Finally, implications for teacher development are considered.

Linguistic Ecologies of South African Classrooms

In South Africa and many other post-colonial countries, centuries of colonial domination, politically and linguistically, have entrenched former colonial languages in hierarchical relations of power with respect to indigenous languages: local languages operate horizontally for everyday social and economic communication while former colonial languages operate vertically as languages of access to prestige, power and academia (Heugh, 2014). Since the advent of democracy in South Africa, attempts have been made to disrupt this linguistic hierarchy and elevate the status and use of indigenous African languages through the constitutional recognition of 11 official languages: the two former colonial languages, English and Afrikaans, and nine African languages, namely Sepedi, Sesotho, Setswana, siSwati, Tshivenda, Xitsonga, isiNdebele, isiXhosa and isiZulu (Republic of South Africa, 1996). Despite these efforts, the twin forces of globalisation and coloniality have contributed to establishing English as the dominant language in the political economy and so too in education.

In line with the Constitution, the Language-in-Education Policy (Department of Education RSA, 1997) aimed to promote multilingualism as a means to overcome the racial and linguistic discrimination and inequalities that were the cornerstones of the former apartheid political system. In terms of the policy, learners are required to learn two official languages as subjects, one of which should be the LoLT, which is English for the majority of learners for reasons to be discussed. A more recent policy directive in the initial stages of implementation is that all learners should also study at least one African language as a subject (Department of Basic Education, RSA, 2013). The Language-in-Education Policy is less clear on the LoLT, simply stating that schools should pursue policies that adopt an 'additive approach to bilingualism' (Department of Education, RSA, 1997: 2). The lack of clear political direction on the question of

LoLT has been strongly criticised by educationists (Heugh, 2002; McKinney, 2017; Plüddemann, 2015) for allowing free rein to entrenched linguistic ideologies and perpetuating educational inequalities.

Under apartheid, schools were segregated according to race and language, with gross inequalities between expenditure on minority 'white' education and education for the majority of 'black' learners, resulting in deep inequalities in educational opportunities. These inequalities have proved difficult to reverse in the democratic era, despite a range of policies aimed at achieving access, equity and redress (Department of Education, RSA, 1996). This is reflected in bimodal patterns of academic achievement, with middle-class learners in formerly 'white', 'coloured' and Indian schools achieving at levels comparable to international norms, while the majority of learners in low-income township and rural schools fail to achieve at even the lowest levels on international scales (Fleisch, 2008). The way the Language-in-Education Policy has played out across the range of classroom contexts and linguistic ecologies has contributed to ongoing inequalities and the poor academic achievement of low-income learners in historically disadvantaged schools.

In theory, school governing bodies (comprised of parents and teachers) may choose any official language as the LoLT, so as to adapt to local linguistic contexts and needs, but in practice that choice is tightly circumscribed by a number of factors, primarily the fact of globalisation and the international dominance of English, and the powerful monolingual ideologies associated with coloniality in South Africa that entrench English LoLT as the norm. Coupled with the very real need to gain proficiency in English for economic access and upward mobility is the common-sense perception that this is best achieved through 'time-on-task' in EMI classrooms. Research that points to the importance of learners' home language/s in learning, for epistemic access, identity affirmation and motivation to engage with learning (Cummins, 2008b; García, 2009a; Macdonald, 1990), has not been widely disseminated and therefore is not appreciated by most parents and teachers. The result is that the majority of schools have opted for an early transition to English LoLT, by the beginning of Grade 4 or even earlier, irrespective of whether the learners have the necessary proficiency in English to cope with EMI across the curriculum. In addition, publishing companies are reluctant to commit to producing teaching materials in indigenous languages in an uncertain market, which further limits practical options for schools.

The Language-in-Education Policy (Department of Education, RSA, 1997) has been enacted differently across the range of linguistic ecologies in South African classrooms. Under apartheid, 'white', so-called 'coloured' and Indian schools were designated English- or Afrikaans-medium and learners had to attend schools that aligned with their race and home language; teachers at these schools also had to conform to designated racial and linguistic classifications. Post-apartheid, these schools have become desegregated and multilingual but they have remained relatively unchanged in terms of language policies and teacher profiles. In English-medium schools, assimilationist policies and what McKinney (2017) has described as 'Anglonormative' attitudes frequently prevail. Few teachers are able to speak African languages, linguistic diversity is cast as a problem and classroom practices frequently close down participation and engagement for learners who are less proficient in English (Makoe & McKinney, 2014). Many former Afrikaans-medium schools have introduced English-medium classes in response to the demand from parents who recognise the economic power of English (Probyn *et al.*, 2002; see also Luckett & Hurst-Harosh, this volume) and to accommodate growing numbers of African language speakers who may have had little prior exposure to Afrikaans, and in any event object to learning Afrikaans for political reasons as it represents apartheid-era oppression. In these schools too, the racial and linguistic profiles of teachers have changed little and while most are proficient speakers of Afrikaans and English, few are able to communicate with African language speakers in their home languages (Plüddemann *et al.*, 2004).

The majority (80%) of learners in South Africa are African language speakers who attend historically disadvantaged township and rural schools (Taylor & Schindler, 2016: 12). Post-apartheid, there has been some movement of African learners to historically advantaged schools, but almost no movement in the reverse direction. As a result, township and rural schools have remained racially and linguistically segregated and learners have little exposure to spoken English outside the classroom.

African languages have strong regional bases and in many parts of the country a particular African language is dominant in the community and school (Heugh, 2002). The exception is the populous and economically dominant province of Gauteng, where historically the development of gold mining from 1886 drew labour from around the country. This resulted in the establishment of multilingual communities which have diversified further in recent years with the influx of refugees and economic migrants from the rest of Africa. The resulting linguistic diversity is reflected in schools where English is frequently the pragmatic choice as LoLT.

Many African teachers are themselves proficient multilinguals and are therefore better positioned than teachers in former English- and Afrikaans-medium schools to engage with learners' home languages. However, this does not have official sanction and so teachers are caught between the perceived obligation to strictly adhere to English and the need to communicate lesson content to learners in the language they can most easily understand. As a result, many teachers in EMI classrooms code-switch to the learners' home language/s for a range of purposes but do so covertly and with conflicted feelings (Probyn, 2009; Setati *et al.*, 2002b). Teacher training has hitherto done little to help teachers to resolve this conflict.

Although there is longstanding research and advocacy for classroom policies and practices that acknowledge and engage with learners' home languages as valuable resources beyond the first years of schooling (Adendorff, 1996; Heugh, 1995; Macdonald, 1990; Setati *et al.*, 2002b), such ideas have yet to gain traction with officialdom. This is a common linguistic scenario in many classrooms in post-colonial countries and has been extensively researched and documented (see, for example, Ferguson, 2003; Lin, 1996; Martin, 1996; Rubagumya, 1994). It is a very different kind of context from that of the Global North, although South and North are linked through the long history of European colonialism that shapes much of Southern linguistic contexts, and which is in turn the subject of increasing critique and research in terms of language policies and classroom practices (see, for example, Heugh, 2014; McKinney, 2017; Probyn, 2005).

In sum, the majority of English and many Afrikaans home language speakers are taught through the medium of their home language, with the attendant advantages. The majority of African language speakers, however, learn through the medium of English despite having limited exposure to English outside the classroom, limited learning resources and consequently poor English proficiency. Thus, the medium of instruction compounds historic socio-economic and political disadvantage in township and rural schools to perpetuate apartheid-era patterns of inequality and social injustice. In this linguistic ecology, EMI for the majority of learners is controversial and politically charged.

Translanguaging Research in South African EMI Classrooms

The relatively recent, widespread and rapid uptake of the term translanguaging to describe language alternation practices in multilingual classrooms has meant that the term has acquired multiple meanings in different contexts, and as such is a concept under development (Lewis *et al.*, 2012b). At times what is identified as translanguaging in classroom research seems little different from what might previously have been described as code-switching. It is necessary therefore to clarify how the terms are distinguished in this chapter.

As is well known, the term *translanguaging* was originally coined to describe a particular bilingual pedagogy in Wales where input and output were varied between English and Welsh, in order to develop bilingual proficiency as well as for the perceived cognitive benefits (Williams, 1996, in Lewis *et al.*, 2012b). The term has been revived and expanded to a range of contexts beyond the classroom, but for the purposes of this chapter the focus is on translanguaging as pedagogy which is usefully defined by Baker (2011: 288) as 'the process of making meaning, shaping experiences, understandings and knowledge through two languages. Both languages are used in an integrated and coherent way to organize and mediate mental processes in learning'. As Lewis *et al.* (2012a) have noted, the emergence of the term 'translanguaging' marks an ideological shift in thinking about bilinguals and bilingualism, from a monoglossic view of bilingualism as the sum of two separate languages or 'two solitudes' (Cummins, 2008b: 65) to a heteroglossic orientation to and positive view of multilingualism and the flexible, systematic use of classroom language resources to mediate learning. Cummins (2008b) has long proposed the interdependence of languages and the transfer of literacy and cognitive proficiency across languages through explicitly 'teaching for transfer' as well as for connecting to learners' lives and affirming identities.

Classroom code-switching, on the other hand, is frequently viewed by participants as a deficit practice, a temporary deviation from a monolingual ideal, in contexts where 'monolingual ideologies hover over the classroom' (Li Wei & Martin, 2009: 119). García and Flores (2012) note with reference to translanguaging:

> These dynamic plurilingual pedagogies should not be confused with the random code-switching that is sometimes prevalent in classrooms … where language use is accidental and haphazard … plurilingual heteroglossic pedagogies are done with intent and are carefully planned. (García & Flores, 2012: 238–239)

Therefore, the differences between code-switching and translanguaging are both ideological and pedagogical: code-switching stems from a monolingual ideology, a belief that languages should be kept separate and that use of the learners' home language/s should only be a strategy of last resort when communications have clearly broken down. Code-switching is thus reactive rather than proactive and is frequently practised covertly in contexts where it has limited or no approval by educational authorities (Ferguson, 2003). Translanguaging, on the other hand, stems from a heteroglossic ideology, the view that within multilingual classrooms languages comprise a common linguistic resource to draw on flexibly, strategically and deliberately to maximise learning opportunities. It is in these senses that the terms are distinguished in this paper.

Earlier Research in EMI Classrooms in South Africa

In South Africa, challenges relating to language and learning, including the media of instruction and teachers' and learners' languaging practices, are matters of longstanding concern for educationists and researchers. Policy choices have been determined as much by politics as by pedagogical principles. Language-in-education was used to assert political dominance by Dutch and later by British colonial rulers, and to resist oppression by both Afrikaner nationalists and the African majority (for full descriptions of the historical background, see Hartshorne, 1992; Heugh, 2002).

Research into classroom language practices in English-medium classrooms where the learners were speakers of indigenous languages arose out of concerns about the negative effects of EMI on teaching and learning (Macdonald, 1990; Probyn, 2005; Setati *et al.*, 2002b). Much of this research focused on the widespread occurrence of classroom code-switching which parallels research in other post-colonial settings (Ferguson, 2003; Lin, 1996; Martin, 1996; Rubagumya, 1994). While code-switching practices have generally been welcomed by researchers as positive strategies for mediating learning in EMI classrooms (Ferguson, 2003), there have been mixed messages from South African education authorities. These mixed messages include some limited acceptance, such as reference in curriculum documents to learners 'code-switching when necessary' when taking part in a conversation or discussion (Department of Basic Education, RSA, 2011: 54), whereas in another policy document it is stated that teachers should 'steer clear of informal code-switching' (Western Cape Government: Education, n.d.: 22).

Another strand of research into language and learning references dual-medium programmes in the 1940s for white English- and Afrikaans-speaking learners who learned through the medium of both languages. Such dual-medium English-Afrikaans programmes fell out of favour with the apartheid government in favour of linguistic and racial segregation, except in some small towns where there were not enough white learners to sustain separate schools. Research at the time provided some of the earliest evidence of the positive cognitive and social effects of such programmes (Malherbe, 1973, in Heugh, 1995). This research evidence has been used to argue for dual-medium or mother tongue based bilingual education (MTBBE) for all learners, including flexible languaging practices in the classroom (Heugh, 1995) to overcome the challenges and inequalities of the sudden switch to English LoLT for the majority of learners.

The above examples serve to illustrate that in South Africa there has been a longstanding concern and involvement in multilingualism in education which prefigures similar concerns in the Global North. In particular, early initiatives described as dual-medium instruction have explored teaching bilingually in ways that work flexibly with languages in the classroom to achieve epistemic access and bilingual proficiency, ways that bear a close resemblance to the original conception of translanguaging as a pedagogical approach in Wales (Lewis *et al.*, 2012b). The concept of translanguaging, embedded in heteroglossic ideologies, appears to offer ways of leveraging the language resources in the classroom to support learning and break out of the current linguistic impasse in EMI classrooms.

Along with the recent interest in translanguaging in multilingual classrooms in the Global North (Creese & Blackledge, 2010; García, 2009a; Li Wei, 2018), there has been a corresponding interest and research in translanguaging in South African classrooms. Makalela (2015) makes the important point that the notion of translanguaging is very much in line with longstanding pre-colonial societal multilingualism and fluid heteroglossic practices in Africa. This he terms 'linguistic ubuntu', drawing on the humanistic African term expressing the interdependence of persons, 'a person is only a person through other people', and applying it to heteroglossic languaging practices (see also Reilly, this volume).

What follows is an overview of a selection of translanguaging research from South Africa, some of which documents unplanned or spontaneous translanguaging in classrooms and some of which documents interventions that have adopted planned translanguaging pedagogies which aim to engage with learners' full linguistic repertoires.

Studies of Spontaneous Translanguaging Practices in EMI Classrooms

South African research on spontaneous translanguaging in multilingual classrooms has built on a well-established body of research on code-switching in African language classrooms which, as mentioned, stemmed from concerns about the challenges of teaching through the medium of English and the negative effects on learning (Adendorff, 1996; Macdonald, 1990; Probyn, 2005; Setati *et al.*, 2002b). In line with research interest in translanguaging in the Global North, and the validation of such practices in EMI contexts, researchers in South Africa have adopted translanguaging lenses in their description of classroom languaging practices. It seems important, though, not simply to rename longstanding code-switching practices but to distinguish between those languaging practices reflecting overall monoglossic orientations to teaching and learning, and those that genuinely adopt more flexible heteroglossic engagement with the full linguistic repertoires that learners bring to the classroom. This marks a shift in the debates about which language/s should function as media of instruction, to how best to activate and engage with learners' full linguistic repertoires in the interests of learning. However, given the constraining force of monoglossic orientations to language and languaging in most EMI classrooms, there are as yet relatively few examples of spontaneous translanguaging practices that can be distinguished from more limited code-switching. Nevertheless, there are some examples described in research studies in South African classrooms and these offer insights as to how translanguaging pedagogies might be realised in classrooms across different linguistic contexts. The key points from these studies are summarised below in order to identify the different contexts, practices and lessons for translanguaging pedagogies.

Makoe and McKinney's (2009) research was conducted in a multilingual urban school in Gauteng province. The school was formerly reserved for white English-speaking learners, but at the time of the research the learner profile had changed to one where the majority of learners were black, from poor and working-class homes and multilingual but not necessarily proficient in English, the LoLT. The research was conducted in a Grade 1 class of 46 learners with six different home languages represented. The research paper focused on one particular learner, Tumi, who assumed the role of teacher's helper and, with the tolerance and support of her teacher, deployed her proficiency in her home language Setswana, as well as in English and Sepedi to support the meaning-making of other less English-proficient learners in the class.

Tumi's languaging is described by Makoe and McKinney (2009) as 'hybrid discursive practices' as she transgressed boundaries between languages and registers and appropriated different identity positions at different points in the lesson. For example, during a word-building literacy exercise, when the teacher asked the class what the meaning of the word 'dog' was, Tumi gave the Sepedi translation of the word. When her friend Lerato was unable to answer the teacher when she repeated the question, Tumi jumped to her feet and, assuming the role of mediator, addressed the class in Sepedi (Lerato's home language): 'Ba go botsisa gore mpšha ke eng. A kere maabane ko holong re bone mpšha' ('The teacher is asking you what a dog is. Do you remember that we saw a dog yesterday at the hall?') (Makoe & McKinney, 2009: 86). The teacher thanked Tumi and continued seamlessly with the lesson. At further points in the lesson, Tumi mediated the teacher's instructions in Sepedi for the benefit of her friend.

It appeared that the teacher had created an enabling heteroglossic environment earlier in the lesson by asking learners to answer a question in isiZulu and then comparing the isiZulu word to the same word in Setswana. Although this research preceded the widespread use of the term 'translanguaging', it appears in fact that Tumi's 'hybrid discursive practices' fit well with current understandings of translanguaging and provide an indication of how learners' multilingual languaging skills might be validated and harnessed to extend opportunities to learn for the whole class, rather than being ignored or at worst stigmatised as often happens in EMI classrooms (see McKinney et al., 2015).

Research by Msimanga and Lelliott (2014) investigated Grade 10 learners' developing conceptual understanding of chemistry in small-group activities in a multilingual EMI science class. The school was located in a low-income linguistically diverse township community where the main home languages of the learners included isiZulu, Sesotho, Xitsonga and Tshivenda. The research found that the teacher and learners tended to stick to English in whole-class talk but the teacher allowed learners to use their home languages when working in small groups, albeit with some reservations on her part. This kind of informal arrangement is fairly typical in EMI classrooms in South Africa (Setati et al., 2002b). The researchers found that the learners mainly used isiZulu, with some Sesotho and English in exploratory talk (Barnes, 1992), as they teased out scientific ideas and meanings in the course of a problem-solving activity on the reactions of acids. Learners moved flexibly across language boundaries, and once their understandings were established in their home languages they were able to articulate and present their findings to the class in English.

The researchers found that in the activity the learners remained on task and were able to reason, make assertions and challenge one another's ideas in ways that they might not have been able to do if restricted to communicating only in English. Although this research does not explicitly refer to translanguaging, it does demonstrate how epistemic access was supported by the softening of boundaries between languages while the learners were working on meaning in small-group work and how learners were able to transfer and present their understandings in English.

A further example of research into spontaneous classroom languaging practices by Probyn (2015) examined the intersection of language and the opportunity to learn science in eight Grade 8 EMI classrooms. The schools were located in low-income rural and township schools in the Eastern Cape province where isiXhosa is the home language of the majority of teachers and learners and learners had little access to English outside the classroom. Five consecutive lessons for each teacher were recorded and analysed to track the construction of science content knowledge over the lessons and the languaging practices that enabled or constrained the construction of science content knowledge.

The research found that in the context where there was little direction or training for teachers in how to cope with the tension between providing access to science content and access to English, there was a range of languaging practices. Two teachers maintained an English-only stance. Five teachers used more English than isiXhosa and tended to code-switch from English to isiXhosa when they realised that the learners did not understand the lesson content, but this comprised only 3–13% of classroom talk. By contrast, one teacher used more isiXhosa (53%) than English in his lessons and set out to deliberately establish conceptual understanding through exploratory talk in the learners' home language and then scaffold the transfer of that understanding to everyday English and then to scientific English. This deliberate and strategic leveraging of the learners' linguistic resources to support opportunities to learn both the science content and the language of wider communication, English, while validating learners' identities and culture, could be described as pedagogical translanguaging and offers a concrete example which could inform much-needed teacher development in similar contexts. However, it should be added that the translanguaging evident in this teacher's practice was a necessary but insufficient condition for the opportunity to learn science, as this was also dependent on the coherence of science content (National Research Council, 2005) in the lessons and the engagement of learners' participation in co-constructing science knowledge through dialogic discourse (Alexander, 2006; Gibbons, 2006).

The above examples of research on spontaneous translanguaging were based on classroom observations across different contexts: a multilingual urban Grade 1 classroom, a multilingual Grade 10 township classroom and a deep rural Grade 8 classroom in a community where isiXhosa was the dominant language. In the first two examples, it was learners who took the initiative in opening up meaning-making opportunities by flexibly using the linguistic resources available to them, with the tacit approval of their teachers. In the third example it was the teacher who deliberately leveraged the learners' home language to support epistemic access, language learning and links to their home knowledge, culture and identity. The question is then how these observed practices might inform the development of context-appropriate translanguaging pedagogies.

Studies of Planned Translanguaging Interventions in EMI Classrooms and Adjacent Spaces

Several research papers have documented innovative planned translanguaging interventions in South African classrooms. For example, Makalela (2015) investigated the effects of translanguaging pedagogies on the reading comprehension skills of Grade 6 learners in a rural school where the common home language was Sepedi. Over an eight-week period, teachers introduced flexible bilingual teaching strategies in English-Sepedi language classes including:

(1) bilingual vocabulary contrasts;
(2) reading the same story in both Sepedi and English with languages alternated for texts and comprehension questions;
(3) reading texts aloud in both languages to compare and contrast linguistic features; and
(4) writing texts bilingually.

Mean scores pre-test and post-test for reading comprehension showed gains for both languages but, interestingly, greater gains for English, the learners' weaker language.

Charamba and Zano (2019) conducted mixed-methods research to assess the impact of a 'translanguaging approach' on teaching a chemistry topic to Grade 10 learners in a rural school in the Free State Province where the dominant home language was Sesotho and the LoLT English. Learners were randomly assigned either to a control or an experimental group, with the control group being taught the topic of chemical change solely through the medium of English while the experimental group was taught through both Sesotho and English. The 'translanguaging informed intervention' included: group tasks written in both languages, i.e. learners engaging in group discussions and writing answers to tasks in their home language and then translating these answers into English; and the provision of learning materials in both languages. The effect of the intervention was assessed with a pre-test and post-test on the topic (both in English) and it was found that while there was no significant difference between the groups in the pre-test, in the post-test the mean score was 38% for the control group and 52% for the experimental group. The authors concluded that the difference in achievement could be attributed to the 'translanguaging informed intervention'. In addition, learners from the experimental group were interviewed to reflect on their experience.

Students claimed that they had found the content easier to understand and were excited to receive learning materials in their home language.

Makalela's (2015) and Charamba and Zano's (2019) research both report on translanguaging interventions in conventional EMI classrooms and make claims as to the positive effects thereof. There is further research reported below that describes translanguaging pedagogies in spaces adjacent to formal classrooms and explores what is possible in working across language boundaries, offering additional insights for mainstream EMI classrooms.

Guzula *et al.* (2016) have described the affordances for learning enabled by heteroglossic and multimodal orientations to learning in two 'established translanguaging spaces' (Guzula *et al.*, 2016: 211): an after-school literacy club for Grade 3–6 learners held in Khayelitsha, a Cape Town township; and a mathematics holiday camp for Grade 11 learners in a rural area in the Eastern Cape Province. In both cases the dominant home language of learners was isiXhosa and English the less familiar language. Students were encouraged to draw on both languages freely, '… disrupting and transgressing the normative view in formally prescribed South African education policy, curriculum and directives to teachers that endeavour to keep named "languages" separate' (Guzula *et al.*, 2016: 215).

In the 'Stars of Today Literacy Club#', translanguaging in both spoken and written forms was encouraged. For example, when discussing the elements of a story, learners were encouraged to offer responses in either isiXhosa or English and then translate the terms for one another. This two-way translation served to include all learners who were on different points on the bilingual continuum and involved negotiation of meaning across languages. In drawing on their full linguistic repertoires in discussions, learners were able to elaborate ideas with more nuanced meaning than they might have been able to do had the discussions been restricted to one language.

In the Grade 11 mathematics holiday camp, the home language of the learners was isiXhosa and they had limited English proficiency, whereas the home language of the mathematics teacher was English, with limited isiXhosa proficiency. In addition, a learning facilitator fluent in both isiXhosa and English was engaged to overcome the linguistic and cultural gap between the learners and the teacher, thus enabling a translanguaging space. As described in the paper, the teacher drew on English, isiXhosa and gesture to develop mathematics concepts, and the learning facilitator at times intervened in isiXhosa; learners were able to work on meaning in familiar registers in isiXhosa during small-group work and then transfer these understandings into academic mathematical English during whole-class talk. Analysis of a teaching episode showed how, by shuttling across languages, one of the learners was able to engage at length in exploratory talk while demonstrating how to solve a mathematical problem for the class on the chalkboard. In the words of the authors, the research 'has shown that translanguaging can be used as an intellectual, social and linguistic resource, enhancing multilingual and multimodal meaning-making ... Also disrupting the existing power and status gap that exists between the two languages, ultimately disrupting Anglonormativity' (Guzula *et al.*, 2016: 223).

McKinney and Tyler (2018) have described the translanguaging pedagogy introduced in an after-school science study group for Grade 9 learners in a Cape Town township school where the dominant home language was isiXhosa and the LoLT English. While learners were observed in class engaging in group discussions in their home language, as has been reported in several of the cited research studies, it emerged in a study group discussion that the learners did not value the exploratory scientific talk in their home language as highly as being able to present scientific statements in English. One of the authors who ran the study group set out to create an alternate space where 'translingual practices were normalized and resources from learners' full semiotic repertoires were welcomed as tools for learning' (McKinney & Tyler, 2018: 8).

An example provided was that of an activity where the learners were given a scientific definition of the term 'molecule', written in formal isiXhosa and asked to translate it into English, reversing the usual experience of receiving scientific definitions in English. Once this task was completed, learners were required to translate the original text again, this time into colloquial isiXhosa. As they worked collaboratively and compared and argued over their different versions of the definition, they drew on their full range of linguistic and semiotic resources and were extended linguistically and conceptually to arrive at precise scientific meanings. At the same time, the dominant Anglonormative ideology experienced in the classroom was overturned and the use of the learners' home language was validated for the high-status domain of science. This was also the case with Charamba and Zano's (2019) study, when learners were provided with bilingual learning materials. This seems an important aspect to pursue: to move beyond translanguaging in classroom talk only, to introducing bilingual texts for learning and assessment, particularly in contexts where learners share a common home language.

This brief overview of a selection of research studies into translanguaging in EMI contexts in South Africa covers a range of stages and linguistic contexts. All are rooted in a common concern for the linguistic and learning challenges faced by the majority of learners who are caught in the tension between the need for epistemic access and the need for upward mobility that English represents. These studies in translanguaging pedagogies offer some alternatives to bridge these tensions, disrupt dominant linguistic ideologies and open up opportunities for learning.

Conclusion and Future Directions

This overview of research into translanguaging in South African EMI classrooms takes into account the linguistic ecologies of classrooms which are very different to those in the Global North in at least two important respects: multilingualism and EMI are the norm in South Africa and so the challenges faced by learners in EMI classrooms are a majority concern central to teaching and learning and educational attainment. In addition, current concerns with increasing multilingualism in classrooms and the related research in the Global North have a long history in South Africa and other post-colonial southern countries.

The examples of research into both spontaneous and planned translanguaging in EMI classrooms that have been included in this overview provide some starting points for opening up discussions about alternative practices which engage with and expand learners' full linguistic repertoires, rather than shutting down what McKinney (2017: xv) has described as 'the most valuable resource a child brings to formal schooling'. However, Guzula *et al.* (2016: 213) draw attention to the 'disturbing lack of impact that this heteroglossic and multimodal view of meaning-making has had on language education, whether in official language-in-education policy, curricula or directives for teachers'. This is demonstrated in documents issued by the Department of Basic Education on an 'English across the curriculum strategy'. While the guidelines issued for teachers recognise that 'English, which is the language of learning and teaching (LoLT) in the majority of schools in our country, is a barrier for learning and thus of learner attainment' (Department of Basic Education, 2012: 2), there is no mention at all of the role of learners' home languages and how these might be mobilised for learning.

The research studies overviewed in this chapter have been based on isolated examples of practice (Makoe & McKinney, 2009; Msimanga & Lelliott, 2014; Probyn, 2015) or short-term experimental projects (Charamba & Zano, 2019; Makalela, 2015) and small-scale out-of-school initiatives (Guzula *et al.*, 2016; McKinney & Tyler, 2018). The next step would seem to be, on the one hand, dissemination and advocacy aimed at shifting entrenched language-in-education ideologies and, on the other hand, systemic interventions in pre-service teacher education. The latter would need to introduce student teachers to the theory and practice of translanguaging for learning in different linguistic contexts, as well as to track such student teachers into their classrooms as newly qualified teachers in order to support and reflect on their classroom practices and developing translanguaging pedagogies. It would also be necessary to assess what adaptations might be necessary in developing clearly articulated, planned and strategic heteroglossic translanguaging pedagogies which are flexible enough to adapt to particular linguistic contexts but share the common aims of affirming and leveraging learners' linguistic resources so as to open up opportunities to learn in EMI classrooms (see, for example, Crisfield *et al.*, this volume). This is central to the pursuit of the long-deferred goals of access, equity and social justice in education in South Africa.

This discussion raises the question as to whether translanguaging pedagogies that are underpinned by heteroglossic ideologies and orientations to multilingualism and languaging are in fact compatible with EMI, or whether they stand in contrast to the monoglossic underpinnings of EMI and as such constitute a parting of the ways, a multilingual turn into something quite different.

Epilogue

Ute Smit

Both English-medium instruction (EMI) and translanguaging (TL) have been 'hot topics' in applied linguistics for quite some time, both in terms of their relevance for students, teachers and educational institutions across the globe as well as when it comes to research undertakings. While EMI research has grown exponentially with the increasing internationalisation of (higher) education since the turn of the century (Dafouz & Smit, 2020; Macaro, 2018; Wilkinson, 2017), the notion of TL has rapidly gained ground in the same time period and is presently widely used when analysing multilingual practices within education (García & Lin, 2017; Lewis et al., 2012a; Mazak & Carroll, 2016). Fundamentally, both research areas address educational realities shaped by monolingual language policies and multilingual social actors; while EMI studies combine macro-, meso- and micro-level perspectives, TL investigations pursue a primarily micro-level interest in meaning-making practices and their implications for the particular educational setting.

In view of the widely acknowledged relevance of such practices for 'doing learning' and participating in education, it is highly welcome to have this edited volume which combines both research topics, thus offering in-depth analyses of various realisations of EMI from the shared perspective of TL. This two-pronged research focus is also remarkable because it means that the chapters of this volume reveal a degree of conceptual coherence seldom found in edited volumes. Although, clearly, each contribution stands on its own, their findings can be carefully pieced together, offering a collage of insights linked to TL in EMI settings. To put it more pointedly, the focus here is on 'translanguaging EMI': the verbal construction pays tribute to the original word form of the notion and recognises its process-stressing semantics, thus supporting its conceptualisation as centrally shaping educational practices and participation (Li Wei & Lin, 2019).

Before suggesting one such collage, I will first provide a brief sketch of the volume in terms of what is covered, how the central concepts are used, and what research interests are pursued.

Translanguaging English-Medium Instruction

This volume offers truly global perspectives: the 11 contributions throw light on educational settings in Southern Europe (Italy), Eurasia (Turkey), Central Asia (Kazakhstan), South Asia (Maldives), Southeast Asia (Cambodia), East Asia (Hong Kong, Japan), East Africa (Kenya) and Southern Africa (Malawi, twice South Africa). In comparison to existing EMI literature, it is noteworthy that Europe is treated rather marginally, placing the focus on Asian and African contexts and also including otherwise little-recorded settings such as Cambodia and Malawi. As these contexts come with diverse sociolinguistic and political-economic backgrounds, the contributions offer a range of multilingual constellations which provide revealing insights into the linguistic repertoires at play in EMI. This diversity is further enhanced by the potpourri of educational settings in the limelight, including primary, secondary and tertiary levels as well as public, private and international institutions. Therefore, the EMI cases at stake constitute a wide field of educational differences, ranging from non-selective public schools in socioeconomically deprived areas in South Africa (Chapter 11) to a private and selective international school in Kenya (Chapter 5); from well-established universities in highly developed countries with a longstanding tradition of using the national language for education (Italy, Chapter 9) to young universities in socio-economically developing countries with disrupted histories of educational language policies (Cambodia, Chapter 8 or Kazakhstan, Chapter 10). Understandably, such varied educational scenarios come with equally different realisations of EMI and of TL practices, which is paid tribute to in the detailed elaborations of the two central concepts in each of the chapters.

An interesting question in this connection is: Why are such repeated conceptualisations of 'translanguaging' and 'English-medium instruction' actually provided? Would it not suffice to have them clarified in the Introduction and elaborated further in the chapters dedicated to theorising EMI and TL, all the more so as there are various other recent publications dealing with the two phenomena, particularly from a theoretical perspective? From a purely academic perspective, then, it could thus be assumed that the resulting conceptualisations, models and frameworks (e.g. Dafouz & Smit, 2020, for EMI; Lin et al., 2020, for TL) offered sufficient theorising, rendering case-specific conceptualisations superfluous.

Why this is not so, however, is that the research area in focus is not 'purely academic', but explicitly applied in the sense of dealing with language-related problems in the 'real world' (Brumfit, 1997). And it is the real world that interferes here, forcing us researchers to deal with different realities and realisations and to adapt our conceptualisations accordingly. The resulting dilemma of dealing, or actually not dealing, with the 'same phenomenon' is exacerbated by the wide range of possible research interests integral to educational linguistics, such as teacher pedagogical practices, student participation and learning, policy implementation at school level or educational ideologies. Given this range of concerns and the situated nature of education, it is thus impossible to provide detailed definitions of EMI and TL that could hold across cases, and it would be naïve to assume that such once-for-all characterisations could be found. Rather, and this I consider a clear strength of the volume, each project needs to identify the phenomena in question in as much detail as possible, thus putting into relief what is at stake for the social actors in the field as well as for the researchers themselves. At the same time, such contextualised explorations clearly profit from the rich literature mentioned above as it offers not only detailed accounts of what the respective phenomenon can consist of and entail, but also shared points of reference that support intellectual exchange.

As implicitly executed throughout this volume, EMI describes educational scenarios which are characterised by regulations of positioning or using English as medium of instruction in settings in which English is not the main language of wider communication. Translanguaging, on the other hand, foregrounds the communicative and educational practices in such settings that draw on the respective multilingual repertoires. Central to both concepts is the understanding that, in contrast to the still widely encountered 'monolingual habitus' of educational institutions (Gogolin, 1994), the characteristics and affordances of multilingualism need to be embraced in education in general and, given its intrinsically multilingual character, even more so in EMI. In sum, then, 'translanguaging EMI' centrally aims to analyse the multilingual practices at the heart of English-medium educational realities, critically evaluating the interrelations between, and tensions arising from, multilingual actors and monolingual regulations.

This core research endeavour of 'translanguaging EMI' materialises in diverse ways, which the contributions to this volume not only showcase in their contextual specificity, but also as regards their research interests. By applying an admittedly coarse brushstroke, three layered areas of interests can be identified (see Figure E.1). Moving from micro to macro, there is, firstly, the focus on TL practices in EMI – pedagogical and/or communicative – and in how far they support content learning and/or language learning in either English or the students' first language/language of wider communication. The second layer of interest combines the micro with the meso as it analyses the interdependence between TL practices and top-down language policies and how they mutually influence one another. Such research can either focus on the policies and practices directly or on how they are experienced and constructed by teachers and/or students as main social actors. Moving to the macro level, the third layer of interest embraces TL as an empowering strategy, critically analysing EMI phenomena from a social justice perspective, ultimately

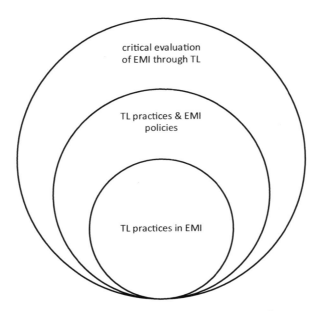

Figure E.1 Layers of research interests in 'translanguaging EMI'

questioning dominant ideologies of education. As already indicated in the metaphors of 'micro to macro' and 'layer', these three types of research interests are not understood in a compartmentalised way, but stand in relation of mutual dependence in terms of both actual 'translanguaging EMI' practices and researchers' interests.

A Collage of Insights

The 11 contributions to this volume are so diverse in their investigative concerns and rich in contextually specific findings that the aim of this very personal 'collage' is certainly not to provide a summary or even overview of all insights gained – the only way to gain that, I'm afraid, is to read the chapters in their entirety. Rather, this section intends to throw light on the potential of TL for English-medium educational settings and will do so with the help of the three layers of research interests captured in Figure E.1.

As indicated by its core position in the graph, the research focus on TL practices in EMI is part and parcel of all studies. Acknowledging the intrinsically discursive and interactional nature of education, it foregrounds how the respective linguistic resources are or should be used in support of the teaching and learning process. In secondary science classes, for instance, the judicious use of Cantonese and English allows Hong Kong teenage students in Chapter 7 to participate in class, to develop science knowledge and how to express it in English, thus underlining the integrated nature of content and language learning (see also Lin, 2016;

Nikula *et al.*, 2016). This supportive role of the L1 is also in focus in the many traditionally monolingual university settings that, despite lower proficiency levels in English as a first foreign language of their students, introduce EMI in recognition of the global role of English as lingua franca in academia, business and trade. A case in point are Turkish higher education institutions (HEIs) (Chapter 1), where TL in class supports students in their learning process in terms of developing understanding, while at the same time acknowledging and profiting from the widely shared bilingual repertoire of Turkish and English. While TL is thus often analysed as supporting the learning process in the target language, it also holds potential for L1 use and development, especially in sociolinguistically more complex scenarios as are depicted in Chapters 6 and 10. The former focuses on primary-level children attending English-medium education in the Maldives, and the latter on university graduates in Kazakhstan. Although dealing with clearly different scenarios, both studies show convincingly that, particularly in multilingual communities, TL can and should be used to enhance L1 learning as regards educational and professional registers and genres so as to support learners in developing situation-appropriate language use. At primary level, for instance, children want to be able to tell stories to family members (Chapter 6), and in work settings, employees need to write professional reports or give convincing presentations to local clients (Chapter 10).

Such insights into the positive role TL has for content and language learning already point towards the next layer of research interests, i.e. the interrelation between TL practices and EMI language policies. Inherent in the widely shared understanding of language policies as dynamic and multi-layered, comprising texts and discourses (e.g. Hornberger, 2012; Hult, 2017; Johnson, 2013), TL practices come with important leverage in terms of implementing and shaping policies – a powerful and dynamic, yet often contested relationship that is at the heart of most of this book's contributions. When first turning to scenarios with a national language of high prestige as an educational language, language policies tend to embrace the beneficial role of English as a medium of education in addition to the established language. TL-focused research then describes EMI implementations and evaluates the degree and type of enacted multilingualism. While all studies underline the TL-inherent advantages mentioned above, Chapter 2 identifies different TL practices across types of learning spaces, hinting at the need for situation-specific policies. The Italian study (Chapter 9) argues for EMI as a multilingual learning space, even or especially so for international students who would also profit from some familiarity with the local language. What is relevant in such multilingual and English as a lingua franca settings, though, is 'the judicious and systematic adoption of translanguaging practices' (p. 140).

Although diverse in themselves, the three settings sketched so far deal with combinations of English and their respective traditionally established and prestigious national languages. This contrasts markedly with the other three studies that fall into the second layer of researching 'translanguaging EMI'. Set in Cambodia, South Africa and Kenya, respectively, the educational scenarios in Chapters 8, 4 and 5 are strongly influenced by a sociolinguistic inequality of languages caused by long and partially traumatic historical developments. Therefore, TL practices in educational contexts do not only have to contend with the more general monolingual expectations of formal schooling, but also with the low prestige of their respective national languages, often considered unfit for educational use. To change such negative attitudes when making EMI a bilingual practice, TL practices must be identified, experienced and accepted as particularly valuable and advantageous. In Cambodia, where English has gained relevance recently, the national language Khmer is seen as acceptable for translanguaging EMI in order to level out the low proficiency levels most Cambodians still have in English. This contrasts markedly with universities in post-colonial settings where English has had a much longer and chequered history which has gone hand-in-hand with a growing status of indigenous languages as identity markers. Against this sociolinguistic background, bilingual EMI policies are not only a reflection of a practically motivated need to draw on English and L1 for educational purposes, but also reflect the ideological expectations to use both English as global language of academia and the local language indexing local identity. While a resulting bilingual policy that would facilitate increased engagement for local students is still a demand rather than a reality in the South African scenario depicted in Chapter 4, Chapter 5 describes the four-year process by which a Kenyan private school developed their originally monolingual EMI policy to a bilingual one, integrating English and Swahili. By systematically combining top-down and bottom-up policies and practices, Swahili could be established as an educational language, used for 'linguistically appropriate practice' and for 'developing global citizenship' (p. 68). Translanguaging as a bundle of pedagogical measures, labelled the 'translanguaging cycle', thus turned the school into a bilingual learning space.

The last two examples already reach into the third layer of research interests of 'translanguaging EMI'. By pursuing an explicitly macro-level endeavour, TL practices are used to argue for a repositioning of 'language in education' to 'languaging education', i.e. to move from a focus on a product view on distinct languages used for specific and often pre-specified educational outcomes, to a process view of social actors employing their complete linguistic repertoires while engaging in co-constructing knowledge. Drawing explicitly on post-colonial theorising, this research interest aims to first identify and then actively change the colonial legacy of uncritically perpetuating the domineering Anglonormative ideology and thereby excluding large parts of the population from education (e.g. Makalela, 2015; McKinney, 2017). Although still a grassroots endeavour, illustrated in good practice examples from mainstream South African schools, Chapter 11 argues convincingly that pedagogical TL has this transformative potential not only for the individual learners, but also for education more generally. So far, however, this potential has not resulted in explicit top-down policies, as is also painfully noticeable at Malawian universities (Chapter 3). The official English-only policy contrasts markedly with the combined use of English and Chichewa that is widely experienced as contextually relevant because 'one language isn't enough' (p. 41). While not a reality yet, a multilingual policy would be a 'win-win game' [with] 'English being an international language, Chichewa being a national language' (p. 41). It can only be hoped that such critical accounts will support the presently largely grassroots process of 'disinventing and (re)constituting languages' (Makoni & Pennycook, 2005) in having an impact on the EMI policy level as well.

In sum, the 11 empirical studies presented in this book not only offer highly welcome insights into the wealth of multilingual practices in supposedly monolingual educational settings, but also provide empirical evidence of the centrality of micro-level practices to meso- and macro-level policies, including all-encompassing ideologies. What is more, the shared research focus on translanguaging EMI holds invaluable conceptual insights for 'translanguaging EMI' and its components, i.e. 'translanguaging' and 'EMI'. Picking up on the previously topicalised dilemma of clearly defining any applied linguistic phenomena, the arguably most fundamental conceptual insight is exactly that they are intrinsically contextualised and need to be conceptualised as such. Thanks to the impressive diversity of realisations, actions and meanings attached to 'translanguaging EMI' in this book, it is hardly possible to even imagine the existence of a comprehensive decontextualised delimitation of what is at stake. Rather, what researchers need to do is to remain as faithful as possible, firstly to the dynamic complexity of what they are studying and, secondly, to their own research concerns. Not surprisingly, this endeavour requires, and is greatly supported by, the rich and interdisciplinary research literature of the past 50 years or so, but – and this is potentially more controversial than it might sound at first – the focus of research attention must remain the 'real-world' phenomenon, rather than a particular model or theoretical framework. So, instead of relying on whatever literature is often quoted and widely used at a certain point in time, insightful analyses of 'translanguaging EMI' need to start with the respective real-world phenomenon and, moving from there, identify as wide a literature base as demanded by their respective research focus. By way of illustration, Chapter 11 makes a strong case for the range of pedagogical uses of TL exactly by drawing on all relevant studies dealing with multilingual practices in South African schools, explicitly those that predated TL as a research framework. Chapter 10, on the other hand, offers a wider conceptualisation of TL by combining it with 'transfer', thus providing a valuable theoretical basis for interpreting language-dependent generic practices reported on by alumni of an EMI programme at a Kazakh university.

The conceptual potential of taking an inclusive rather than exclusive view becomes particularly rife when turning to the relationship proposed between investigations of bilingual practices undertaken from the perspectives of TL versus code-switching. Without wanting to downplay the theoretical differences between these research paradigms (for discussions, see, for example, García & Li Wei, 2014; Lin *et al.*, 2020; MacSwan, 2017), the point at stake here is that both research traditions address bilingual practices in educational settings. Given the long history of code-switching research in particular, the respective body of research is sizable and, as illustrated in Chapters 4 and 7, also valuable for research that is embedded in the TL framework. By keeping in mind the applied linguistic intention of revealing the ins and outs of multilingual practices in particular educational sites, it seems thus more constructive to take an inclusive approach and benefit from both research traditions by identifying situation-relevant findings and insights realised within both the TL and code-switching approaches (see also Smit, 2019).

When turning to 'EMI', a conceptual concern worth mentioning is its scope. Given the broad range of possible realities, this is done best by exclusion, i.e. by focusing on possible EMI scenarios not featured in this book. Besides Kachru's (1992) inner circle countries (see, for example, Jenkins & Mauranen, 2019), the most notable absence is the truly international higher educational setting where English functions as the only lingua franca (e.g. Smit, 2010). In other words, the contributions to this book largely exclude scenarios where English is the main language for communication in the wider society or on campus, scenarios where communicators rely on English as the only shared language instead of having two or more at their disposal. Put differently, the prototypical case of English-medium education in multilingual university settings, or EMEMUS for short (Dafouz & Smit, 2020), catering for internationally mobile students is not in focus here. Instead, the book is concerned with EMI in educational communities across all levels of education that are multilingual in English and one or more other languages. Clearly, this EMI focus underlines the investigative focus of the book to throw light on TL practices in multilingual groups faced with a top-down monolingual policy.

While the EMI settings included in this book are diverse along dimensions such as educational level and type, geographical location or languages involved, it is highly interesting to note that what seems to be a major dividing factor is whether English comes with a legacy of colonialism. In the cases where it does – and that includes all cases of EMI at primary and secondary levels – the investigative focus goes beyond the first research layer of Figure E.1 and suggests ways of changing educational policy or, possibly even, education at large. Ideally, the desired EMI policies should embrace the local language(s) explicitly and systematically, actively support increased student participation and improved learning in both languages, and possibly even aim for dissolving EMI towards 'something quite different' (p. 172). Such fundamental policy challenges and envisaged changes do not seem so pressing in EMI settings free of the burden of Anglophone colonialism, however. Responding exclusively to the much younger historically grown role of English as main global language of academia, business and trade, EMI tends to be understood as a practical necessity or, in comparison with higher education in the national language, as an educational opportunity. To make the most of that, the use of the national language(s) is considered positive in terms of providing content and/or language learning support, such as when the English proficiency levels are fairly low. In these cases, then, EMI is certainly uncontested as an important educational policy, particularly in higher education.

What Next?

As indicative of exciting research, the empirical and conceptual insights sketched above suggest further research interests in connection with the practice–policy interface in English-medium education in multilingual settings, such as:

- Working with a contextualised understanding of TL in support of analysing 'real-world' multilingual practices, future research should follow the lead identified here of (a) remaining conceptually open to integrating other relevant ideas and (b) using all relevant literature, irrespective of their conceptual framing.
- Seeing that this book is not concerned with truly international EMI realisations – or prototypical cases of what Dafouz and Smit (2020) call EMEMUS – it would be very interesting to pay concerted research interest to TL in such settings, and investigate actual practices across different TL spaces, by particularly paying attention to their pedagogical potential.
- As indicated in the 'translanguaging cycle' (Chapter 5), TL can be used as a pedagogical strategy in long-term policy planning and implementation. It would be highly revealing to see what this long-term process could look like in a different setting and what agents, conceptualisations and procedures would make it happen and to what ends.
- The positive examples of combining TL as either communicative or pedagogical practice in content teaching with language-focused classes open an interesting area for future interdisciplinary work, involving applied linguistics, second language teaching and educational research.

I trust that this volume will inspire more such contextually detailed, conceptually rich and empirically exciting studies into 'translanguaging EMI'.

Conclusion

This volume has presented a wide range of studies from across the globe, all exploring what may transpire at the crossroads of *translanguaging* and *English-medium instruction* (EMI). Clearly, our stance as editors, together with our authors, is that the juxtaposition of translanguaging and EMI is a positive recognition of both the realities of English-taught programmes as well as the everyday realities of multilingual individuals in the classroom. Still, we acknowledge that while this volume contributes to an expanded view of translanguaging as theory and pedagogy in EMI contexts, there is still much more to be done in the field – especially considering the special circumstances of the axiomatic place of English in EMI classrooms with students whose first language is not likely to be English (Macaro, 2018; Pecorari & Malmström, 2018).

Jaspers (2019: 101) argues that while researchers have 'rightly disagreed much with the idea that the one "good" type of language (teaching) is monolingual', it is not enough to then merely advocate that all fluid, plurilingual practices in the classrooms are ideal. He calls for a more 'critical spirit' (Jaspers, 2019: 101) that does not limit the value of diverse linguistic repertoires to the improvement of learning outcomes, but rather opens up for a move away from a dichotomous view of 'worthwhile and less worthwhile fluid language' in education (Jaspers, 2019: 100). Further, as Jaspers (2018: 9) has pointed out, 'at the end of the road, pupils will be evaluated for their skills in a monolingual, academic type of language'. Assessment, therefore, can and should not be overlooked when considering pedagogical practices that make use of a range of linguistic resources. Simply allowing for the use of multiple languages in the classroom, then, would not be enough to advance a social justice agenda in education (see Jaspers, 2018), nor would it necessarily be appropriate to term it *translanguaging*. For example, Hedman (2018; see also Ganuza & Hedman, 2017) suggests that use of the term 'pedagogical translanguaging' should be reserved for educational contexts where multilingual language practices reflect heteroglossic, rather than monoglossic, ideologies. We recognise and accept the need for more critical explorations of the intersections of translanguaging and EMI.

In the epilogue to this volume, Smit outlines several key areas for future research. Here, we add to these suggestions with areas within EMI that we, together with our authors, have identified as warranting further, critical exploration:

- effective implementation of EMI policies legitimising translanguaging practices;
- translanguaging as the medium of instruction;
- pedagogical translanguaging approaches in EMI teacher training courses;
- stakeholder beliefs about translanguaging in relation to native speakerism;
- recognition of the use and value of languages other than English and the local language in EMI classrooms;
- varieties of English (accepted and/or promoted) in the EMI classroom;
- how ideologies and hierarchies may be represented in teaching materials for EMI;
- content learning/student outcomes in EMI settings where translanguaging is pedagogically legitimised versus in EMI contexts where translanguaging is not included in the pedagogy;
- explorations of multimodal data including non-verbal communication in EMI classrooms, such as lesson observations using videos;
- navigating translanguaging practices in the workplace upon graduation from EMI programmes;
- translanguaging and assessment in the EMI classroom.

Final Words

We would like to end this chapter with an acknowledgment to all of the authors and reviewers who have joined us on this journey. We feel fortunate to have worked with such wonderful scholars from around the globe and appreciate all of their hard work every step of the way. We look forward to the new studies inspired by this volume as well as the new directions awaiting research in the fields – and crossroads – of translanguaging and EMI.

BethAnne Paulsrud, Zhongfeng Tian and Jeanette Toth

References

Ackerley, K., Guarda, M. and Helm, F. (eds) (2017) *Sharing Perspectives on English-Medium Instruction*. Bern: Peter Lang.

Adamson, J.L. and Coulson, D. (2014) Pathways towards success for novice academic writers in a CLIL setting: A study in an Asian EFL context. In R. Al-Mahrooq, V.S. Thakur and A. Roscoe (eds) *Methodologies for Effective Writing Instruction in EFL and ESL Classrooms* (pp. 151–171). Hershey: IGI Global.

Adamson, J.L. and Coulson, D. (2015) Translanguaging in English academic writing preparation. *International Journal of Pedagogies and Learning* 10 (1), 24–37.

Adamson, J.L. and Fujimoto-Adamson, N. (2012) Translanguaging in self-access language advising: Informing language policy. *SISAL (Studies in Self-access Learning)* 3 (1), 59–73.

Adamson, J.L., Brown, H. and Fujimoto-Adamson, N. (2012) Revealing shifts and diversity in understandings of self-access language learning. *Journal of University Teaching and Learning Practice* 9 (1), 1–16.

Adendorff, R.D. (1996) The functions of code switching among high school teachers and students in KwaZulu and implications for teacher education. In K.M. Bailey and D. Nunan (eds) *Voices from the Language Classroom: Qualitative Research in Second Language Education* (pp. 388–406). Cambridge: Cambridge University Press.

Aga Khan Academies (2018) What makes us unique. *Aga Khan Academies* website. See http://www.agakhanacademies.org/general/what-makes-us-unique (accessed 27 January 2019).

Airey, J. (2012) 'I don't teach language': The linguistic attitudes of physics lecturers in Sweden. *AILA Review* 25, 64–79.

Alexander, R. (2006) *Towards Dialogic Teaching: Rethinking Classroom Talk* (3rd edn). Cambridge: Dialogos.

Ali, N.L. (2013) A changing paradigm in language planning: English-medium instruction policy at the tertiary level in Malaysia. *Current Issues in Language Planning* 14 (1), 73–92.

Alidou, H., Boly, A., Brock-Utne, B., Satina Diallo, Y., Heugh, K. and Wolff, H.E. (2006) Optimizing learning and education in Africa – the language factor: A stock-taking research on mother tongue and bilingual education in Sub-Saharan Africa. *ADEA 2006 Biennial Meeting, Libreville Gabon*. Paris: ADEA.

Allard, E.C. (2017) Re-examining teacher translanguaging: An ecological perspective. *Bilingual Research Journal* 40 (2), 116–130.

Andersson, I., Kagwesage, A.M. and Rusanganwa, J. (2013) Negotiating meaning in multilingual group work: A case study of higher education in Rwanda. *International Journal of Bilingual Education and Bilingualism* 16 (4), 436–450.

Antia, B.E. and Dyers, C. (2019) De-alienating the academy: Multilingual teaching as decolonial pedagogy. *Linguistics and Education*, 51, 91–100.

Anton, M. and DiCamilla, F. (1998) Socio-cognitive functions of L1 collaborative interaction in the L2 classroom. *Canadian Modern Language Review* 54 (3), 314–342.

Arthur, J. and Martin, P. (2006) Accomplishing lessons in postcolonial classrooms: Comparative perspectives from Botswana and Brunei Darussalam. *Comparative Education* 42 (2), 177–202.

Bagwasi, M.M. (2017) A critique of Botswana's language policy from a translanguaging perspective. *Current Issues in Language Planning* 18 (2), 199–214.

Baijnath, M. (2017) Engaging with transformation of the humanities curriculum at an English-medium research-intensive South African university: Decolonisation and academic agency in an era of uncertainty. Master's dissertation, University of Cape Town.

Baker, C. (2011) *Foundations of Bilingual Education and Bilingualism* (5th edn). Bristol: Multilingual Matters.

Baker, C. and Wright, W.E. (2017) *Foundations of Bilingual Education and Bilingualism* (6th edn). Bristol: Multilingual Matters.

Ballantyne, K. and Rivera, C. (2014) *Research Summary: Language Proficiency for Academic Achievement in the International Baccalaureate Diploma Program.* Washington, DC: International Baccalaureate Organisation.

Barnard, R. and McLellan, J. (eds) (2014) *Code-switching in University English-Medium Classes: Asian Perspectives.* Bristol: Multilingual Matters.

Barnes, D. (1992) *From Communication to Curriculum.* Harmondsworth: Penguin.

Beelen, J. and Jones, E. (2015) Redefining internationalization at home. In A. Curaj, L. Matei, R. Pricopie, J. Salmi and P. Scott (eds) *The European Higher Education Area* (pp. 59–72). New York: Springer.

Blackledge, A. and Creese, A. (2010) *Multilingualism: A Critical Perspective.* London and New York: Continuum.

Bolton, K., Botha, W. and Bacon-Shone, J. (2017) English-medium instruction in Singapore higher education: Policy, realities and challenges. *Journal of Multilingual and Multicultural Development* 38 (10), 913–930.

Borg, S. (2016) *English Medium Instruction in Iraqi Kurdistan: Perspectives from Lecturers at State Universities.* London: British Council.

Boun, S. (2014) A critical examination of language ideologies and identities of Cambodian foreign-trained university lecturers of English. PhD thesis, University of Texas at San Antonio.

Bradley, J., Moore, E., Simpson, J. and Atkinson, L. (2018) Translanguaging space and creative activity: Theorising collaborative arts-based learning. *Language and Intercultural Communication* 18 (1), 54–73.

Braun, V. and Clarke, V. (2006) Using thematic analysis in psychology. *Qualitative Research in Psychology* 3 (2), 77–101.

Brown, H. and Adamson, J.L. (2012) Connecting disciplines at Japanese university: Adapting EAP to local academic culture. In D. Schaffer and M. Pinto (eds) *Proceedings of the 19th Annual KOTESOL International Conference* (pp. 123–134). Seoul: KOTESOL.

Brown, H. and Adamson, J.L. (2014) Localizing EAP in light of the rise of English-medium instruction at Japanese universities. *OnCue Journal* 6 (3), 5–20 (JALT College and University Educators SIG Journal).

Brown, H. and Iyobe, B. (2014) The growth of English medium instruction in Japan. In N. Sonda and A. Krause (eds) *JALT 2013 Conference Proceedings* (pp. 9–19). Tokyo: JALT.

Brumfit, C.J. (1997) How applied linguistics is the same as any other science. *International Journal of Applied Linguistics* 7 (1), 86–94.

Burgess, C. (2014) To globalise or not to globalise? 'Inward-looking youth' as scapegoats for Japan's failure to secure and cultivate 'global human resources'. *Globalisation, Societies and Education* 13 (4), 487–507.

Camó, A.C. and Ballester, E.P. (2015) The effects of using L1 translation on young learners' foreign language vocabulary learning. *ELIA: Estudios de Lingüística Inglesa Aplicada* 15, 109–134.

Canagarajah, A.S. (2005) Introduction. In A.S. Canagarajah (ed.) *Reclaiming the Local in Language Policy and Practice* (pp. xiii–xxx). Mahwah, NJ: Lawrence Erlbaum.

Canagarajah, A.S. (2006) TESOL at forty: What are the issues? *TESOL Quarterly* 40 (1), 9–34.

Canagarajah, A.S. (2011) Codemeshing in academic writing: Identifying teachable strategies of translanguaging. *The Modern Language Journal* 95 (3), 401–417.

Canagarajah, A.S. (2013a) *Translingual Practice: Global Englishes and Cosmopolitan Relations*. Abingdon and New York: Routledge.

Canagarajah, A.S. (2013b) Skilled migration and development: Portable communicative resources for transnational work. *Multilingual Education* 3 (8), 1–19.

Candas, P. (2011) Analyzing student practice in language resource centres of the Louis Pasteur University in Strasbourg: Is planning really central to self-directed learning? *Innovation in Language Learning and Teaching* 5 (2), 191–204.

Carder, M. (2007) *Bilingualism in International Schools: A Model for Enriching Language Education*. Clevedon: Multilingual Matters.

Carder, M. (2018) *Second Language Learners in International Schools*. London: University College of London Institute of Education.

Carroll, K.S. and van den Hoven, M. (2016) Translanguaging within higher education in the United Arab Emirates. In C.M. Mazak and K.S. Carroll (eds) *Translanguaging in Higher Education: Beyond Monolingual Ideologies* (pp. 139–154). Bristol: Multilingual Matters.

CDC and HKEAA (2007a) *Science Education Key Learning Area Biology Curriculum and Assessment Guide (Secondary 4–6)*. Hong Kong: HKSAR Government Printer.

CDC and HKEAA (2007b) *Science Education Key Learning Area Chemistry Curriculum and Assessment Guide (Secondary 4–6)*. Hong Kong: HKSAR Government Printer.

CDC and HKEAA (2007c) *Science Education Key Learning Area Physics Curriculum and Assessment Guide*. Hong Kong: HKSAR Government Printer.

Celic, C. and Seltzer, K. (2011) *Translanguaging: A CUNY-NYSIEB Guide for Educators*. New York: Graduate Center, City University of New York, CUNY-NYSIEB.

Cenoz, J. and Gorter, D. (2011) Focus on multilingualism: A study of trilingual writing. *The Modern Language Journal* 95 (3), 356–369.

Centre for Language Studies (1999) *Sociolinguistic Surveys of Four Malawian Languages with Special Reference to Education*. Zomba and Lilongwe: Centre for Language Studies and GTZ.

Centre for Language Studies (2006) *Language Mapping Survey for Northern Malawi*. Zomba: Centre for Language Studies.

Centre for Language Studies (2009) *Language Mapping Survey for the Central and Southern Regions of Malawi: Language and their Dialects*. Zomba: Centre for Language Studies.

Chalmers, H. (2019) *The Role of the First Language in English Medium Instruction*. Oxford: Oxford University Press.

Chan, J.Y.H. (2014) Fine-tuning language policy in Hong Kong education: Stakeholders' perceptions, practices and challenges. *Language and Education* 28 (5), 459–476.

Chandler, D.P. (1993) *A History of Cambodia*. Chiang Mai: Silkworm Books.

Chang, H., Ngunjiri, F.W. and Hernandez, K-A.C. (2013) *Collaborative Autoethnography*. Walnut Creek: Left Coast Press.

Chang, S. (2019) Beyond the English box: Constructing and communicating knowledge through translingual practices in the higher education classroom. *English Teaching and Learning* 43, 23–40.

Charamba, E. and Zano, K. (2019) Effects of translanguaging as an intervention strategy in a South African chemistry classroom. *Bilingual Research Journal* 42 (3), 291–307.

Chavula, J. (2019) *How Does the English Only Medium Work in the Classroom? Survey Report*. See http://langdev.mw/downloads/How%20Does%20The%20English%20Only%20Medium%20Work%20In%20The%20Classroom.pdf (accessed July 2019).

Chellin, G. (2018) Translanguaging in higher education: An investigation of English-medium instruction (EMI) at the University of Padova. Unpublished MA thesis, University of Padova.

Childs, M. (2016) Reflecting on translanguaging in multilingual classrooms: Harnessing the power of poetry and photography. *Educational Research for Social Change (ESRC)* 5 (1), 22–40.

Chilora, H.G. (2000) School language policy research and practice in Malawi. *Comparative and International Education Society (CIES) 2000 Conference*, 8–12 March, San Antonio, TX.

Chimbutane, F. (2011) *Rethinking Bilingual Education in Postcolonial Contexts*. Bristol: Multilingual Matters.

Chumak-Horbatsch, R. (2012) *Linguistically Appropriate Practice*. Toronto: University of Toronto Press.

Clayton, S. (2008) The problem of 'choice' and the construction of the demand for English in Cambodia. *Language Policy* 7 (2), 143–164.

Clayton, T. (1995) Restriction or resistance? Educational development in French colonial Cambodia. *Education Policy Analysis Archives* 3 (19), 1–12.

Clayton, T. (2002) Language choice in a nation under transition: The struggle between English and French in Cambodia. *Language Policy* 1 (1), 3–25.

Clayton, T. (2006) *Language Choice in a Nation under Transition: English Language Spread in Cambodia*. New York: Springer.

Cogo, A. (2009) Accommodating difference in ELF conversations: A study of pragmatic strategies. In A. Mauranen and E. Ranta (eds) *English as a Lingua Franca: Studies and Findings* (pp. 254–273). Newcastle upon Tyne: Cambridge Scholars Press.

Coleman, J.A. (2006) English-medium teaching in European higher education. *Language Teaching* 39 (1), 1–14.

Coleman, J., Hultgren, A.K., Li Wei, Tsui, C. and Shaw, P. (2018) Forum on English-medium instruction. *TESOL Quarterly* 52 (3), 701–720.

Conteh, J. (2018) Translanguaging as pedagogy – a critical review. In A. Creese and A. Blackledge (eds) *The Routledge Handbook of Language and Superdiversity* (pp. 473–487). London: Routledge.

Cook, V. (2001) Using the first language in the classroom. *Canadian Modern Language Review* 57 (3), 402–423.

Copland, F. and Creese, A. (2015) *Linguistic Ethnography: Collecting, Analysing and Presenting Data*. Thousand Oaks, CA: Sage.

Coronel-Molina, S.M. and Samuelson, B.L. (2017) Language contact and translingual literacies. *Journal of Multilingual and Multicultural Development* 38 (5), 379–389.

Corson, D. (1990) *Language Policy Across the Curriculum*. Clevedon: Multilingual Matters.

Costa, F. and Coleman, J.A. (2013) A survey of English-medium instruction in Italian higher education. *International Journal of Bilingual Education and Bilingualism* 16 (1), 3–19.

Coyle, D., Hood, P. and Marsh, D. (2010) *CLIL: Content and Language Integrated Learning*. Cambridge: Cambridge University Press.

Creese, A. and Blackledge, A. (2010) Translanguaging in the bilingual classroom: A pedagogy for learning and teaching? *The Modern Language Journal* 9, 103–115.

Creese, A. and Blackledge, A. (2015) Translanguaging and identity in educational settings. *Annual Review of Applied Linguistics* 35, 20–35.

Crisfield, E. (2018) What is ethical bilingual education? *Crisfield Educational Consulting*, blog post, 1 May. See https://www.crisfieldeducationalconsulting.com/single-post/2018/05/01/What-is-ethical-bilingual-education (accessed 27 January 2019).

Cross, R. (2016) Language and content 'integration': The affordances of additional languages as a tool within a single curriculum space. *Journal of Curriculum Studies* 48 (3), 388–408.

Cumming-Potvin, W. (2009) Social justice, pedagogy and multiliteracies: Developing communities of practice for teacher education. *Australian Journal of Teacher Education* 34 (3), 82–99.

Cummins, J. (1979) Cognitive/academic language proficiency, linguistic interdependence, the optimum age question, and some other matters. *Working Papers on Bilingualism* 19, 121–129.

Cummins, J. (2000) *Language, Power and Pedagogy: Bilingual Children in the Crossfire.* Clevedon: Multilingual Matters.

Cummins, J. (2005a) A proposal for action: Strategies for recognizing heritage language competence as a learning resource within the mainstream classroom. *The Modern Language Journal* 80 (4), 585–592.

Cummins, J. (2005b) Teaching for cross-language transfer in dual language education: Possibilities and pitfalls. *TESOL Symposium on Dual Language Education*, Boğaziçi University, Istanbul.

Cummins, J. (2008a) BICS and CALP: Empirical and theoretical status of the distinction. In B. Street and N. Hornberger (eds) *Encyclopedia of Language and Education, Vol. 2: Literacy* (pp. 71–83). Netherlands: Springer Science and Business Media.

Cummins, J. (2008b) Teaching for transfer: Challenging the two solitudes assumption in bilingual education. In J. Cummins and N.H. Hornberger (eds) *Encyclopedia of Language and Education, Vol. 5* (2nd edn, pp. 65–75). New York: Springer.

Cummins, J., Hu, S., Markus, P. and Montero, M.K. (2015) Identity texts and academic achievement: Connecting the dots in multilingual school contexts. *TESOL Quarterly* 49 (3), 555–581.

Dafouz, E. and Smit, U. (2020) *ROAD-MAPPING English Medium Education in the Internationalised University.* Cham: Palgrave Macmillan.

Dafouz, E., Huettner, J. and Smit, U. (2016) University teachers' beliefs of language and content integration in English-medium education in multilingual university settings. In T. Nikula, E. Dafouz, P. Moore and U. Smit (eds) *Conceptualising Integration in CLIL and Multilingual Education* (pp. 123–144). Bristol: Multilingual Matters.

Dalziel, F. (2020) EMI and translanguaging: Student language use in an Italian English-taught programme. In L. Mastellotto and R. Zanin (eds) *EMI and Beyond: Internationalizing Curricula in Higher Education.* Bolzano: Bolzano University Press.

Daryai-Hansen, P., Barfod, S. and Schwarz, L. (2016) A call for (trans)languaging: The language profiles at Roskilde University. In C.M. Mazak and K.S. Carroll (eds) *Translanguaging in Higher Education: Beyond Monolingual Ideologies* (pp. 29–49). Bristol: Multilingual Matters.

Dearden, J. (2014) *English as a Medium of Instruction: A Growing Global Phenomenon.* London: British Council.

DePalma, M.J. and Ringer, J.M. (2011) Toward a theory of adaptive transfer: Expanding disciplinary discussions of 'transfer' in second-language writing and composition studies. *Journal of Second Language Writing* 20 (2), 134–147.

Department of Basic Education, RSA (2010) *The Status of the Language of Learning and Teaching (LoLT) in South African Public Schools: A Quantitative Overview.* Pretoria: Department of Basic Education.

Department of Basic Education, RSA (2011) *National Curriculum Statement (NCS) Curriculum and Assessment Policy Statement: English First Additional Language.* Pretoria: Department of Basic Education.

Department of Basic Education, RSA (2012) *Manual for Teaching English across the Curriculum 2013.* Pretoria: Department of Basic Education.

Department of Basic Education, RSA (2013) *The Incremental Introduction of African Languages in South African Schools.* Pretoria: Department of Basic Education.

Department of Education (1997) *Education White Paper 3: A Programme for the Transformation of Higher Education.* See https://www.gov.za/sites/default/files/gcis_document/201409/18207gen11960.pdf (accessed 26 August 2019).

Department of Education, RSA (1996) *South African Schools Act No. 84 of 1996.* Pretoria: Government Printer.

Department of Education, RSA (1997) *Language-in-Education Policy.* Pretoria: Department of Education.

Deumert, A. (2018) Let's shuffle: An epistemology of dance and decoloniality. *Diggit Magazine*, 27 September. See https://www.diggitmagazine.com/column/let-s-shuffle-epistemology-dance-disruption-and-decoloniality (accessed 24 August 2019).

Dewilde, J. (2017) Multilingual young people as writers in a global age. In B. Paulsrud, J. Rosén, B. Straszer and Å. Wedin (eds) *New Perspectives on Translanguaging and Education* (pp. 56–71). Bristol: Multilingual Matters.

Dimova, S., Hultgren, A.K. and Jensen, C. (eds) (2015) *English-medium Instruction in European Higher Education.* Berlin: De Gruyter Mouton.

Doiz, A. and Lasagabaster, D. (2016) Teachers' beliefs about translanguaging practices. In C.M. Mazak and K.S. Carroll (eds) *Translanguaging in Higher Education: Beyond Monolingual Ideologies* (pp. 157–176). Bristol: Multilingual Matters.

Doiz, A., Lasagabaster, D. and Sierra, J.M. (2011) Internationalisation, multilingualism and English-medium instruction. *World Englishes* 30 (3), 345–359.

Doiz, A., Lasagabaster, D. and Sierra, J.M. (eds) (2013) *English-Medium Instruction at Universities: Global Challenges.* Bristol: Multilingual Matters.

D'warte, J. (2018) Recognizing and leveraging the bilingual meaning-making potential of young people aged six to eight years old in one Australian classroom. *Journal of Early Childhood Literacy* 20 (2), 1–31.

Early, M. and Norton, B. (2014) Revisiting English as medium of instruction in rural African classrooms. *Journal of Multilingual and Multicultural Development* 35 (7), 647–691.

Echevarria, J., Vogt, M. and Short, D. (2017) *Making Content Comprehensible for English Learners: The SIOP Model* (5th edn). Boston, MA: Pearson.

Efurosibina, A. (1994) English and indigenous languages in Kwara State (Nigeria): The bottom-line attitudinal factors. *Multilingua: Journal of Cross-Cultural and Interlanguage Communication* 13 (3), 253–284.

ELFA Transcription Guide (2004) *ELFA Transcription Guide (7/2004)* (A. Mauranen, Director). See http://www.helsinki.fi/elfa/elfacorpus/ (accessed 20 July 2019).

Erling, E.J., Adinolfi, L. and Hultgren, A.K. (2017) *Multilingual Classrooms: Opportunities and Challenges for English Medium Instruction in Low and Middle Income Contexts.* UK: British Council/Open University/Education Development Trust.

Evans, D. (2014) *Language and Identity: Discourse in the World.* London and New York: Bloomsbury Academic.

Evans, S. (2008) Classroom language use in Hong Kong's reformed English-medium stream. *Journal of Multilingual and Multicultural Development* 29 (6), 483–498.

Fenton-Smith, B., Humphreys, P. and Walkinshaw, I. (eds) (2017) *English Medium Instruction in Higher Education in Asia-Pacific: From Policy to Pedagogy.* Cham: Springer International.

Ferguson, G. (2003) Classroom code-switching in post-colonial contexts: Functions, attitudes and policies. *AILA Review* 14, 38–51.

Ferguson, G. (2009) What next? Towards an agenda for classroom code-switching research. *International Journal of Bilingual Education and Bilingualism* 12 (2), 231–241.

Fleisch, B. (2008) *Primary Education in Crisis: Why South African Schoolchildren Underachieve in Reading and Mathematics.* Cape Town: Juta.

Flores, N. and García, O. (2013) Linguistic third spaces in education: Teachers' translanguaging across the bilingual continuum. In D. Little, C. Leung and P. Van Avermaet (eds) *Managing Diversity in Education: Languages, Policies, Pedagogies* (pp. 243–256). Bristol: Multilingual Matters.

Flynn, E., Hoy, S., Lea, J. and Garcia, M. (2019) Translanguaging through story: Empowering children to use their full language repertoire. *Journal of Early Childhood Literacy* (online).

Fraser, N. (2008) *Scales of Justice: Reimagining Political Space in a Globalized World.* Cambridge: Polity Press.

Fujimoto-Adamson, N. and Adamson, J.L. (2018) From EFL to EMI: Hybrid practices in English as a medium of instruction in Japanese tertiary contexts. In Y. Kırkgöz and K. Dikilitaş (eds) *Key Issues in English for Specific Purposes* (pp. 201–221). Dordrecht: Springer.

Gacheche, K. (2010) Challenges in implementing a mother tongue-based language-in-education policy: Policy and practice in Kenya. *POLIS* 4, 1–45.

Gallagher, F. and Colohan, G. (2017) T(w)o and fro: Using the L1 as a language teaching tool in the CLIL classroom. *Language Learning Journal* 45 (4), 485–498.

Gambushe, W. (2017) English an African language? Hay' khona! (Nope). See http://mulosige.soas.ac.uk/english-african-language-against/ (accessed 26 August 2019).

Ganuza, N. and Hedman, C. (2017) Ideology versus practice: Is there a space for pedagogical translanguaging in mother tongue instruction? In B. Paulsrud, J. Rosén, B. Straszer and Å Wedin (eds) *New Perspectives on Translanguaging in Education* (pp. 208–225). Bristol: Multilingual Matters.

García, O. (2009a) *Bilingual Education in the 21st Century: A Global Perspective.* Malden, MA: Wiley-Blackwell.

García, O. (2009b) Education, multilingualism and translanguaging in the 21st century. In A.K. Mohanty, M. Panda, R. Phillipson and T. Skutnabb-Kangas (eds) *Multilingual Education for Social Justice: Globalising the Local* (pp. 140–158). New Delhi: Orient Blackswan.

García, O. (2009c) Emergent bilinguals and TESOL: What's in a name? *TESOL Quarterly* 43 (2), 322–326.

García, O. (2014) Countering the dual: Transglossia, dynamic bilingualism and translanguaging in education. In R. Rubdy and L. Alsagoff (eds) *The Global-Local Interface and Hybridity: Exploring Language and Identity* (pp. 100–118). Bristol: Multilingual Matters.

García, O. and Flores, N. (2012) Multilingual pedagogies. In M. Martin-Jones, A. Blackledge and A. Creese (eds) *The Routledge Handbook of Multilingualism* (pp. 232–246). London: Routledge.

García, O. and Kano, N. (2014) Translanguaging as process and pedagogy: Developing the English writing of Japanese students in the US. In J. Conteh and G. Meier (eds) *The Multilingual Turn in Languages Education: Opportunities and Challenges* (pp. 258–277). Bristol: Multilingual Matters.

García, O. and Kleifgen, J.A. (2018) *Educating Emergent Bilinguals: Policies, Programs, and Practices for English Learners* (2nd edn). New York: Teachers College Press.

García, O. and Kleyn, T. (eds) (2016) *Translanguaging with Multilingual Students: Learning from Classroom Moments.* New York: Routledge.

García, O. and Li Wei (2014) *Translanguaging: Language, Bilingualism and Education.* New York: Palgrave Macmillan.

García, O. and Li Wei (2015) Translanguaging, bilingualism, and bilingual education. In W.E. Wright, S. Boun and O. García (eds) *Handbook of Bilingual and Multilingual Education* (pp. 223–240). Malden, MA: John Wiley.

García, O. and Lin, A.M.Y. (2017) Translanguaging in bilingual education. In O. García, A.M.Y. Lin and S. May (eds) *Bilingual and Multilingual Education* (3rd edn, pp. 117–130). Cham: Springer.

García, O. and Sylvan, C.E. (2011) Pedagogies and practices in multilingual classrooms: Singularities in pluralities. *The Modern Language Journal* 95 (3), 385–400.

García, O., Sylvan, C. and Witt, D. (2011) Pedagogies and practices in multilingual classrooms: Singularities in pluralities. *The Modern Language Journal* 95 (3), 385–400.

García, O., Lin, A.M.Y. and May, S. (2017) *Bilingual and Multilingual Education*. Cham: Springer International.

Gardner, D. and Miller, L. (1999) *Establishing Self-access*. Cambridge: Cambridge University Press.

Gardner, S. (2012) Global English and bilingual education. In M. Martin-Jones, A. Blackledge and A. Creese (eds) *The Routledge Handbook of Multilingualism* (pp. 247–264). Abingdon: Routledge.

Gibbons, P. (2006) *Bridging Discourses in the ESL Classroom: Students, Teachers and Researchers*. London: Continuum.

Gogolin, I. (1994) *Der Monolinguale Habitus der Multilingualen Schule*. Münster and New York: Waxmann.

Gogolin, I. (1997) The 'monolingual habitus' as the common feature in teaching in the language of the majority in different countries. *Per Linguam* 13 (2), 38–49.

Goodman, B.A. (2014) Implementing English as a medium of instruction in a Ukrainian University: Challenges, adjustments, and opportunities. *International Journal of Pedagogies and Learning* 9 (2), 130–141.

Goodman, B.A. (2016) The ecology of language and translanguaging in a Ukrainian university. In C.M. Mazak and K.S. Carroll (eds) *Translanguaging in Higher Education: Beyond Monolingual Ideologies* (pp. 50–69). Bristol: Multilingual Matters.

Gordon, L.R. (2014) Disciplinary decadence and the decolonisation of knowledge. *Africa Development* 39 (1), 81–92.

Gotti, M. (2015) Code-switching and plurilingualism in English-medium education for academic and professional purposes. *Language Learning in Higher Education* 5 (1), 83–103.

Green, J.H. (2015) Teaching for transfer in EAP: Hugging and bridging revisited. *English for Specific Purposes* 37 (1), 1–12.

Grimshaw, T. (2015) Critical perspectives on language in international education. In M. Hayden, J. Thompson and J. Levy (eds) *The SAGE Handbook of Research in International Education* (2nd edn, pp. 215–232). London: Sage.

Groff, C. (2016) Multilingual policies and practices in Indian higher education. In C.M. Mazak and K.S. Carroll (eds) *Translanguaging Practices in Higher Education: Beyond Monolingual Ideologies* (pp. 121–140). Bristol: Multilingual Matters.

Grosfoguel, R. (2013) The structure of knowledge in westernized universities: Epistemic racism/sexism and the four genocides of the long 16th century. Human Architecture. *Journal of the Sociology of Self-Knowledge* 11 (1), 73–90.

Grosjean, F. (2010) *Bilingual: Life and Reality*. Cambridge, MA: Harvard University Press.

Guarda, M. (2018) 'I just sometimes forget that I'm actually studying in English': Exploring student perceptions on English-medium instruction at an Italian university. *Rassegna Italiana di Linguistica Applicata (RILA)* 2/3, 129–144.

Guzula, X., McKinney, C. and Tyler, R. (2016) Languaging-for-learning: Legitimising translanguaging and enabling multimodal practices in third spaces. *Southern African Linguistics and Applied Language Studies* 34 (3), 211–226.

Haim, O. (2015) Investigating transfer of academic proficiency among trilingual immigrant students: A holistic tri-directional approach. *The Modern Language Journal* 99 (4), 696–717.

Hansen, D.T. (2001) Teaching as a moral activity. In V. Richardson (ed.) *Handbook of Research on Teaching* (pp. 826–857). Washington, DC: American Educational Research Association.

Hartshorne, K. (1992) *Crisis and Challenge: Black Education 1910–1990*. Cape Town: Oxford University Press.

Hayden, M., Thompson, J. and Levy, J. (eds) (2007) *The SAGE Handbook of Research in International Education*. Los Angeles, CA: Sage.

Heaton, J.B. (1975) *Composition Through Pictures*. Harlow: Longman.

Hedman, C. (2018) Epilog: Transspråkande som pedagogisk praktik [Epilogue: Translanguaging as a pedagogical practice]. In B. Paulsrud, J. Rosén, B. Straszer and Å. Wedin (eds) *Transspråkande i Svenska Utbildningssammanhang [Translanguaging in Swedish Education Contexts]* (pp. 265–271). Lund: Studentlitteratur.

Hélot, C. (2011) Christine Hélot. *NNEST of the Month*, blog post, 31 August. See https://nnestofthemonth.wordpress.com/2011/08/ (accessed 7 January 2019).

Heugh, K. (1995) The multilingual school: Modified dual medium. In K.A. Heugh, A. Siegruhn and P. Plüddemann (eds) *Multilingual Education for South Africa*. Johannesburg: Heinemann.

Heugh, K. (2002) The case against bilingual and multilingual education in South Africa: Laying bare the myths. *Perspectives in Education* 20 (1), 171–196.

Heugh, K. (2013) Multilingual education policy in South Africa constrained by theoretical and historical disconnections. *Annual Review of Applied Linguistics* 33, 215–237.

Heugh, K. (2014) Multilingualism, the 'African lingua franca' and the 'new linguistic dispensation'. In H. McIlwraith (ed.) *Language Rich Africa: Policy Dialogue. The Cape Town Language and Development Conference: Looking Beyond 2015*. See www.langdevconferences.org.

Heugh, K. (2015) Epistemologies in multilingual education: Translanguaging and genre – companions in conversation with policy and practice. *Language and Education* 29 (3), 280–285.

Higgins, C. and Jo, K. (2016) Ethics and education. *Oxford Bibliographies*, 31 March. See http://www.oxfordbibliographies.com/view/document/obo-9780199756810/obo-9780199756810-0142.xml?rskey = oLIfJp&result = 3&q = Ethics + and + Education#obo-9780199756810-0142-div1-0002 (accessed 26 January 2019).

Hong Kong Education Bureau (2009) *Fine-tuning the Medium of Instruction for Secondary Schools*. See http://sc.legco.gov.hk/sc/www.legco.gov.hk/yr08-09/english/panels/ed/papers/ed0115cb2-623-1-e.pdf (accessed 1 September 2018).

Hornberger, N. (1991) Extending enrichment bilingual education: Revisiting typologies and redirecting policy. In O. García (ed.) *Bilingual Education: Essays in Honour of Joshua A. Fishman* (pp. 215–234). Philadelphia, PA: John Benjamins.

Hornberger, N.H. (ed.) (2012) *Educational Linguistics: Critical Concepts in Linguistics, Vols 1–6*. London and New York: Routledge.

Hornberger, N.H. and Link, H. (2012) Translanguaging and transnational literacies in multilingual classrooms: A biliteracy lens. *International Journal of Bilingual Education and Bilingualism* 15 (3), 261–278.

Huiskamp, J. (2016) 'I am an accomplished speaker of Chibrazi': Chibrazi language and identity. BA thesis, Leiden University.

Hult, F.M. (2017) Discursive approaches to policy. In S. Wortham, D. Kim and S. May (eds) *Discourse and Education* (pp. 111–121). Cham: Springer.

Hultgren, A.K. (2018) The Englishization of Nordic universities: What do scientists think? *European Journal of Language Policy* 10, 77–96.

Hultgren, A.K., Jensen, C. and Dimova, S. (2015) English-medium instruction in European higher education: From the north to the south. In S. Dimova, A.K. Hultgren and C. Jensen (eds) *English-Medium Instruction in European Higher Education* (pp. 1–11). Berlin: Walter de Gruyter.

Hurst, E. (forthcoming) Hierarchies and coloniality: Students' language ideologies and attitudes in Cape Town. In S. Hedid (ed.) *Young Speakers Facing Socio-Societal Mobility in African Cities*. Montreal, Canada: Agence Universitaire de la Francophonie.

Hurst, E. and Mona, M. (2017) Translanguaging as a socially just pedagogy. *Education as Change* 21 (2), 126–148.

Hurst, E., Madiba, M. and Morreira, S. (2017) Surfacing and valuing students' linguistic resources in an English-dominant university. In D. Palfreyman and C. van der Walt (eds) *Academic Biliteracies: Multilingual Repertoires in Higher Education* (pp. 76–95). Bristol: Multilingual Matters.

Husu, J. and Tirri, K. (2007) Developing whole school pedagogical values – a case of going through the ethos of 'good schooling'. *Teacher and Teacher Education* 23 (4), 390–401.

IBA (2009) *Making the PYP Happen: A Curriculum Framework for International Primary Education*. Cardiff: International Baccalaureate Association.

Imoto, Y. (2013) Japan: Internationalisation in education and the problem of introspective youth. In P.-T.J. Hsieh (ed.) *Education in East Asia* (pp. 127–152). London: Bloomsbury.

ISC Research (2018) *Global Opportunities Report 2018*. See https://www.iscresearch.com/services/global-report/ (accessed 28 January 2019).

Ishikawa, M. (2011) Redefining internationalization in higher education: Global 30 and the making of global universities in Japan. In D.B. Willis and J. Rappleye (eds) *Reimagining Japanese Education: Borders, Transfers, Circulations and the Comparative* (pp. 193–223). Oxford: Symposium Books.

Jacobson, R. and Faltis, C. (eds) (1990) *Language Distribution Issues in Bilingual Schooling*. Clevedon: Multilingual Matters.

Jalasi, E.M. (1999) Semantic shift in Chichewa among Chancellor College students. BA thesis, University of Malawi.

Jarvis, S. and Pavlenko, A. (2008) *Crosslinguistic Influence in Language and Cognition*. New York: Routledge.

Jaspers, J. (2018) The transformative limits of translanguaging. *Language & Communication* 58 (1), 1–10.

Jaspers, J. (2019) Authority and morality in advocating heteroglossia. *Language, Culture and Society* 1 (1), 83–105.

Jenkins, J. and Mauranen, A. (eds) (2019) *Linguistic Diversity on the EMI Campus: Insider Accounts of the Use of English and Other Languages in Universities within Asia, Australasia, and Europe*. London: Routledge Taylor & Francis.

Jiang, L., Jun Zhang, L. and May, S. (2019) Implementing English-medium instruction (EMI) in China: Teachers' practices and perceptions, and students' learning motivation and needs. *International Journal of Bilingual Education and Bilingualism* 22 (2), 107–119.

Johnson, D.C. (2013) *Language Policy*. New York: Palgrave.

Jones, B. (2017) Translanguaging in bilingual schools in Wales. *Journal of Language, Identity & Education* 16 (4), 199–215.

Kachru, B.B. (ed.) (1992) *The Other Tongue: English Across Cultures* (2nd edn). Urbana, IL: University of Illinois Press.

Kagwesage, A.M. (2013) Coping with English as language of instruction in higher education in Rwanda. *International Journal of Higher Education* 2 (2), 1–12.

Källkvist, M. and Hult, F.M. (2016) Discursive mechanisms and human agency in language policy formation: Negotiating bilingualism and parallel language use at a Swedish university. *International Journal of Bilingual Education and Bilingualism* 19 (1), 1–17.

Kamanga, C. (2014) Who speaks Chibrazi, the urban contact vernacular of Malawi? *Language Matters* 45 (2), 257–275.

Kamanga, C. (2016) A descriptive analysis of Chibrazi, the urban contact vernacular language of Malawi: A focus on the lexicon and semantic manipulation. PhD thesis, University of Pretoria.

Kamtukule, V. (2019) *Report on Rationale for the Current Language Policy*. See http://www.langdev.mw/downloads/Rationale%20for%20the%20Current%20Language%20Policy.pdf (accessed July 2019).

Kamwangamalu, N. (2015) The sociolinguistic and language education landscapes of African commonwealth countries. In A. Yiakoumetti (ed.) *Multilingualism and*

Language in Education: Sociolinguistic and Pedagogical Perspectives from Commonwealth Countries (pp. 1–18). Cambridge: Cambridge University Press.

Kamwendo, G. (2003) Is Malawi guilty of spoiling the Queen's language? *English Today* 2, 30–33.

Kamwendo, G. (2008) The bumpy road to mother tongue instruction in Malawi. *Journal of Multilingual and Multicultural Development* 29 (5), 353–363.

Kamwendo, G. (2015) The straight for English policy in Malawi: The road not to be taken. In L. Miti (ed.) *The Language of Instruction Question in Malawi* (pp. 29–40). Cape Town: CASAS.

Kayambazinthu, E. (1998) The language planning situation in Malawi. *Journal of Multilingual and Multicultural Development* 19 (5 & 6), 369–439.

Kayambazinthu, E. (2000) Sociolinguistic theories: Some implications from Malawian data. *Journal of Humanities* 14, 9–47.

Kerfoot, C. and Hyltenstam, K. (2017) Introduction: Entanglement and orders of visibility. In C. Kerfoot and K. Hyltenstam (eds) *Entangled Discourses: South-North Orders of Visibility*. New York: Routledge.

Khote, N. and Tian, Z. (2019) Translanguaging in culturally sustaining systemic functional linguistics: Developing a heteroglossic space with multilingual learners. *Translation and Translanguaging in Multilingual Contexts* 5 (1), 5–28.

Kim, J., Kim, E.G. and Kweon, S. (2018) Challenges in implementing English-medium instruction: Perspectives of humanities and social sciences professors teaching engineering students. *English for Specific Purposes* 51, 111–123.

Kim, K.-R. (2011) Korean professor and student perceptions of the efficacy of English-medium instruction. *Linguistic Research* 28 (3), 711–741.

Kirkpatrick, A. (2017) The languages of higher education in East and Southeast Asia: Will EMI lead to Englishisation? In B. Fenton-Smith, P. Humphreys and I. Walkinshaw (eds) *English Medium Instruction in Higher Education in Asia-Pacific* (pp. 21–36). Cham: Springer.

Kishindo, P.J. (2015) The bird that was not allowed to fly: The case of the mother tongue language-in-education policy in Malawi. In L. Miti (ed.) *The Language of Instruction Question in Malawi* (pp. 9–28). Cape Town: CASAS.

Klimpfinger, T. (2007) 'Mind you sometimes you have to mix': The role of code-switching in English as a lingua franca. *VIEWS* 16 (2), 36–61.

Kotzé, E. (2014) The emergence of a favourable policy landscape. In L. Hibbert and C. van der Walt (eds) *Multilingual Universities in South Africa: Reflecting Society in Higher Education* (pp. 15–27). Bristol: Multilingual Matters.

Kretzer, M. and Kumwenda, J. (2016) Language policy in Malawi: A study of its contexts, factors for its development and consequences. *Journal of Language and Literature* 27 (1), 20–38.

Kuteeva, M. (2018) Researching English-medium instruction at Swedish universities: Developments over the past decade. In K. Murata (ed.) *English-Medium Instruction from an English as a Lingua Franca Perspective: Exploring the Higher Education Context* (pp. 46–63). Abingdon: Routledge.

Kvale, S. (1996) *InterViews*. Thousand Oaks, CA: Sage.

Kym, I. and Kym, M.H. (2014) Students' perceptions of EMI in higher education in Korea. *Journal of Asia TEFL* 11 (2), 35–61.

Langman, J. (2014) Translanguaging, identity, and learning: Science teachers as engaged language planners. *Language Policy* 13 (2), 183–200.

Lasagabaster, D. (2013) The use of the L1 in CLIL classes: The teachers' perspective. *Latin American Journal of Content and Language Integrated Learning* 6 (2), 1–21.

Law Commission (2010) *Report of the Law Commission on the Review of Education Act*. Lilongwe: Government of Malawi.

Lee, E. and Canagarajah, S. (2018) The connection between transcultural dispositions and translingual practices in academic writing. *Journal of Multicultural Discourses* 14 (1), 14–28.

Lehohla, P. (2012) *Census 2011: Census in Brief*. Pretoria: Statistics South Africa.

Lekera, C.F. (1994) Chirunga language: A preliminary description. BA thesis, Chancellor College.

Lemke, J.L. (1990) *Talking Science: Language, Learning and Values*. Norwood, NJ: Ablex.

Lemke, J. (2016) Translanguaging and flows. Unpublished manuscript, Department of Communication, University of California.

Levine, G.S. (2011) *Code Choice in the Language Classroom*. Bristol: Multilingual Matters.

Lewis, G., Jones, B. and Baker, C. (2012a) Translanguaging: Developing its conceptualisation and contextualisation. *Educational Research and Evaluation* 18 (7), 655–670.

Lewis, G., Jones, B. and Baker, C. (2012b) Translanguaging: Origins and development from school to street and beyond. *Educational Research and Evaluation* 18 (7), 641–654.

Li Wei (2011) Moment analysis and translanguaging space: Discursive construction of identities by multilingual Chinese youth in Britain. *Journal of Pragmatics* 43 (5), 1222–1235.

Li Wei (2014) Translanguaging knowledge and identity in complementary classrooms for multilingual minority ethnic children. *Classroom Discourse* 5 (2), 158–175.

Li Wei (2018) Translanguaging as a practical theory of language. *Applied Linguistics* 39 (1), 9–30.

Li Wei and García, O. (2016) From researching translanguaging to translanguaging research. In K. King, Y.J. Lai and S. May (eds) *Encyclopedia of Language and Education, Vol. X: Research Methods in Language and Education* (pp. 227–240). Cham: Springer International.

Li Wei and Lin, A.M.Y. (2019) Translanguaging classroom discourse: Pushing limits, breaking boundaries. *Classroom Discourse* 10 (3–4), 209–215.

Li Wei and Martin, P. (2009) Conflicts and tensions in classroom codeswitching: An introduction. *International Journal of Bilingual Education and Bilingualism* 12 (2), 117–122.

Li Wei and Wu, C.J. (2009) Polite Chinese children revisited: Creativity and the use of code-switching in the Chinese complementary school classroom. *International Journal of Bilingual Education and Bilingualism* 12 (2), 193–211.

Li, S. and Luo, W. (2017) Creating a translanguaging space for high school emergent bilinguals. *CATESOL Journal* 29 (2), 139–162.

Lin, A.M.Y. (1996) Bilingualism or linguistic segregation? Symbolic domination, resistance and code-switching in Hong Kong schools. *Linguistics and Education* 8 (1), 49–84.

Lin, A.M.Y. (2005) Critical, transdisciplinary perspectives on language-in-education policy and practice in postcolonial contexts: The case of Hong Kong. In A.M.Y. Lin and P.W. Martin (eds) *Decolonization, Globalization: Language-in-education Policy and Practice* (pp. 38–54). Clevedon: Multilingual Matters.

Lin, A.M.Y. (2006) Beyond linguistic purism in language-in-education policy and practice: Exploring bilingual pedagogies in a Hong Kong science classroom. *Language and Education* 20 (4), 287–305.

Lin, A.M.Y. (2016) *Language Across the Curriculum & CLIL in English as an Additional Language (EAL) Contexts: Theory and Practice*. Cham: Springer.

Lin, A.M.Y. and He, P. (2017) Translanguaging as dynamic activity flows in CLIL classrooms. *Journal of Language, Identity & Education* 16 (4), 228–244.

Lin, A.M.Y. and Lo, Y.Y. (2017) Translanguaging and the triadic dialogue in content and language integrated learning (CLIL) classrooms. *Language and Education* 31 (1), 26–45.

Lin, A.M.Y. and Wu, Y. (2015) 'May I speak Cantonese?': Co-constructing a scientific proof in an EFL junior secondary science classroom. *International Journal of Bilingual Education and Bilingualism* 18 (3), 289–305.

Lin, A.M.Y., Wu, Y. and Lemke, J.L. (2020) 'It takes a village to research a village': Conversations between Angel Lin and Jay Lemke on contemporary issues in translanguaging. In S.M.C. Lau and S. Van Viegen (eds) *Plurilingual Pedagogies: Critical and Creative Endeavors for Equitable Language in Education* (pp. 47–74). Cham: Springer International.

Little, D. (1995) Learning as dialogue: The dependence of learner autonomy on teacher autonomy. *System* 23 (2), 175–181.

Ljosland, R. (2010) Teaching through English: Monolingual policy meets multilingual practice. *Hermes* 45, 99–113.

Lo, Y.Y. (2014) L2 learning opportunities in different academic subjects in content-based instruction – evidence in favour of 'conventional wisdom'. *Language and Education* 28 (2), 141–160.

Lo, Y.Y. and Macaro, E. (2012) The medium of instruction and classroom interaction: Evidence from Hong Kong secondary schools. *International Journal of Bilingual Education and Bilingualism* 15 (1), 29–52.

Lo, Y.Y. and Macaro, E. (2015) Getting used to content and language integrated learning: What can classroom interaction reveal? *Language Learning Journal* 43 (3), 239–255.

Long, M.H. (1983) Native speaker/non native speaker conversation and the negotiation of comprehensible input. *Applied Linguistics* 4 (2), 126–141.

Luckett, K. (1993) National additive bilingualism: Towards the formulation of a language plan for South African schools. *South African Journal of Applied Language Studies* 2 (1), 38–60.

Luckett, K. and Shay, S. (2017) Reframing the curriculum: A transformative approach. *Critical Studies in Education* 61 (1), 50–65.

Luckett, K., Morreira, S. and Baijnath, M. (2019) Recontextualization, identity and self-critique in a post-apartheid university. In L. Quinn (ed.) *Decolonizing the Curriculum* (pp. 23–43). Stellenbosch: African Sun Media.

Lüpke, F. (2015) Denorthernising multilingualism and multilingualism research framing language in the north. *VOICES from around the World: Special Issue on Multilingualism in the Global South* 3, 3–5.

Lyster, R. (2007) *Learning and Teaching Languages Through Content: A Counterbalanced Approach.* Philadelphia, PA: John Benjamins.

Macaro, E. (2018) *English Medium Instruction: Content and Language in Policy and Practice.* Oxford: Oxford University Press.

Macaro, M., Curle, S., Pun, J., An, J. and Dearden, J. (2018) A systematic review of English medium instruction in higher education. *Language Teaching* 51 (1), 36–76.

Macdonald, C.A. (1990) *Crossing the Threshold into Standard Three in Black Education: The Consolidated Main Report of the Threshold Project.* Pretoria: Human Sciences Research Council.

MacSwan, J. (2017) A multilingual perspective on translanguaging. *American Educational Research Journal* 54 (1), 167–201.

Makalela, L. (2013) Translanguaging in *Kasi-Taal*: Rethinking old language boundaries for new language planning. *Stellenbosch Papers in Linguistics Plus* 42, 111–125.

Makalela, L. (2015) Translanguaging as a vehicle for epistemic access: Cases for reading comprehension and multilingual interactions. *Per Linguam* 31 (1), 15–29.

Makalela, L. (2016a) Ubuntu translanguaging: An alternative framework for complex multilingual encounters. *Southern African Linguistics and Applied Language Studies* 34 (3), 187–196.

Makalela, L. (2016b) Translanguaging practices in a South African institution of higher learning: A case of Ubuntu multilingual return. In C.M. Mazak and K.S. Carroll (eds) *Translanguaging in Higher Education: Beyond Monolingual Ideologies* (pp. 88–106). Bristol: Multilingual Matters.

Makalela, L. (2018) *Shifting Lenses: Multilanguaging, Decolonisation and Education in the Global South.* Cape Town: Centre for Advanced Studies of African Society (CASAS).

Makoe, P. and McKinney, C. (2009) Hybrid discursive practices in a South African multilingual classroom: A case study. *English Teaching: Practice and Critique* 8 (2), 80–95.

Makoe, P. and McKinney, C. (2014) Linguistic ideologies in multilingual South African suburban schools. *Journal of Multilingual and Multicultural Development* 35 (7), 658–673.

Makoni, S. and Mashiri, P. (2006) Critical historiography: Does language planning in Africa need a construct of language as part of its theoretical apparatus? In S. Makoni and A. Pennycook (eds) *Disinventing and Reconstituting Languages* (pp. 62–89). Clevedon: Multilingual Matters.

Makoni, S. and Pennycook, A. (2005) Disinventing and (re)constituting languages. *Critical Inquiry in Language Studies* 2 (3), 137–156.

Makoni, S. and Pennycook, A. (2007) Disinventing and reconstituting languages. In S. Makoni and A. Pennycook (eds) *Disinventing and Reconstituting Languages* (pp. 1–41). Clevedon: Multilingual Matters.

Makoni, S. and Pennycook, A. (2010) *Disinventing and Reconstituting Languages.* Clevedon: Multilingual Matters.

Malawi Government (2013) *New Education Act.* Lilongwe: Government of Malawi.

Martin, J.R. and White, P.R.R. (2005) *The Language of Evaluation: Appraisal in English.* Basingstoke: Palgrave Macmillan.

Martin, P.W. (1996) Code-switching in the primary classroom: One response to the planned and unplanned language environment in Brunei. *Journal of Multilingual and Multicultural Development* 17 (2–4), 128–144.

Martin, P.W. (2005) Bilingual encounters in the classroom. In J.-M. Dewale, A. Housen and Li Wei (eds) *Bilingualism: Beyond the Basic Principles* (pp. 67–87). Clevedon: Multilingual Matters.

Maseko, P. (2014) Multilingualism at work in South African higher education: From policy to practice. In L. Hibbert and C. van der Walt (eds) *Multilingual Universities in South Africa: Reflecting Society in Higher Education* (pp. 28–48). Bristol: Multilingual Matters.

Matiki, A.J. (2001) The social significance of English in Malawi. *World Englishes* 20 (2), 201–218.

Maton, K. (2014) *Knowledge and Knowers: Towards a Realist Sociology of Education.* Abingdon: Routledge.

May, S. (2014) Introducing the 'multilingual turn'. In S. May (ed.) *The Multilingual Turn: Implications for SLA, TESOL and Bilingual Education* (pp. 1–6). New York: Routledge.

Mazak, C.M. (2016) Introduction: Theorizing translanguaging practices in higher education. In C.M. Mazak and K.S. Carroll (eds) *Translanguaging in Higher Education: Beyond Monolingual Ideologies* (pp. 1–10). Bristol: Multilingual Matters.

Mazak, C.M. and Carroll, K.S. (eds) (2016) *Translanguaging in Higher Education: Beyond Monolingual Ideologies.* Bristol: Multilingual Matters.

Mazak, C.M. and Herbas-Donoso, C. (2014) Translanguaging practices and language ideologies in Puerto Rican university science education. *Critical Inquiry in Language Studies* 11 (1), 27–49.

Mazak, C.M. and Herbas-Donoso, C. (2015) Translanguaging practices at a bilingual university: A case study of a science classroom. *International Journal of Bilingual Education and Bilingualism* 18 (6), 698–714.

Mazak, C.M., Mendoza, F. and Mangonéz, L.P. (2016) Professors translanguaging in practice: Three cases from a bilingual university. In C.M. Mazak and K.S. Carroll (eds) *Translanguaging in Higher Education: Beyond Monolingual Ideologies* (pp. 70–90). Bristol: Multilingual Matters.

Mazzaferro, G. (ed.) (2018) *Translanguaging as Everyday Practice*. Cham: Springer International.

McKinney, C. (2017) *Language and Power in Post-colonial Schooling: Ideologies in Practice*. New York: Routledge.

McKinney, C. and Tyler, R. (2018) Disinventing and reconstituting language for learning in school science. *Language and Education* 33 (2), 141–158.

McKinney, C., Carrim, H., Marshall, A. and Layton, L. (2015) What counts as language in South African schooling? Monoglossic ideologies and children's participation. *AILA Review* 28, 103–126.

McMillan, B.A. and Rivers, D.J. (2011) The practice of policy: Teacher attitudes toward 'English only'. *System* 39 (2), 251–263.

Menken, K. and García, O. (eds) (2010) *Negotiating Language Policies in Schools: Educators as Policymakers*. New York: Routledge.

Merino, J.A. and Lasagabaster, D. (2015) CLIL as a way to multilingualism. *International Journal of Bilingual Education and Bilingualism* 21 (1), 79–92.

MEXT (Ministry of Education, Culture, Sports, Science and Technology) (2011) *Daigaku ni okeru kyouikunaiyou to no kaikakujokyou (Heisei 23 nen ban) [Regarding the Current Situation of Educational Contents at Universities (as of 2011)]*. See https://www.mext.go.jp/a_menu/koutou/daigaku/04052801/1341433.htm (accessed 28 September 2016).

Miller, S. and Pennycuff, L. (2008) The power of story: Using storytelling to improve literacy learning. *Journal of Cross-Disciplinary Perspectives in Education* 1 (1), 36–43.

Ministry of Education (2002) *Language Policy for Higher Education*. See http://www.dhet.gov.za/Management%20Support/Language%20Policy%20for%20Higher%20Education.pdf (accessed 26 August 2019).

Ministry of Education (2003) *Development of Indigenous Languages as Mediums of Instruction in Higher Education*. See http://www.dhet.gov.za/Management%20Support/The%20development%20of%20Indigenous%20African%20Languages%20as%20mediums%20of%20instruction%20in%20Higher%20Education.pdf (accessed 26 August 2019).

Ministry of Education (2008) *Report of the Ministerial Committee on Transformation and Social Cohesion and the Elimination of Discrimination in Public Higher Education Institutions*. See https://www.ukzn.ac.za/wp-content/miscFiles/publications/ReportonHEandTransformation.pdf (accessed 26 August 2019).

Miti, L. (2015) In search of an inclusive language of instruction policy in Malawi. In L. Miti (ed.) *The Language of Instruction Question in Malawi* (pp. 4–5). Cape Town: CASAS.

Mohamed, N. (2016) Language of instruction and the development of biliteracy skills in children: A case study of a pre-school in the Maldives. In V. Murphy and M. Evangelou (eds) *Early Childhood Education in English for Speakers of Other Languages* (pp. 187–194). London: British Council.

Mohamed, N. (2019) From a monolingual to a multilingual nation: Analysing the language education policy in the Maldives. In A. Kirkpatrick and A. Liddicoat (eds) *The Routledge International Handbook of Language Education Policy in Asia* (pp. 414–426). London: Routledge.

Montgomery, D.P., Sparks, J. and Goodman, B. (2019) 'What kind of paper do you want from us?': Developing genre knowledge in one Kazakhstani university postgraduate school. *Journal of Learning Development in Higher Education* 15, 1–27.

Moody, S., Chowdhury, M. and Eslami, Z. (2019) Graduate students' perceptions of translanguaging. *English Teaching & Learning* 43 (1), 85–103.

Moore, P.J. (2017) Unwritten rules: Code choice in task-based learner discourse in an EMI context in Japan. In B. Fenton-Smith, P. Humphreys and I. Walkinshaw (eds) *English*

Medium of Instruction in Asia-Pacific: From Policy to Pedagogy (pp. 299–320). Cham: Springer.

Mortimer, E. and Scott, P. (2003) *Meaning Making in Secondary Science Classrooms.* Maidenhead: Open University Press.

Moto, F. (2001) Language and societal attitudes: A study of Malawi's 'new language'. *Nordic Journal of African Studies* 10 (3), 320–343.

Motta, A. (2017) Nine and a half reasons against the monarchy of English. In K. Ackerley, M. Guarda and F. Helm (eds) *Sharing Perspectives on English-Medium Instruction* (pp. 95–110). Bern: Peter Lang.

Msimanga, A. and Lelliott, A. (2014) Talking science in multilingual contexts in South Africa: Possibilities and challenges for engagement in learners' home languages in high school classrooms. *International Journal of Science Education* 36 (7), 1159–1183.

Msonthi, J. (1997) Parents' attitude towards multilingual education in the lower primary school (Standard 1–4: The Malawian experience). BEd thesis, Chancellor College.

Mtenje, A. (2013) Developing a language policy in an African country: Lessons from the Malawi experience. In H. McIlwraith (ed.) *Multilingual Education in Africa: Lessons from the Juba Language-in-Education Conference* (pp. 95–102). London: British Council.

NCHE (National Council for Higher Education) (2014) *Standards for Accreditation of Malawi's Higher Education Institutions.* Lilongwe: NCHE.

NCHE (National Council for Higher Education) (2015) *Minimum Standards for Higher Education Institutions.* Lilongwe: NCHE.

National Research Council (2005) *How Students Learn: Science in the Classroom.* Washington, DC: National Academies Press.

National Statistical Office (1998) *Population and Housing Census: Analytical Report.* Lilongwe: NSO.

Nazarbayev, N. (2007) *A New Kazakhstan in a New World: Address by the President of the Republic of Kazakhstan Mr. Nursultan Nazarbayev to the Republic of Kazakhstan*, 1 March. See https://www.zakon.kz/83346-poslanie-prezidenta-respub-liki.html (accessed 24 August 2019).

Nazarbayev University (2018) *Strategy 2018–2030*, 1 December. See https://nu.edu.kz/wp-content/uploads/2016/07/2_NU-Strategy_ENG_2030-1.pdf (accessed 24 August 2019).

Nikula, T., Dafouz, E., Moore, P. and Smit, U. (eds) (2016) *Conceptualising Integration in CLIL and Multilingual Education.* Bristol: Multilingual Matters.

Nyarigoti, N. and Ambiyo, S. (2014) Mother tongue in instruction: The role of attitude in the implementation. *International Journal of Research in Social Sciences* 4 (1), 77–87.

Nyasa Times (2014) Malawi Std 1 pupils to start learning in English in all subjects. *Nyasatimes*, 5 March. See https://www.nyasatimes.com/malawi-std-1-pupils-to-start-learning-in-english-all-subjects/ (accessed 5 January 2019).

Otheguy, R., García, O. and Reid, W. (2015) Clarifying translanguaging and deconstructing named languages: A perspective from linguistics. *Applied Linguistics Review* 6 (3), 281–307.

Otheguy, R., García, O. and Reid, W. (2018) A translanguaging view of the linguistic system of bilinguals. *Applied Linguistics Review* 10 (4), 625–651.

Ouane, A. and Glanz, C. (2010) *Why and How Africa Should Invest in African Languages and Multilingual Education.* New York: UNESCO Institute for Lifelong Learning.

Palfreyman, D.M. and van der Walt, C. (eds) (2017) *Academic Biliteracies: Multilingual Repertoires in Higher Education.* Bristol: Multilingual Matters.

Palmer, D.K., Martínez, R.A., Mateus S.G. and Henderson, K. (2014) Reframing the debate on language separation: Toward a vision for translanguaging pedagogies in the dual language classroom. *The Modern Language Journal* 98 (3), 757–772.

Paris, D. (2012) Culturally sustaining pedagogy: A needed change in stance, terminology, and practice. *Educational Researcher* 41 (3), 93–97.

Parmegiani, A. and Rudwick, S. (2014) isiZulu-English bilingualisation at the University of KwaZulu-Natal: An exploration of students' attitudes. In L. Hibbert and C. van der Walt (eds) *Multilingual Universities in South Africa: Reflecting Society in Higher Education* (pp. 107–122). Bristol: Multilingual Matters.

Paulsrud, B. (2019) Just a little plus: The CLIL student perspective. In L.K. Sylvén (ed.) *Investigating Content and Language Integrated Learning: Insights from Swedish High Schools* (pp. 285–300). Bristol: Multilingual Matters.

Paulsrud, B. and Toth, J. (2020) English as a medium of instruction. In S. Laviosa and M. González-Davies (eds) *The Routledge Handbook of Translation and Education* (pp. 143–155). Abingdon: Routledge.

Paulsrud, B. and Zilliacus, H. (2018) Flerspråkighet och transspråkande i lärarutbildningen [Multilingualism and translanguaging in teacher education]. In B. Paulsrud, J. Rosén, B. Straszer and Å. Wedin (eds) *Transspråkande i Svenska Utbildningssammanhang [Translanguaging in Swedish Education Contexts]* (pp. 27–48). Lund: Studentlitteratur.

Paulsrud, B., Rosén, J., Straszer, B. and Wedin, Å. (eds) (2017a) *New Perspectives on Translanguaging and Education*. Bristol: Multilingual Matters.

Paulsrud, B., Rosén, J., Straszer, B. and Wedin, Å. (2017b) Perspectives on translanguaging in education. In B. Paulsrud, J. Rosén, B. Straszer and Å. Wedin (eds) *New Perspectives on Translanguaging in Education* (pp. 10–19). Bristol: Multilingual Matters.

Pecorari, D. and Malmström, H. (2018) At the crossroads of TESOL and English medium instruction. *TESOL Quarterly* 52 (3), 497–515.

Pérez-Milan, M. (2015) Language education policy in late modernity: (Socio)linguistic ethnographies in the European Union language policy. *Language Policy* 14 (2), 99–107.

Pérez-Milan, M. (2016) Language and identity in linguistic ethnography. In S. Preece (ed.) *The Routledge Handbook of Language and Identity* (pp. 83–97). London: Routledge.

Pérez-Vidal, C. (2015) Languages for all in education: CLIL and ICLHE at the crossroads of multilingualism, mobility and internationalism. In M. Juan-Garau and J. Salazar-Noguera (eds) *Content-Based Language Learning in Multilingual Educational Environments* (pp. 31–50). Cham: Springer International.

Phan, H.L. (2013) Issues surrounding English, the internationalisation of higher education and national cultural identity in Asia: A focus on Japan. *Critical Studies in Education* 54, 160–175.

Phillipson, R. (1988) Linguicism: Structures and ideologies in linguistic imperialism. In T. Skutnabb-Kangas and J. Cummins (eds) *Minority Education: From Shame to Struggle* (pp. 339–358). Clevedon: Multilingual Matters.

Phillipson, R. (1992) *Linguistic Imperialism*. Oxford: Oxford University Press.

Phillipson, R. (2003) *English-only Europe?: Challenging Language Policy*. London: Routledge.

Phillipson, R. (2015) English as threat or opportunity in English-medium higher education. In S. Dimova, A.K. Hultgren and C. Jensen (eds) *English-Medium Instruction in European Higher Education* (pp. 19–42). Berlin: De Gruyter Mouton.

Piller, I. (2016) *Linguistic Diversity and Social Justice: An Introduction to Applied Sociolinguistics*. Oxford: Oxford University Press.

Pinker, S. (1994) *The Language Instinct*. New York: William Morrow & Co.

Plüddemann, P. (2015) Unlocking the grid: Language-in-education policy realisation in post-apartheid South Africa. *Language and Education* 29 (3), 186–199.

Plüddemann, P., Braam, D., October, M. and Wababa, Z. (2004) *Dual-Medium and Parallel-Medium Schooling in the Western Cape: From Default to Design*. PRAESA Occasional Papers No. 17. Cape Town: PRAESA, University of Cape Town.

Poza, L.E. (2017) Translanguaging: Definitions, implications, and further needs in burgeoning inquiry. *Berkeley Review of Education* 6 (2), 101–128.

Probyn, M. (2005) Language and the struggle to learn: The intersection of classroom realities, language policy, and neocolonial and globalization discourses in South African schools. In P.W. Martin and A.M.Y. Lin (eds) *Decolonisation, Globalization: Language-in-Education Policy and Practice* (pp. 153–172). Clevedon: Multilingual Matters.

Probyn, M. (2009) Smuggling the vernacular into the classroom: Conflicts and tensions in classroom code-switching in South Africa. *International Journal of Bilingual Education and Bilingualism* 12 (2), 123–136.

Probyn, M. (2015) Pedagogical translanguaging: Bridging discourses in South African science classrooms. *Language and Education* 29 (3), 218–234.

Probyn, M., Murray, S., Botha, L., Botya, P., Brooks, M. and Westphal, V. (2002) Minding the gaps – an investigation into language policy and practice in four Eastern Cape districts. *Perspectives in Education* 20 (1), 29–46.

Reilly, C. (2019) Attitudes towards English as a medium of instruction in Malawian universities. *English Academy Review* 36 (1), 32–45.

Reinders, H. and Lewis, M. (2006) An evaluative checklist for self-access materials. *ELT Journal* 60 (3), 272–278.

Reinders, H., Hacker, P. and Lewis, M. (2004) The language advisor's role: Identifying and responding to needs. *Language Learning Journal* 30, 30–34.

Republic of South Africa (1996) *The Constitution of the Republic of South Africa.* Pretoria: Republic of South Africa.

Risager, K. (2012) Language hierarchies at the international university. *International Journal of the Sociology of Language* 216, 111–130.

Rivera, A.J. and Mazak, C.M. (2017) Analyzing student perceptions on translanguaging: A case study of a Puerto Rican university classroom. *HOW* 24 (1), 122–138.

Rivers, D.J. (2014) *Resistance to the Known.* London: Palgrave Macmillan.

Robinson, E., Tian, Z., Martinez, T. and Qarqeen, A. (2018) Teaching for justice: Introducing translanguaging in an undergraduate TESOL course. *Journal of Language and Education* 4 (3), 77–87.

Rose, H. and Galloway, N. (2019) *Global Englishes for Language Teaching.* Cambridge: Cambridge University Press.

Rose, H. and McKinley, J. (2018) Japan's English-medium instruction initiatives and the globalization of higher education. *Higher Education* 75 (1), 111–129.

Rosén, J. and Wedin, Å. (2015) *Klassrumsinteraktion och Flerspråkighet: Ett Kritiskt Perspektiv [Classroom Interaction and Multilingualism: A Critical Perspective].* Stockholm: Liber.

Rubagumya, C. (1994) Introduction. In C. Rubagumya (ed.) *Teaching and Researching Language in African Classrooms* (pp. 1–5). Clevedon: Multilingual Matters.

Savin-Baden, M. (2007) *Learning Spaces: Creating Opportunities for Knowledge Creation in Academic Life.* Maidenhead: McGraw Hill.

Sebidi, K. and Morreira, S. (2017) Accessing powerful knowledge: A comparative study of two first year sociology courses in a South African university. *Critical Studies in Teaching and Learning (CriSTaL)* 5 (2), 33–50.

Seedhouse, P. (2004) Conversation analysis methodology. *Language Learning* 54 (S1), 1–55.

Setati, M., Adler, J., Reed, Y. and Bapoo, A. (2002a) Incomplete journeys: Code-switching and other language practices in mathematics, science and English language classrooms in South Africa. *Language and Education* 16 (2), 128–149.

Setati, M., Adler, J., Reed, Y. and Bapoo A. (2002b) Code-switching and other language practices in mathematics, science and English language classrooms in South Africa. In J. Adler and Y. Reed (eds) *Challenges of Teacher Development: An Investigation of Take-up in South Africa* (pp. 72–93). Pretoria: Van Schaik.

Shohamy, E.G. (2006) *Language Policy: Hidden Agendas and New Approaches.* London: Routledge.

Shohamy, E. (2013) A critical perspective on the use of English as a medium of instruction at universities. In A. Doiz, D. Lasagabaster and J.M. Sierra (eds) *English-Medium Instruction at Universities: Global Challenges* (pp. 196–210). Bristol: Multilingual Matters.

Simango, S.R. (2015) Learning English or learning in English: Some thoughts on the language question in the Malawian classroom. In L. Miti (ed.) *The Language of Instruction Question in Malawi* (pp. 41–60). Cape Town: CASAS.

Skelton, M. (2007) International-mindedness and the brain – the difficulties of 'becoming'. In M. Hayden, J. Thompson and J. Levy (eds) *The SAGE Handbook of Research in International Education* (pp. 379–389). London: Sage.

Skutnabb-Kangas, T. (2000) *Linguistic Genocide in Education – Or Worldwide Diversity and Human Rights?* Mahwah, NJ: Lawrence Erlbaum.

Skutnabb-Kangas, T. and Phillipson, R. (1999) Linguicide. In B. Spolsky and R.E. Asher (eds) *Concise Encyclopedia of Educational Linguistics* (p. 48). Oxford: Pergamon Press.

Smit, U. (2010) *English as a Lingua Franca in Higher Education: A Longitudinal Study of Classroom Discourse, Vol. 2*. Vienna: Mouton de Gruyter.

Smit, U. (2019) Classroom discourse in EMI: On the dynamics of multilingual practices. In K. Murata (ed.) *English-Medium Instruction from an English as a Lingua Franca Perspective* (pp. 99–122). London: Routledge.

Söderlundh, H. (2013) Applying transnational strategies locally: English as a medium of instruction in Swedish higher education. *Nordic Journal of English Studies* 13 (1), 113–132.

South African Freedom Charter (1955) *The Freedom Charter*. See http://www.historical-papers.wits.ac.za/inventories/inv_pdfo/AD1137/AD1137-Ea6-1-001-jpeg.pdf (accessed 1 July 2020).

Spear, G. and Mocker, D. (1984) The organising circumstance: Environmental determinants in self-directed learning. *Adult Education Quarterly* 35 (1), 52–77.

Spolsky, B. (2004) *Language Policy*. Cambridge: Cambridge University Press.

Stake, R.E. (1995) *The Art of Case Study Research*. Thousand Oaks, CA: Sage.

Stigger, E. (2018) Introduction: Internationalization in higher education. In E. Stigger, M. Wang, D. Laurence and A. Bordilovskaya (eds) *Internationalization within Higher Education: Perspectives from Japan* (pp. 1–19). Singapore: Springer.

Stroupe, R. (2014) Commentary on code-switching in two Japanese contexts. In R. Barnard and J. McLellan (eds) *Code-switching in University English-Medium Classes: Asian Perspectives* (pp. 76–90). Bristol: Multilingual Matters.

Swain, M. and Lapkin, S. (2000) Task-based second language learning: The uses of the first language. *Language Teaching Research* 4 (3), 251–274.

Swain, M. and Lapkin, S. (2013) A Vygotskian perspective on immersion education: The L1/L2 debate. *Journal of Immersion and Content Based Language Education* 1 (1), 101–129.

Tarnopolsky, O.B. and Goodman, B.A. (2014) The ecology of language in classrooms at a university in eastern Ukraine. *Language and Education* 28 (4), 383–396.

Tastanbek, S. (2019) Kazakhstani pre-service teacher educators' beliefs on translanguaging. Master's thesis, Nazarbayev University.

Tayjasanant, C. and Robinson, M.G. (2014) Code-switching in universities in Thailand and Bhutan. In R. Barnard and J. McLellan (eds) *Code-switching in University English-Medium Classes: Asian Perspectives* (pp. 92–117). Bristol: Multilingual Matters.

Taylor, N. and Schindler, J. (2016) *Education Sector Landscape Mapping: South Africa*. Johannesburg: JET Education Services.

Thesen, L. (2014) Risk as productive: Working with dilemmas in the writing of research. In L. Thesen and L. Cooper (eds) *Risk in Academic Writing: Postgraduate Students, their Teachers and the Making of Knowledge* (pp. 1–24). Bristol: Multilingual Matters.

Thompson, G. and Atkinson, L. (2010) Integrating self-access into the curriculum: Our experience. *Studies in Self-Access Learning Journal* 1 (1), 47–58.

Tian, Z. and Link, H. (eds) (2019) Positive synergies: Translanguaging and critical theories in education. *Translation and Translanguaging in Multilingual Contexts* 5 (1) (Special issue).

Timammy, R. and Oduor, J.A.N. (2016) The treatment of Kiswahili in Kenya's education system. *University of Nairobi Journal of Language and Linguistics* 5, 174–194.

Toth, J. (2018a) English-medium instruction for young learners in Sweden. A longitudinal case study of a primary school class in a bilingual English-Swedish school. PhD thesis, Stockholm University.

Toth, J. (2018b) Transspråkande i engelskspråkig ämnesundervisning [Translanguaging in English-medium content instruction]. In B. Paulsrud, J. Rosén, B. Straszer and Å. Wedin (eds) *Transspråkande i Svenska Utbildningssammanhang [Translanguaging in Swedish Educational Contexts]* (pp. 243–263). Lund: Studentlitteratur.

Toth, J. and Paulsrud, B. (2017) Agency and affordance in translanguaging for learning: Case studies from English-medium instruction in Swedish schools. In B. Paulsrud, J. Rosén, B. Straszer and Å. Wedin (eds) *New Perspectives on Translanguaging and Education* (pp. 189–207). Bristol: Multilingual Matters.

Tremain, S. (2005) Foucault, governmentality and critical disability theory: An introduction. In S. Tremain (ed.) *Foucault and the Government of Disability* (pp. 1–24). Ann Arbor, MI: University of Michigan Press.

Unamuno, V. (2014) Language dispute and social change in new multilingual institutions in Chaco, Argentina. *International Journal of Multilingualism* 11 (4), 409–429.

UNESCO (United Nations Educational, Scientific and Cultural Organization) (2016) *If You Don't Understand, How Can You Learn? Global Education Monitoring Report.* Paris: UNESCO.

Universitaly (2019) *L'università italiana a portata di click.* See https://www.universitaly.it/index.php/public/cercacorsiInglese (accessed 31 November 2019).

van der Walt, C. (2013) *Multilingual Higher Education: Beyond English Medium Orientations.* Bristol: Multilingual Matters.

van der Walt, C. (2015) Bi/multilingual higher education: Perspectives and practices. In W.E. Wright, S. Boun and O. García (eds) *Handbook of Bilingual & Multilingual Education* (pp. 354–371). New York: Wiley Blackwell.

van Lier, L. (2004) *The Ecology and Semiotics of Language Learning.* Dordrecht: Kluwer Academic.

Velasco, P. and García, O. (2014) Translanguaging and the writing of bilingual learners. *Bilingual Research Journal* 37 (1), 6–23.

Vogel, S. and García, O. (2017) Translanguaging. In G. Noblit (ed.) *Oxford Research Encyclopedia of Education* (pp. 1–21). Oxford: Oxford University Press.

Wächter, B. and Maiworm, F. (eds) (2015) *English-Taught Programmes in European Higher Education: The State of Play in 2014.* Bonn: Lemmens.

Wang, W. and Curdt-Christiansen, X.L. (2019) Translanguaging in a Chinese–English bilingual education programme: A university-classroom ethnography. *International Journal of Bilingual Education and Bilingualism* 22 (3), 322–337.

Wannagat, U. (2007) Learning through L2 – content and language integrated learning (CLIL) and English as medium of instruction (EMI). *International Journal of Bilingual Education and Bilingualism* 10 (5), 663–682.

Wenger, E. (1998) *Communities of Practice: Learning, Meaning, and Identity.* New York: Cambridge University Press.

Western Cape Government: Education (n.d.) *Language Strategy 2015–2019.* See https://wcedonline.westerncape.gov.za/documents/MathLanguageStrat/WCED-LanguageStrategy-2015-2019.pdf (accessed 24 June 2020).

Wilkinson, R. (2013) English-medium instruction at a Dutch university: Challenges and pitfalls. In A. Doiz, D. Lasagabaster and J.M. Sierra (eds) *English-Medium Instruction at Universities: Global Challenges* (pp. 3–24). Bristol: Multilingual Matters.

Wilkinson, R. (2017) Trends and issues in English-medium instruction in Europe. In K. Ackerley, M. Guarda and F. Helm (eds) *Sharing Perspectives on English-medium Instruction* (pp. 35–75). Bern: Peter Lang.

Williams, C. (1994) Arfarniad o ddulliau dysgu ac addysgu yng nghyd-destun addysg uwchradd ddwyieithog [Evaluation of teaching and learning methods in the context of bilingual secondary education]. Unpublished PhD thesis, University of Wales.

Williams, C. (2000) Bilingual teaching and language distribution at 16+. *International Journal of Bilingual Education and Bilingualism* 3 (2), 129–148.

Williams, C. (2002) Ennill iaith: Astudiaeth o sefyllfa drochi yn 11–16 oed [A language gained: A study of language immersion at 11–16 years of age]. Bangor: School of Education.

Williams, E. (2011) Language policy, politics and development in Africa. In H. Coleman (ed.) *Dreams and Realities: Developing Countries and the English Language* (pp. 39–56). London: British Council.

Wright, W.E. (2019) *Foundations for Teaching English Language Learners: Research, Theory, Policy, and Practice* (3rd edn). Philadelphia, PA: Caslon.

Wright, W.E. and Li, X. (2006) Catching up in math? The case of newly-arrived Cambodian students in a Texas intermediate school. *TABE Journal* 9 (1), 1–22.

Yip, D.Y., Tsang, W.K. and Cheung, S.P. (2003) Evaluation of the effects of medium of instruction on the science learning of Hong Kong secondary students: Performance on the science achievement test. *Bilingual Research Journal* 27 (2), 295–331.

Yip, D.Y., Coyle, D. and Tsang, W.K. (2007) Evaluation of the effects of the medium of instruction on science learning of Hong Kong secondary students: Instructional activities in science lessons. *Education Journal* 35 (2), 77–107.

Yonezawa, A. (2011) The internationalization of Japanese higher education: Policy debates and realities. In S. Marginson, S. Kaur and E. Sawir (eds) *Higher Education in the Asia-Pacific* (pp. 329–342). Dordrecht: Springer.

Yoxsimer Paulsrud, B. (2014) English-medium instruction in Sweden: Perspectives and practices in two upper secondary schools. PhD thesis, Stockholm University.

Zentella, A.C. (1997) *Growing Up Bilingual*. Malden, MA: Blackwell.

Zhu Hua, Li Wei and Lyons, A. (2017) Polish shop(ping) as translanguaging space. *Social Semiotics* 27 (4), 411–433.

Zúñiga, C. (2016) Between language as problem and resource: Examining teachers' language orientations in dual-language programs. *Bilingual Research Journal* 39 (3–4), 339–353.

Index